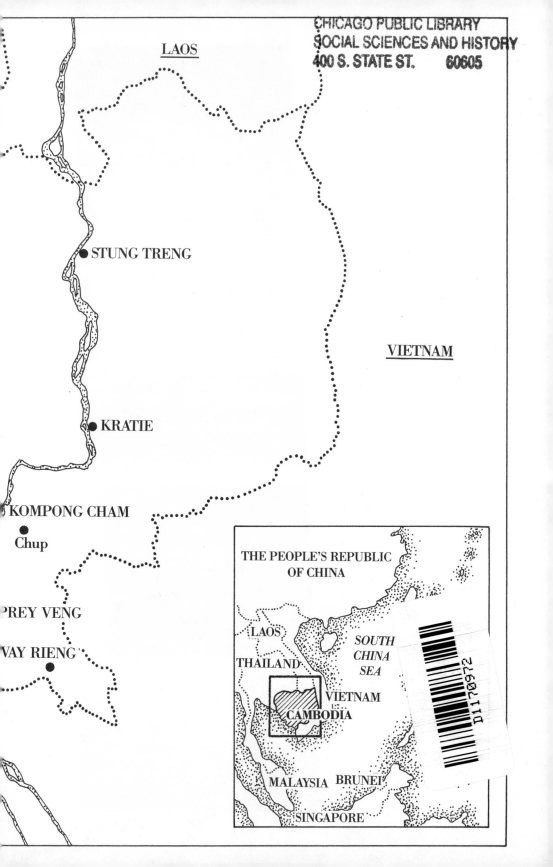

LAOS

● STUNG TRENG

VIETNAM

● KRATIE

KOMPONG CHAM

● Chup

PREY VENG

VAY RIENG ●

THE PEOPLE'S REPUBLIC
OF CHINA

LAOS

THAILAND

SOUTH
CHINA
SEA

VIETNAM
CAMBODIA

MALAYSIA   BRUNEI

SINGAPORE

Sihanouk

Milton Osborne captures vividly the vainglorious personality of the most remarkable political survivor of the post-colonial era.
Professor Michael Leifer, London School of Economics

A steady, penetrating look at one of Asia's most flamboyant and enduring figures.
David Chandler, Monash University

Also by Milton Osborne

BOOKS

The French Presence in Cochinchina and Cambodia: Rule and Response (1859–1905), 1969

Region of Revolt: Focus on Southeast Asia, 1970, revised and expanded edition 1971

Politics and Power in Cambodia: The Sihanouk Years, 1973

River Road to China: The Mekong River Expedition, 1866–1873, 1975

Before Kampuchea: Preludes to Tragedy, 1979

Southeast Asia: An illustrated introductory history, 1979, revised and expanded editions 1983, 1985, 1988, 1990; Japanese edition 1987

RESEARCH MONOGRAPHS

Singapore and Malaysia, 1964

Strategic Hamlets in South Viet-Nam: A Survey and a Comparison, 1965

SIHANOUK

Prince of light, prince of darkness

MILTON OSBORNE

UNIVERSITY OF HAWAII PRESS
HONOLULU

© Milton Osborne 1994
All Rights Reserved

Published in North America by
University of Hawaii Press
2840 Kolowalu Street
Honolulu, Hawaii 96822

Published in Australia by
Allen & Unwin Pty Ltd
9 Atchison Street
St Leonards, NSW 2065

Printed in Singapore

Library of Congress Cataloging-in-Publication Data

Osborne, Milton E.
Sihanouk: prince of light, prince of darkness/Milton E. Osborne.

   p. cm.
  Includes bibliographical references and index.
  ISBN 0–8248–1638–2. —ISBN 0–8248–1639–0 (pbk.)
  1. Norodom Sihanouk, Prince. 1922– . 2. Cambodia—
Kings and rulers—Biography. I. Title.

DS554.83. N6084 1994
959.604'092–dc20
[B]
                                            93–48520
                                            CIP

REF.

Contents

Preface

This book is a critical, unauthorised biography of Norodom
Sihanouk of Cambodia. The account I provide of Sihanouk's life
is critical, both in the technical sense of being concerned with
judgment and in the more everyday sense, since it is my contention
that there has been much in Sihanouk's life that is open to
criticism. The biography is unauthorised and I have made no
approach to Sihanouk for his assistance since I felt that to do so
could compromise my ability to write in the frank terms that I have.

In writing the book I have drawn on a wide range of material,
most particularly the voluminous writings and speeches of the
prince himself. Like any student of modern Cambodian history, I
am particularly indebted to recent publications by David Chandler
and Ben Kiernan. David Chandler's *The Tragedy of Cambodian History,
Politics, War and Revolution since 1945* and *Brother Number One:
A Political Biography of Pol Pot*, and Ben Kiernan's *How Pol Pot Came
to Power* have opened new vistas to all who have an interest in
Cambodia's tragic history. Both in the text and in the endnotes to
the chapters of this book I have endeavoured to make clear when
their ideas have shaped what I have written. My debt to other
authors and sources will be clear from the endnotes and bibliography. I owe the title of the book to the late Donald Lancaster,
whom I first heard describe Sihanouk in Manichean fashion in
1966.

My aim in this book has been to provide an account of
Sihanouk's life, presented, essentially, in chronological form. The
'core' period of Sihanouk's life, the time from the early 1950s until

his overthrow in 1970, was the subject of a book I wrote over twenty years ago: *Politics and Power in Cambodia: The Sihanouk Years.* In this book, I attempt to cover a broader canvas but, as must be the case with any biography, concentration on the man leads to necessary selectivity in the description of the events against which his life has been led. The book is not, therefore, a history of Cambodia during Sihanouk's lifetime. Neither is this book the definitive biography of Sihanouk, for which further archival research and additional interviews with key participants will be essential.

I shall not attempt to list all those with whom, over many years, I have discussed Cambodia and Sihanouk. My own interest in and knowledge of Cambodia began in 1959, when I was posted to Phnom Penh as a member of the Australian foreign service. From that time on, over more than 30 years, dozens of people have been generous with their time and advice as I have sought to extend my knowledge and understanding of a country that has sustained more than its share of tragedy during the twentieth century. My gratitude to all, and most particularly to those Cambodians who have treated me as a friend, is deep and sincere. I must, however, make an exception to offer explicit thanks to David Chandler, who read my manuscript in an earlier version and, as he has always done, offered wise suggestions for improvement. And, at a more personal level, I was able to work on this book in London in 1992–93 in ideal conditions because of Karina Campbell's generosity. Beyond the acknowledgment of my debt to so many, I must, as always, make clear that I alone am responsible for what appears in this book and for the judgments it contains.

Milton Osborne
November 1993

A simplified genealogy of the Cambodian Royal Family
showing Prince Sihanouk's descent

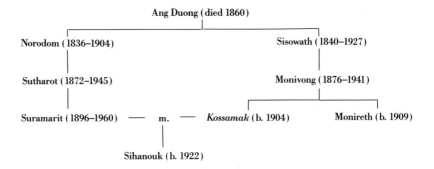

Note: Female figure in italics.

A simplified genealogy of the male descent of the Sisowath
branch of the Cambodian Royal Family

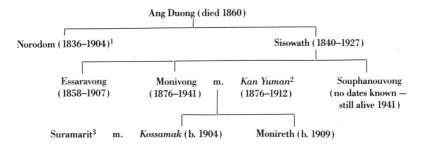

Notes: Female figures are in italics.
1. For details of this branch see next chart.
2. Kan Yuman was a descendant of King Norodom, but details of her exact relationship to that king are unclear.
3. Suramarit was a Norodom prince, a grandson of Norodom I.

A simplified genealogy of the male descent of the Norodom branch of the Cambodian Royal Family

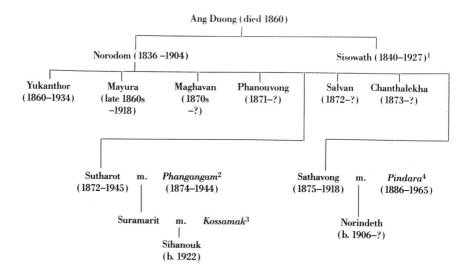

J'ai été, c'est vrai, un chef d'Etat autoritaire, ou plus exactement un mélange de Soekarno d'Indonésie et de Nasser d'Egypte, mais je n'ai jamais concurrencé un Amin Dada d'Ouganda, ni un Macias N'Guema de Guinée équitoriale, encore moins leur maître à tous en cruauté, un Pol Pot du Kampuchea dit 'démocratique'. Je n'ai jamais non plus été ce 'roitelet' insignifiant et farfelu qu'ont dépeint certains journaux français de droite, qui voyaient en moi une sorte de 'roi nègre' . . . à peau jaune.

. . . Je suis un homme, tout simplement, avec ses qualités et ses défauts. Je ne suis ni plus ni moins vertueux que mes frères humains, crées, dit la Genesis, à l'image de Dieu, mais devant assumer l'héritage du péché originel.

It is true that I have been an authoritarian head of state, or more exactly a blend of Sukarno of Indonesia and Nasser of Egypt. But I have never been in the same class as Amin Dada of Uganda or Macias N'Guema of Equitorial Guinea, even less their undisputed master of cruelty, Pol Pot of so-called Democratic Kampuchea. Neither have I been this insignificant and feckless 'little king' depicted by some right-wing French newspapers, which see me as a kind of 'negro king' . . . with yellow skin.

. . . Quite simply, I am a man, with his good points and his bad. I am neither more nor less virtuous than my brother men, created, in the words of 'Genesis', in the image of God, but having to assume the inheritance of original sin.

Norodom Sihanouk, *Souvenirs doux et amers*, p. 23

1

All in one lifetime

In November 1991, after nearly thirteen years in gilded exile, Prince Norodom Sihanouk returned to Cambodia. Sixty-nine years old—70 by Cambodian reckoning—he had lost none of his fabled ebullience, but the passage of years showed in his thinning hair, his pudgy frame and the stress lines on his face. The contrast between the giant idealised portraits erected in Phnom Penh and the reality of his appearance was striking. The portraits showed a prince twenty, even 30 years younger than the old man afflicted by mild diabetes and high blood pressure who had come home, convinced he could play a part in healing the wounds of protracted civil war.

The capital to which Sihanouk returned was sharply different from the one he had left hastily in the early days of January 1979. Then, Sihanouk, his Khmer Rouge 'minders' and a crowd of Chinese diplomats and officials hurriedly flew out of a nearly deserted Phnom Penh just ahead of an invading Vietnamese army bent on overthrowing Pol Pot's tyrannous regime. Nearly four years before, the bulk of Phnom Penh's population had been brutally driven out of the city when the Khmer Rouge came to power in April 1975. After that climactic event, Phnom Penh had been close to a ghost town, peopled by a few thousand Khmer Rouge and those who laboured for them.

The new masters of the city subjected it to selective vandalism, some on an almost incredible scale. The large Roman Catholic cathedral was totally demolished so that where it had stood became an empty grass-covered space, which bore not a trace of the former building. A wing of the National Bank had been blown up, since the bank represented all the evils of urban capitalism against which the Khmer Rouge had fought; for years afterward, banknotes from Lon Nol's defeated Khmer Republic blew about the capital's largely empty streets. But much of the city remained untouched while Pol Pot ruled: the royal palace, the national museum, the central *phnom*, the small hill from which the city took its name, all these were still standing, if neglected.

Now, in late 1991, Sihanouk returned to a city bustling with life, but a very different city nonetheless from that over which he had ruled, under various titles, for nearly 30 of his 69 years. Phnom Penh remained a city of tree-lined boulevards, the royal palace had been refurbished to receive him and the villas built decades before to architectural models from the south of France still stood as incongruous reminders of colonial times. But despite the superficial signs of economic activity, Phnom Penh and Cambodia as a whole were in crisis. The years of war throughout the 1980s, following as they did the massive demographic disruption and death toll of the Pol Pot years, had rendered Cambodia a broken-backed state. The country was unable to feed itself, with barely any exports of its own to sell to the outside world.

Despite superficial signs of economic recovery, Cambodia, and most particularly Phnom Penh, was a mendicant. Corruption had become a way of life for a privileged few who flaunted their wealth as peasants uprooted from the countryside still squatted, whole families to a single room, in some of the former villas of the rich. Basic supplies of water and electricity could barely meet demand. Health services were in chaos and disease was rampant and, because of the widespread use of mines during the protracted civil war, Cambodia had the tragic distinction of having more amputees proportionate to its population than any other country in the world. To all this was added the fact that the country's infrastructure was in ruins. Weary and guilt-ridden by Cambodia's agony, the permanent members of the United Nations Security Council had forced a settlement on the warring parties which had fought throughout the 1980s. Now the international community hoped that Sihanouk would again be able to play a unifying role as he had done, with qualified success, in earlier years.

'Cambodia is Sihanouk' was once a common judgment, and for years it seemed a valid one. Indeed, for all but specialist observers of Cambodian politics in the 1950s and 1960s there seemed no other major figures on the Cambodian political stage. All others were bit players, it appeared. No-one, not even the specialists, paid attention to an obscure leftist school teacher, Saloth Sar, who, under his revolutionary name of Pol Pot, was to wreak such savage vengeance on those aspects of Cambodia he hated and despised. Rather, it was Sihanouk who for decades, whether as king, prime minister or chief of state, symbolised Cambodia and, periodically, captured the international headlines.

That he did so reflected many things, most importantly Sihanouk's deeply held sense of his own indispensability. His mood swings between strident insistence on the correctness of *his* policies and *his* solutions and the readiness to threaten withdrawal from office, or even from the country, when he was opposed, were two sides of the same personality trait. Backed all too often by sycophantic advisers who would not, or dared not, contradict his decisions, Sihanouk in his heyday seemed set endlessly to dominate Cambodian politics both domestically and in the international sphere.

Consider the record. Once he emerged from the chrysalis of French control after the Second World War, he first overcame the democratically inclined politicians who sought to curb his kingly power and then went on to campaign for his country's independence from France. The stuff of legend was beginning to be made: Sihanouk addressing appeals to the international community during flying visits to Montreal, Washington and Tokyo; Sihanouk in self-imposed 'exile', first in Bangkok, then in Siemreap; Sihanouk at the head of a highly publicised, if marginally important, military campaign against rebels in the northwest of Cambodia—his bespoke field boots were to grace the Norodom Sihanouk Museum in Phnom Penh for years to come.

As he threw himself into frenetic political activity, Sihanouk discovered his talent for impassioned rhetoric. He also recognised the importance of the written word for his international audience. From the early 1950s, marathon speeches and an endless stream of articles, bearing his name but frequently written by a stable of French advisers and journalists, became twin trademarks. As a speaker he could grip an audience as he spoke in Khmer, French or English, or a combination of all three. None who saw and heard his performance during the visit to Cambodia by Indonesia's President Sukarno would ever forget the 'double act' of these two

3

charismatic orators. Sukarno spoke in English to an assembled audience of the curiously named Royal Cambodian Socialist Youth. As Sukarno paused between ever more intense denunciations of 'imperialism', Sihanouk translated extemporaneously into Khmer, his voice rising in pitch to match Sukarno's increasing passion. The climax to Sukarno's speech was a ringing eulogy of Sihanouk and his achievements. Glowing with satisfaction but overwhelmed by the excess of flattery, Sihanouk ceased translating and collapsed into the high-pitched giggle that was one of his most distinctive personal characteristics.

By the time of Sukarno's visit in 1959 Sihanouk was a well-known international figure, the prince who had been king and who was the dominant politician in his country. But given the fickle nature of the international press, it seems certain that he would not have received so much attention if his personal, particularly his amatory life had not been so colourful and if his ego had not been so ready to respond either fulsomely or fiercely to praise or criticism.

Yet while Sihanouk's personal life has been colourful in Western terms, it is well to remember that this has not, in itself, been a preoccupation for his compatriots. For most of them, his alliances, both brief and sustained, with many women were not a cause for criticism. To have taken many women to his bed was a sign of the virility for which Cambodian kings were traditionally admired. What did come to worry the official classes of Phnom Penh was the free rein Sihanouk later gave to his most favoured consort, Monique, for the greed she and her family clique displayed in the late 1960s played an essential part in Sihanouk's overthrow in March 1970.

Long before that event the international press, particularly the 'peek and tell' picture magazines in France, had found in Sihanouk a perfect subject for their reportage. Here was a king who played the clarinet and the saxophone and led a band of princes who performed his compositions at *soirées dansantes* that lasted until dawn before the exhausted guests were allowed to slip away. Here was a king who loved women.

Well before Sihanouk demonstrated his readiness to pursue political policies that ran counter to French wishes, he had shown his independence in matters of the heart. Soon after he was placed on the throne in 1941, the French *résident supérieur* in Cambodia, Gautier, pressed him to marry a wealthy commoner. Apparently, Gautier and the governor-general of Indochina, Admiral Decoux, thought that such a marriage would ensure that Sihanouk would follow the subservient model provided by the Vietnamese ruler, Bao Dai, who had married the daughter of a rich southern Vietnamese landowner and showed no inclination to question French control of his country. Whether or not at the time he felt resentment at being urged to act like Bao Dai, Sihanouk has retrospectively made clear his firm dismissal of Bao Dai as a role model. For Sihanouk, Bao Dai has been nothing more than a 'playboy', a term which, when commentators have applied it to the prince himself, has caused him to erupt in terrible rages.

So, contrary to French urgings, Sihanouk pursued his own amatory program. It has been extensive, and not all authorities agree on just how many alliances Sihanouk has contracted over the years. As important as noting the women who have shared his bed is the need to take account of the parts played by some of his children in the shaping of his life, both political and personal. Although he has seldom been close to any of his male children, his affection for some of his daughters has been important. He doted on Kantha Bopha, a daughter who died in the early 1950s and whose death reinforced Sihanouk's determination to devote himself to continuing a political career. His affection for Bopha Devi and Botum Bopha was clearly real: it has lasted with the former and it heightened his passionate dislike of the Khmer Rouge who killed the latter. But of all the factors associated with his personal life, none has been more important than his decision, reached finally in the late 1960s, to opt for a sole relationship with Monique, the daughter of a Franco-Italian father and a Cambodian mother, who captivated Sihanouk when he first saw her in a Phnom Penh beauty contest in 1951.

By the mid-1960s, Sihanouk had held almost unfettered power for more than a decade. In part his apparent political pre-eminence reflected the genuine awe and affection in which he was held within Cambodia, particularly by the peasants in the countryside. Very importantly, too, Sihanouk had been ready until the early 1960s to heed the wise advice given him by his elder advisers. But by 1965 the Cambodian 'oasis of peace', which he constantly proclaimed his country to be, was sliding towards increasing involvement in the war being fought next door in Vietnam. At the same time the first public signs were emerging of leftist political dissent that ultimately climaxed in the Khmer Rouge's coming to power a decade later.

Yet it was at this acutely critical time that Sihanouk embarked on the most bizarre of his passions. Like Kenneth Grahame's Toad, Sihanouk had earlier progressed through a series of 'fads'; amateur dramatics, horse riding, cooking, music and the promotion of sport. Then, no less disastrously than was the case with Toad and his motor cars, Sihanouk embraced the making of 'feature' films. From 1966 until his overthrow in 1970, Sihanouk devoted much of his energy to the production of films, which he scripted, directed and acted in. He also composed the musical scores for some. Artistically they were of an embarrassingly amateurish standard, despite the puffery that surrounded their presentation in Phnom Penh. The films' subject matter was an extraordinary mix of fantasy and the portrayal of human weakness.

But did any of this matter, or should Sihanouk's films be regarded as no more than a foible, an indulgence of the kind allowed Western politicians as was the case with Eisenhower's golf or Reagan's disinclination to master the details of affairs of state?

In Cambodia's case the prince's passion for film-making *did* matter, for it came at a time when the Cambodian state was poised to slide into disaster. The conservative politicians who had seen their interests protected by alliance with Sihanouk were no longer convinced that his policies served those interests. The men and women of the left, after years of being hounded by Sihanouk's security police, were planning a move into full-scale resistance. And peasant discontent with a range of Phnom Penh's policies led to outbreaks of major rural unrest.

As the situation deteriorated, Sihanouk increasingly agonised publicly over the state of the country and the role he should play. His speeches became more and more gloomy until, in April 1967, he made a fateful statement: 'I act according to my conscience which is absolutely clear. Let those who disapprove of me come and take my place or do away with me.' Three years were to pass before his opponents on the right took him at his word, but in the meantime the prince showed himself ready to sanction the use of violence to bolster his position. Still making films, Sihanouk reacted to reports of rebellion and disaffection in the harshest fashion. The politically conscious population in Phnom Penh was not greatly surprised when Sihanouk announced that he had personally called for the mass execution of hill people in northeastern Cambodia who had allied themselves with the growing communist-led insurgency in that region. And they had no doubt that Sihanouk had approved of another harsh order. This was an instruction that resulted in loads of severed heads being brought from Battambang province to Phnom Penh as evidence that the peasant rebellion in the northwest of the kingdom was being suppressed.

Most dramatically of all, Phnom Penh throughout 1967 was abuzz with the news that three of Sihanouk's most outspoken leftist parliamentary critics had disappeared. There was a widespread belief that they had been murdered on his orders. There were many theories about how they had died. The most widely held view was that, after being savagely beaten, they had been buried up to their necks and then had their heads crushed beneath the tracks of a bulldozer. The presumption that this had taken place was given greater force by the fact that it was a modern version of a traditional Cambodian punishment by which criminals and enemies were literally ploughed into the ground. Only six years later did it become clear that these men were still alive.

From late 1967 onwards the pace of decline accelerated. Sihanouk was still in the saddle, but uncertainly, with his feet no longer in the stirrup irons. In March 1970, while he was absent from Cambodia, Sihanouk's right-wing opponents mounted the *coup d'état* that was to usher in the terrible tragedies of the 1970s: the bitter civil war; Sihanouk's becoming first a dupe and then a prisoner of the Khmer Rouge; Cambodia transformed into a country that was part concentration camp and part charnel house.

In the most honest of all his many writings, Sihanouk has revealed the psychological trauma of his years as a prisoner of the Khmer Rouge after Pol Pot came to power, when, never sure whether he would live or die, he watched his brutish guards amusing themselves by torturing monkeys to death outside the house in which he was confined. He did not know what was happening throughout the country as he was held prisoner, nor that five of his children and fourteen grandchildren had become victims of the Pol Pot tyranny.

When Cambodia's liberation came through Vietnam's invasion, Sihanouk still had one more task to perform on behalf of those who had been his captors for nearly three years. Only days after fleeing Phnom Penh, a physically and emotionally exhausted Sihanouk appeared before the United Nations Security Council to denounce the Vietnamese invasion of his country. His appearance before the world body was followed by a dramatic escape from Khmer Rouge control and his subsequent exile in Peking and Pyongyang.

7

Sihanouk was not nor is Cambodia, but for a lifetime he has remained as the principal actor on his country's stage. Others have sought to share that position with him, but their roles have never matched his for longevity. Yet some of those other players deserve more attention than they have usually received and the cast is enormous when one reviews the prince's more than 50 years as a public figure. Son Ngoc Thanh, for instance, was an early campaigner for Cambodian independence in the 1930s. After wartime exile in Japan he was briefly prime minister of Cambodia before the French reasserted control over the kingdom in 1945. His career later included time spent as a law student in France, as a leader of an anti-Sihanouk rebel force along the Thai–Cambodian border and, ultimately, as one of the plotters who overthrew the prince in 1970.

Assorted members of the royal family parade as near-permanent figures in Cambodia's continuing drama. Sihanouk's father, Suramarit, never came to the fore, despite his period as king following Sihanouk's abdication in 1955. But Kossamak, his mother, was always a major influence on him and a powerful figure in her own right. She was venerated by her son, and the suggestion in a Western news magazine that she profited from brothels built on land she owned led to one of Sihanouk's more pyrotechnic displays of rage. Prince Sirik Matak, Sihanouk's cousin, who was once a trusted ally and then became a dedicated political opponent, deserves particular mention as one of the key figures in the 1970 coup. He gained high office immediately afterward, only to be executed in one of the first acts of the Khmer Rouge after they seized power in April 1975. Some of Sihanouk's children played their parts in the long-running drama. Sons such as Naradipo and Ranariddh have moved in and out of their father's favour, but only his daughters seem to have managed to hold his affection for prolonged periods.

For years, until his downfall in 1970, a group of senior advisers was closely associated with Sihanouk. In the 1950s and '60s their names recur in cabinet after cabinet: Penn Nouth, who stood by Sihanouk in good times and bad for more than 30 years; Son Sann, the courtly adviser on economic affairs who fell out with Sihanouk in the late 1960s and who later became the unlikely leader of a resistance group in the 1980s; Nhiek Tioulong, the bluff Sino-Cambodian whose devotion to Sihanouk led to his agreeing to play the part of an ageing roué in Sihanouk's first feature film, *Apsara*; General Lon Nol, the man who commanded Sihanouk's armed forces before overthrowing the prince and then, crippled, militarily incompetent and in thrall to astrologers and mystics, lost the war against the Khmer Rouge; Kou Roun, Sihanouk's sinister minister of the interior who controlled the secret police and ended his career as a night watchman in Paris.

Then there were and are Sihanouk's enemies on the left. With a few exceptions they are shadowy figures. Even after intensive research the most important of them, Pol Pot, is a man whose career is more easily described than his motivations are explained. Perhaps a determination totally to transform a society, even at extraordinary human cost, can be dimly understood by an outsider who does not share the beliefs of those presiding over the transformation. But to understand, let alone empathise with the decisions Pol Pot and his associates took during the years they controlled Cambodia ultimately defies rational analysis. The cost of the Cambodian holocaust was staggering. No-one will ever be sure just how many died between 1975 and 1979, but solid arguments exist for the assessment that between 500 000 and 1 000 000 Cambodians died during those years who would otherwise have lived if the Pol Pot regime had not been in power. Perhaps as many as 200 000 died as the result of executions. After due weight has been given to ideology, fear of Vietnamese invasion and pervasive paranoia, the governance of Cambodia under Pol Pot and his lieutenants is more readily condemned than understood.

The international media briefly paid attention to Pol Pot's lieutenant, Khieu Samphan, when he was beaten by a mob on his return to Phnom Penh in November 1991, but he, like his colleague Ieng Sary, is only dimly remembered by the world at large as a close associate of Pol Pot. Names such as Son Sen and Ta Mok are even less familiar to those without a professional interest in Cambodia. The same is true of Hou Youn and Hu Nim, two prominent leftists of the 1960s who were eventually consumed by the revolution they supported, the latter executed after torture in the gruesome prison slaughterhouse at Toul Sleng in Phnom Penh's suburbs. One of the many paradoxes of modern Cambodian history is that Sihanouk should have been the victim of men who wreaked terrible havoc on their countrymen but who are scarcely known outside the borders of Cambodia. An even greater paradox, not least for Sihanouk, is the fact that he returned to work in tandem with men who were part of the system that killed his children.

Outside Cambodia, the list of foreign leaders who have played a part in Sihanouk's life is extensive and politically eclectic. Some of the relationships that Sihanouk established with foreign leaders played an important part in shaping Cambodia's post–Second World War history. Others have involved more form than substance. The political friendship that developed between Sihanouk and Zhou Enlai, from the 1955 Bandung Conference onwards, was to have long-term consequences, ultimately helping to ensure Sihanouk's survival as a major figure on the international stage. Despite the warm admiration Sihanouk displayed towards Charles de Gaulle, it is far from clear that the French leader ever did much that altered Cambodian political developments one way or another. That said, Sihanouk has always responded warmly to the courtesies accorded him by successive French governments. One of the more puzzling, even bizarre, relationships Sihanouk has maintained over many years is that which he has with the octogenarian and authoritarian North Korean leader, Kim Il-Sung. A more unlikely association it is difficult to imagine.

For every personal international association marked by the trappings of warmth and friendship, there has been another characterised by enmity and despite. After an initial friendly view of Sukarno, Sihanouk and his courtiers came to see him as an ill-behaved boor, whom the prince denounced as a 'scatter-brained old man fond of virgins'. The closer to home Sihanouk came, the more likely it was that foreign leaders would become the object of his criticism or scorn. He could not abide President Ngo Dinh Diem of South Vietnam, while the Laotian king and successive Thai leaders were objects of bitter commentary.

But whether they were friendly or not—with American leaders they were usually the latter—the relationships Sihanouk has had and still has with the political leaders of other countries are a further testimony to the rich diversity of his remarkable life and to his never-ending thirst for recognition as a figure of importance on the world stage.

Yet how much of Sihanouk's career has, in fact, been an illusion, a series of dramatic episodes in which his energy and flamboyance have hidden the fact that he could rarely shape events rather than react to them? A dispassionate view bolsters the conclusion that Sihanouk was only rarely able to choose courses of action rather than trim his sails to winds he could not control. What is remarkable is the extent to which he has made the most of limited opportunities and in so doing remained in power for so long. Even more remarkable is the fact that he has returned to Cambodia to play a final role in his country's politics against all odds.

Through the 1950s and 1960s Sihanouk was the leader of a small country—the size of Oklahoma, with a population of less than 7 million—menaced by much larger neighbours, which in both historical and contemporary terms sought to exercise some degree of domination over Cambodia. Worse, his years as leader of Cambodia coincided with the steady growth of the Second Indochina War. That war and the competing interests of the countries that fought in it accorded little importance to Cambodia's concerns. The manner in which Sihanouk sought to promote those concerns remains one of the most controversial aspects of his career.

An equally controversial issue is his handling of domestic affairs, for long before the final years of his rule, when external difficulties and demands compounded Cambodia's internal problems, there can be no doubt that Sihanouk's actions and his decisions contributed to the political malaise that finally tore Cambodia apart.

Could anyone else have done better? That question will lie behind this book's examination of a richly varied political career, and of a personal life deeply tinged with tragedy and, on more than a few occasions, lightened by manic comedy.

Notes

I visited Phnom Penh in 1981 when it was still possible to see the full effects of the Khmer Rouge's selective vandalism. For a survey of the years in which Sihanouk held power, see my *Politics and Power in Cambodia: The Sihanouk Years*, Melbourne, 1973. A more detailed analytical coverage is provided in David Chandler's recent and valuable *The Tragedy of Cambodian History: Politics, War and Revolution Since 1945*, New Haven, 1991. I witnessed Sukarno's address in Phnom Penh in 1959. Useful, if frequently highly critical commentary on Sihanouk's early life is provided in Charles Meyer's *Derrière le sourire khmer*, Paris, 1971. Chapter 5 in my *Before Kampuchea: Preludes to Tragedy*, Sydney, 1979, deals in detail with Sihanouk's film-making. Sihanouk made his gloomy statement in a speech on 7 April 1967. I was in Phnom Penh in December 1967, when the fate of the three deputies was a matter for fevered discussion among the Cambodian elite. Sihanouk's own account of his years as a prisoner is given in his *Prisonnier des Khmers Rouges*, Paris, 1986. For details of the political figures mentioned, see Chandler, *Tragedy*, Ben Kiernan, *How Pol Pot Came to Power: A History of Cambodian Communism, 1930–1975*, London, 1985, and Osborne, *Politics*. David Chandler's biography of Pol Pot, *Brother Number One: a Political Biography of Pol Pot*, Westview, Colorado, 1992, gives the most detailed, available account of the Khmer Rouge leader's life.

Sihanouk made his critical comment on Sukarno in a radio speech on 26 September 1967. (According to information given to David Chandler by Charles Meyer, Sihanouk's long-time French adviser, the prince's dislike of President Sukarno may have been heightened by the Indonesian leader's expressing a wish to sleep with Sihanouk's consort, Monique.) See, also, Norodom Sihanouk with Bernard Krisher, *Charisma and Leadership: The Human Side of the Great Leaders of the Twentieth Century*, Tokyo, 1990, in which, pp. 34–5, Sihanouk hints at Sukarno's carnal interest in Monique and refers to the Indonesian leader asking the prince's permission to marry his daughter, Bopha Devi.

2

Unexpected king

The throne which Norodom Sihanouk mounted in 1941 had a history that stretched back to the days of the great Angkorian empire, when Cambodian power extended over much of present-day mainland Southeast Asia. But with the abandonment of Angkor in the fifteenth century, Cambodia progressively lost territory to its more vigorous western and eastern neighbours, Thailand and Vietnam. By the end of the eighteenth century there seemed little prospect that Cambodia would survive as an independent state. During the early decades of the nineteenth century it was scarcely that, as Thailand and Vietnam contended for dominance over the pitifully weak Cambodian court, Vietnam gaining the ascendancy in the 1830s.

The memory of this period has remained deeply impressed in Cambodian consciousness, for while the Vietnamese exercised control over the kingdom, ruling for a time through a puppet queen, they sought to transform the country into an approximation of their own. The prerogatives of the royal family were attacked, an attempt was made to substitute the Vietnamese style of provincial administration for the existing Cambodian structure, and Cambodian officials were ordered to dress in the same manner as Vietnamese mandarins. At the same time, large numbers of Cambodian peasants were forced into harsh *corvée* labour as the Vietnamese developed the canal and drainage system in their southern provinces. Finally, as the Vietnamese exercised control over Cambodia they acted against Buddhism, the national religion which commanded the respect of prince and peasant alike. By desecrating pagodas and persecuting monks, the Vietnamese struck at a central element of Cambodian identity.

The harshness of the regime the Vietnamese imposed on Cambodia sparked a major rebellion in 1840, which for a time seemed likely to threaten Vietnam's control. But although the force of the rebellion faded the following year, renewed Thai interest in the affairs of its eastern neighbour spelt an end to the exclusive influence that the Vietnamese court at Hue had been able to exercise over Cambodian affairs. Between 1841 and 1848, Thailand gradually asserted its influence over Cambodia, backing the accession to the throne of its chosen nominee, King Ang Duang. He was the last Cambodian to rule free of direct foreign control until 1953.

Although Cambodian chroniclers and historians have celebrated Ang Duang's rule as a period of high achievement, his actions were still constrained by his dual vassalage to the Thai and Vietnamese courts. His awareness of these constraints led him to make tentative efforts to secure assistance from France to bolster his country's independence. These efforts led eventually to the imposition of a French protectorate over Cambodia in 1863, three years after Duang's death.

By 1863 France had established a firm colonial presence in southern Vietnam (Cochinchina), the base from which it was eventually to gain control of the whole of Indochina. Seen from Saigon, the French regarded Cambodia as a potentially worrisome neighbour. Poorly informed though they were about much in the weak kingdom, the French colonisers knew enough to be aware that Norodom, the man named to be Ang Duang's successor, was a prince who had spent much of his life as a part-guest, part-hostage at the Thai court in Bangkok. The French feared, with some reason, that Norodom saw the king of Thailand as the authority upon whom he must rely to assure his legitimate assumption of the Cambodian throne. But beyond this, and quite without justification, the eager imperialists in Saigon conjured up fantastic theories that cast the Thais in the role of surrogates for France's imperial rivals, the British. The best evidence suggests that far from orchestrating Thai actions to advance their colonial ambitions, British influence at the Thai court was restricted to the presence of an English bandmaster.

Largely in response to French pressure, and still concerned not to anger the Thai king, Norodom grudgingly signed a protectorate treaty with France in August 1863. Under the treaty's terms, Noro-

14

dom ceded control of his country's foreign relations to France in return for French protection of Cambodia, recognition of the king's sovereignty, and a pledge to assist him to maintain order within the kingdom. After one abortive attempt to disengage from the treaty, Norodom accepted its terms and was finally crowned king of Cambodia in June 1864. He was Sihanouk's great-grand-father, a man whom the prince has idealised throughout his life as a great Cambodian patriot.

Norodom was to reign for 40 years and to found the Norodom branch of the Cambodian royal family. Unbiased commentators testified to his lively intelligence and his deep sense of the dignity of kingship. But for most of the French officials who dealt with Norodom throughout his long reign the king was an oriental despot. They deplored his linking of 'the refinements of European comfort to the luxury of Asia . . .

> Filipino bands and Cambodian orchestras;
> Carriages of all sorts and two hundred and fifty elephants, driven and looked after by numerous slaves;
> A flotilla of steam-driven vessels and innumerable boats of all sorts;
> A Filipino bodyguard and a Cambodian bodyguard . . .
> Finally, and to crown everything, a harem made up of four hundred women, which becomes larger each year through the recruitment of young girls carried on in Siam through the intermediary of an Indian, Ibrahim, who is an English subject.

Most of all, the Frenchmen who steadily increased their involve-ment in the administration of Cambodia throughout the nine-teenth century reacted against what they saw as the king's financial profligacy. In particular, they deplored Norodom's determination to try and preserve his prerogatives in relation to the levying of taxes. When, in the 1880s, the French forced Norodom to agree to new arrangements that would lead to the costs of French 'protection' over Cambodia being met by France's taking over control of the collection of taxes on alcohol and opium, they were suddenly confronted by a nationwide rebellion led and supported by the king's provincial officials. Whether Norodom inspired the rebellion, as many French officials believed, remains unproven. Certainly he would have supported its aim of minimising French influence. But in the longer term the rebellion of 1885–86 made the French even more determined to exert control over the details of administration in Cambodia. Most fundamentally, the French concluded that the next Cambodian king would have to be a man unquestionably amenable to their interests.

They had long had a suitable candidate in mind, Norodom's

half-brother, Sisowath. Born in 1840, like Norodom a son of Ang Duang but by a different mother, Sisowath early adopted a Herodian role. When it seemed possible that Norodom would die from illness in 1875, Sisowath assured the most senior French official in Cambodia that if he gained the throne he would be ready to institute whatever reforms the French desired. Time and again in succeeding years Sisowath demonstrated his willingness to work with the French to advance their aims. Yet it was not until 1897 that he was finally given a firm promise that he would succeed Norodom.

The best evidence suggests that Norodom opposed such an outcome, hoping that one of his sons would succeed him. The likelihood of this happening was further diminished by the outspoken anti-French activities of two of those sons, Duong Chacr and Yukanthor, each of whom was sent into exile as punishment. When Norodom died a bitter man, worn out by his losing struggle against French control, Sisowath, the man whom Norodom had many times denounced for being 'two-faced', reaped his reward and mounted the throne in 1904. He was still king when his great-grandson, Norodom Sihanouk, was born eighteen years later.

When Sihanouk was born on 31 October 1922, Cambodia was already marked by a paradox that was to have long-term political consequences. French control of the kingdom had never been stronger, so that in the 1920s and '30s French officials saw no contradiction in describing the Cambodian ruler as an 'absolute monarch' who 'had to submit all his decisions to the representative of the French government' for approval. Yet despite there being no question as to where temporal power lay, the prestige of the Cambodian monarch among the majority of his compatriots was probably higher in the early decades of the twentieth century than it had been for many generations. Given the importance that Sihanouk was later to reap from his kingly status, the nature of this paradox requires explanation.

Largely without thought for the consequences of their actions, the French created conditions during Norodom I's reign that led to his subjects seeing him as embodying the splendour of kingship more grandly than had been possible for his ancestors during much of the long period of secular decline that had characterised Cambodian history after the fall of Angkor. By the closing years of Norodom's reign the king was still seen by most of his countrymen as a near divine being, a status that was reinforced by the wealth of his material possessions grouped in and around his palace in Phnom Penh. The palace itself was a far cry from the wooden buildings that had housed the Cambodian court when the first French visitors came to Cambodia in the 1850s. By the time Sisowath came to the throne in 1904, the palace complex in Phnom Penh consisted of an impressive series of pavilions. More buildings were added during Sisowath's lifetime, including a vast throne hall, and the whole complex was surrounded by a high crenellated wall.

Within the complex and associated with it were some particularly striking and unusual features that owed nothing to the traditionally styled architecture of fantasy. Alongside the royal chapel, the Silver Pagoda, so called because its floor is paved with silver, is an equestrian statue of Norodom. The fact that this statue had once celebrated Napoleon III and then had its head replaced by a representation of Norodom's did not prevent its becoming a votive object for the king and his court. Not far from the Silver Pagoda was another gift from France that, for a period, was Norodom's favourite structure within the palace grounds. This was the reassembled Victorian-baroque villa that had first been erected for the Empress Eugénie's use at the opening of the Suez Canal. The palace, the king's elephants and carriages and later his motor cars, the host of servants, musicians and dancers—all these lent material weight to the symbolic position the king occupied as 'the living incarnation, the august and supreme personification of nationality'.

Superficially, the first two decades of the twentieth century seemed to justify the French claim that their control of Cambodia had restored a decaying kingdom and provided the Cambodian king with all the marks of dignity that his position required. Below the surface appearance of unchanging calm the reality was more complex. The life lived by the king and his officials, the French administrators, and the Chinese merchants who dominated commerce in the capital was sharply different from the lot of the peasants in the countryside. And for the French, as the dominant political force in Cambodia, an awareness of what was happening in the rural regions may well have been declining as the twentieth century progressed. As David Chandler has tellingly pointed out, the provision by 1909 of typewriters to all French officials responsible for provincial administration in Cambodia and the fact that tours of inspection by these officials were increasingly made by car had two linked effects. The preparation of reports for the head-quarters administration in Phnom Penh and Hanoi consumed more and more time and tours of inspection of the provinces became swifter and seldom took in areas that were not served by roads.

That much took place in rural Cambodia that was hidden from the French was underlined by the so-called 1916 Affair. Late in 1915, and increasingly in the early part of 1916, thousands of Cambodian peasants trooped into Phnom Penh to complain to the king about the taxes and *corvées* they were forced to meet. Once heard by the king, the peasants dispersed and returned to their villages. Despite the large number of participants in the protests, there were only isolated instances of violence, none of which was directed against the French.

Two points stand out in any evaluation of the significance of the affair. First, it was to the king rather than the French admin-istration that the peasants brought their complaints, and it was on the urging of the king that the peasants returned to their villages. Despite the protectorate's having been in force for more than five decades, rural Cambodians still saw the king as the source of power within the kingdom. Second, the affair emphasised how little the French administrators in Cambodia knew about what was happen-ing in the rural areas. They had no forewarning of the protests and were never able to pinpoint their immediate cause, let alone connect the events to the actions of particular leaders.

In a period of heightened concern brought on by the war raging in Europe, it was perhaps inevitable that some officials tried to link the affair with the supposed activities of German agents masterminding events from neutral Bangkok. Not even patriotic fervour could sustain acceptance of this wildly improbable propo-sition. While historians are still puzzled by aspects of the 1916 Affair, the fact that it took place alerts us to the difficulty of knowing the true nature of the rural life of the Cambodian peas-antry. What can be said with certainty is that for many peasants their daily existence involved a harsh grind of long physical labour, indebtedness to Chinese rice merchants and the ever-present risk of being robbed or murdered by the bandits who roamed the countryside.

Not only the French knew little of peasant life. Few members of the large royal family knew or cared about events outside the capital. For the most part, the male members of the royal family lived indolent lives, some occupying senior positions in the traditional Cambodian administration or in rare cases becoming officers in the French armed forces. Life for the royal princesses was more constrained. Not until King Sisowath's reign were adult princesses permitted to appear unaccompanied in public. Previously they had been forbidden from marrying a man lower in rank than them-selves, a rule that led to frequent scandals as princesses smuggled 'men of the people', as the French officials called them, into the palace as their lovers.

The lives of the various members of the Cambodian royal family were a source of continuing concern and fascination for the French officials who worked in Cambodia. To a degree that now seems unrealistic, succeeding generations of French administrators wor-ried that one or another prince might be plotting to undermine French control of the kingdom. The explanation for this concern, and for the interest the royal family evoked more generally, needs to take account of a number of factors. At the broadest level, French officials in Indochina were much less assured of the dura-bility of their colonial rule than has usually been recognised. In part their concerns reflected the persistent patterns of resistance that the French encountered in Vietnam, by far the most important of their Indochinese colonial possessions. And although there was no comparable resistance in Cambodia or Laos before the Second World War, there was always a fear in French minds that unrest in Vietnam would spill over into the remainder of Indochina.

In part, too, the almost paranoid French preoccupation with the possibility that their control in Cambodia might be threatened related to the failure of most of them to gain any understanding of the nature of Cambodian society, whether that of the peasantry or of the royal and official classes. French officials were conscious that they had never been able to sheet home responsibility for the rebellion of 1885–86. The sudden emergence of the 1916 Affair remained a mystery to them, just as the murder of *Résident* Bardez in 1925 by an angry group of peasants stunned the French because they had no expectation that violence would occur. When to this sense of unease was added concerns generated by the still-fresh memories of France's huge losses in the First World War, one has a picture of a colonial society in the 1920s and '30s in which apparent confidence was in many ways an illusion.

There was another reason for French preoccupation with the Cambodian royal family. Quite simply, many of those who served France in Indochina were snobs, less-than-convinced supporters of republican ideas and not infrequently anti-Semites. The adminis-trators and their wives revelled in the opportunity to be associated with a royal court, even if it was the court of a 'native' king. The endless correspondence of successive French *résidents supérieurs* in Phnom Penh discussing the merits of various candidates for the throne evinces a fascination with royalty that went beyond the actual political needs of preserving France's position in Cambodia. Yet, when that fact is noted, there was nevertheless a further reason for the attention the officials paid to the royal family. Without doubt, the French decision to place Sisowath on the throne in 1904 rather than one of Norodom's sons did lay the foundations for intra-royal family rivalry that, at least in part, contributed to Sihanouk's being named king in 1941.

Once on the throne, Sisowath made clear his concern that one of his sons should succeed him. In 1906, during a visit to Paris, he advanced the claims of his eldest son, Essaravong, but this prince died the following year. Next Sisowath proposed to the governor-general of Indochina that the succession should eventually pass to Monivong, a son who had attended a French military academy and had been commissioned as a lieutenant in the French Foreign Legion in 1908. The French authorities in Indochina made no promises to the king and Monivong did little to advance his own cause once he returned to Cambodia. Briefly filling various positions in the Cambodian administration, he soon opted to remove himself from Phnom Penh and to live quietly but comfortably in a country villa.

Over the next fifteen years, quantities of ink flowed in discussions between Paris, Phnom Penh and Hanoi on what to do when Sisowath died. Monivong's star waxed and waned. French officials considered him a man 'of very ordinary intelligence'. But he was not suspected of being disloyal, as were some members of the Norodom branch of the royal family. Prince Norodom Yukanthor was still in exile in Bangkok and another Norodom, Mayura, had been exiled to Vietnam in 1913 for presumed readiness to plot the overthrow of French rule. Nevertheless, and despite the French concerns raised by Yukanthor's and Mayura's 'disloyalty', an apparently firm French decision was made in 1916 that Sisowath's successor should be a Norodom. The prince designated was Sutharot, another of Norodom I's sons, who had been born in 1876.

For nearly eleven years Sutharot seemed assured of mounting the Cambodian throne. Yet his accession did not come to pass and the reasons for this remain unclear. That there was a change of heart on the part of two of the most important French officials concerned with the succession is apparent enough from the archival evidence, but what moved them is debatable. In the case of the *résident supérieur* in Cambodia, Baudoin, intriguing but inconclusive evidence exists that an important reason for his change of mind was a payment from Sisowath of a substantial bribe. Whatever the true explanation, with Monivong's accession to the throne in 1927 Sutharot ceased, in French eyes at least, to be a contender for the Cambodian throne. Instead, Sutharot's own son Suramarit now became one of those viewed by the colonial authorities as a possible candidate. For Suramarit this honour was to come much later, in 1955, when he succeeded his son after Sihanouk's abdication. His importance for modern Cambodian history stems less from that later role than from the fact that, in what Sihanouk has called a Romeo and Juliet alliance, he had married a Sisowath princess and that he and Princess Kossamak became Sihanouk's parents in 1922.

Sihanouk has given us a relatively frank account of his childhood, one that is rather less marked by the special pleading frequently found in the autobiographical writings dealing with his later years. He had a lonely upbringing as the only child of increasingly estranged parents. His father emerges from Sihanouk's description of his early years as an amiably dedicated womaniser, kindly enough to his son in a distant fashion, but hardly concerned with his day-to-day development. In his behaviour, Suramarit was probably little different from most Cambodian princes of his generation. Not surprisingly, his son later showed similar inclinations in his dealings with his own male children. Kossamak, Sihanouk's mother, was more interested in her son and became a major influence in his adult life. But in his early years, and in response to the advice of an astrologer, she consigned his upbringing to an aged relative. In turn, the relative entrusted Sihanouk's care to an old female servant—a *nana* Sihanouk calls her in his description of his childhood, a trusted domestic, he suggests, like one of the female house slaves depicted in *Gone with the Wind*. He does not tell us of another aspect of this very early period of his life that some other commentators claim to have been the case: the fact that until he was five his *nana* dressed him as a girl. Whether or not this was so, Sihanouk from his earliest years was involved in a pattern that was to continue throughout his life. He lived in a world in which the word and comforting presence of women was a dominant feature.

Sihanouk commenced his formal education in a Phnom Penh primary school, the Ecole François Baudoin, with French as the medium of instruction. He was, in his own account, a solitary child, younger than many of his classmates but already showing the very real talent for music that he has preserved throughout his life. Estimates of his early academic abilities vary; at least one school contemporary suggested that the grades recorded in his school reports owed as much to a Gallic desire to please as to the reality of his achievements. In addition to Sihanouk's interest in and aptitude for music, he had, even before he entered his teens, developed a love of the cinema. This love or interest—Sihanouk himself has called it a passion—was to continue into the 1960s, when his preoccupation with film making became a political liability. In the 1930s, the young prince's preoccupation with the screen had another and more immediate effect. Concerned with the amount of time the young Sihanouk devoted to attending the cinema in Phnom Penh, his parents decided to enrol him in the *lycée* with the best reputation throughout Indochina, the Lycée Chasseloup-Laubat in Saigon.

In Saigon Sihanouk undertook a classic French secondary school education. At his father's behest, he lodged as a boarder with a French customs official of Indian descent, the relative of an official who worked in the royal palace in Phnom Penh. There is no suggestion that the official and his family were other than kind to their young *pensionnaire,* but equally there is no indication that Sihanouk's Saigon hosts were able to fill the gap of parental love and care that he might have received from a more united family than his own. No deep psychological skill is required to recognise that the combination of estranged parents and relatively early separation from his home heightened Sihanouk's sense of lonely vulnerability. There is an almost pathetic eagerness to Sihanouk's account of his friendships—one senses they were the first he truly had—with two of his fellow students in Saigon. Interestingly, neither of the friends was a Cambodian. Although both came from families resident in Cambodia, one was an ethnic Vietnamese, the other an ethnic Chinese.

Sihanouk did not entirely lose touch with his royal relatives during his time as a *lycéen* in Saigon. Returning to Phnom Penh, he continued to indulge his interest in music, a talent that his father shared. He joined with other princes and princesses in acting in Cambodian-language versions of classic French plays, and was a

Boy Scout under the direction of his mother's brother, his uncle Prince Monireth. He has also noted wryly that he saw King Monivong handling, or failing to handle, affairs of state. The picture he leaves of Monivong is a graphic one. The king, in his 60s, surrounded himself with the women of his household and his many offspring. He took no interest in the details of administration. He signed the papers brought to him for validation without bothering to read them while lying in a hammock. His predecessors, Sihanouk recalls, were nothing more than 'parrots' trained by the French to say 'yes'.

Sihanouk had no sense that the next king to whom papers would be brought for signature would be himself. Nor should he have. As the 1930s drew to a close the French were once again debating who should succeed to the throne. Although other names were considered, the French authorities increasingly directed their attention to the merits of Sihanouk's father, Suramarit, and his uncle, Monireth.

If one picks a path through the incomplete and sometimes contradictory evidence, a relatively clear picture emerges of how it was that neither Suramarit nor Monireth gained the Cambodian throne and how, instead, Sihanouk—to his great surprise—found that he was to be Monivong's successor.

By the mid-1930s, Suramarit was under consideration as a successor to King Monivong. As debate about the desirability of once more having a Norodom on the Cambodian throne continued among senior French officials, Suramarit met this requirement. He had, moreover, shown a greater interest in public affairs in the 1930s than had been the case previously. Those French officials who favoured Monireth's candidacy argued for his worthiness as a French-trained military officer with a reputation for being straightforward, even blunt. In the light of the contending claims put forward on behalf of the two princes, the French minister of the Colonies, Georges Mandel, summoned both of them to Paris so that he could choose between them. Having met them, there is no firm evidence that he made a choice; instead he postponed the decision.

Members of the Sisowath branch of the royal family contest this view, claiming that Mandel did, indeed, assure Monireth that he would succeed his father. Complicating attempts to unravel fact from assertion are various stories based on oral tradition that circulated among the always gossip-ridden royal family and their clients and which were still to be heard in Phnom Penh in the 1960s. Both Norodoms and Sisowaths claimed there had been attempts to bribe French officials and a strong oral tradition persisted that there was a falling out between King Monivong and his son Monireth because of the latter's choice of a wife. (Monireth had married the vivacious and handsome Rosette Poc, the daughter of a senior official, who had previously had been the mistress of a number of Frenchmen.) Whatever truth may be contained in these suggestions—and none can be confirmed by documentary evidence—major political and military events in both France and Indochina were to have a more important bearing on the surprising decision that placed Sihanouk on the throne.

By the time it had become clear that Monivong's death was imminent, France had surrendered to Nazi Germany and the Pétainist regime was established in Vichy. More immediately of concern to French officials in Indochina was the increasing menace to their authority posed by the Japanese. Starting with Vichy's agreement to allow Japanese transit through Indochina and following an arrangement that permitted Japan to station troops in northern Vietnam, the Japanese had further undermined France's colonial position by cooperating with the Thai government to ensure the return to Thai control of two western Cambodian provinces and a part of Laos to which Bangkok laid claim. For Governor-General Decoux, who had embraced the aims of the Vichy regime, protecting French interests in Indochina now became crucial. This fact became the key consideration in the selection of Sihanouk to succeed Monivong when the king died on 23 April 1941.

In his defence of his wartime actions, *A la barre de l'Indochine*, Decoux writes of the reasons of 'high policy' that he took into consideration in supporting Sihanouk's selection for the throne. Although not elaborated further, these words can only be taken to mean the concerns the governor-general had for the maintenance of France's position in Indochina. But what part did other factors play?

Easiest to assess and dismiss as having no major importance is Sihanouk's own suggestion that he gained the throne because Decoux's wife found him charming. That such an encounter might have played a small part in determining Decoux's selection of Sihanouk cannot be totally discounted, but the problems facing Decoux as he sought to preserve French sovereignty over its possessions in Indochina were too great to be seriously affected by his wife's finding Sihanouk *mignon*.

What, then, of the dynastic factor that has been given considerable importance by Cambodian commentators? Was Decoux, who places much weight on this consideration in his apologia for his period as governor-general, being disingenuous? Did he really believe that a prime reason for choosing Sihanouk was to end the rivalry between Norodoms and Sisowaths that had existed since the nineteenth century? After all, Monireth, like Sihanouk, could claim joint descent from the two branches of the royal family, and Suramarit had played his part in reducing rivalry by marrying a Sisowath.

A considered answer would take account of the following points. A concern to have an easily controlled youth on the Cambodian throne, rather than have even the marginal risk of an older man who might stand in the way of the implementation of some French policies, was without doubt the main reason for the choice of Sihanouk. This said, to discount completely the issue of dynastic rivalry would be too simple. The abundant archival evidence that French officials were concerned by the rivalry between the two branches of the Cambodian royal family seems quaint in a late-twentieth-century world. But the existence of that rivalry clearly preoccupied French administrators for many decades. As with all important political events, no single explanation is ever satisfactory, and in the case of Sihanouk's accession to the Cambodian throne the judgment that *realpolitik* was Decoux's main concern does not mean he had no other considerations in mind. To suggest that the extensive correspondence in which he and other officials weighed the merits of possible contenders for the Cambodian throne and the implications of a Norodom rather than a Sisowath succession was a mere charade is not justified. That official French hypocrisy was also present is abundantly apparent from the archival records. In a 'Note' prepared in the Ministry of the Colonies in Paris fourteen days before King Monivong died, an anonymous civil servant offered a gloss on Sihanouk's claims to the throne that mixed an accurate comment on his descent from both the Norodom and Sisowath branches of the royal family with a baldly fabricated account of his parents' supposed marital harmony. 'Prince Sihanouk,' the 'Note' observed, 'is viewed favourably in Cambodian circles and benefits, among both the mass of the people and the elite, from the sympathy inspired by his parents whose family life is particularly appreciated by a nation attached to domestic virtues.'

Nevertheless, whatever the balance of motives in French minds, there can be no doubt that the office of king remained important for members of the Cambodian royal family throughout the first four decades of the twentieth century, and beyond. Exactly what the throne represented to those who sought it is no easy matter to define, particularly for a non-Cambodian. Later in his life, Sihanouk repeatedly stressed the unifying political role of the Cambodian throne. These were surely not the terms in which Sisowath, Monivong or even Sihanouk himself thought of the position of king when they assumed it. Rather, it seems that the members of the royal family viewed the throne as an institution still holding a mystical attraction, the ultimate dignity and honour to which a Cambodian prince might aspire. At the same time, whatever limitations the French had placed on the king's temporal power in the kingdom at large by the beginning of the 1940s, his power within the closed world of the court remained of great importance: favourites could be promoted and largesse distributed. In these circumstances it should be no surprise that there was competition for the throne and that this competition was given added vigour by the dynastic rivalries within a factious and sprawling royal family.

When, following Monivong's death and Sihanouk's selection as his successor, Monireth received the news that he had been passed over, he was, Decoux records, 'notably discontent'. As for Sihanouk, he has said that 'My first reaction was of fear, of fright: I broke down in tears'. Five months later, at the time of his coronation in September 1941, Sihanouk's apprehension at the role he now confronted was captured in the official photograph of the young king in his full kingly regalia. Staring fixedly at the camera, his face is doleful as he faces the future. Perhaps he was reflecting on the conclusion reached by the court astrologers when he was elevated to the throne: that his would be a glorious reign but that in the end this would avail him nothing.

Notes

The best general introduction to Cambodian history is David Chandler's valuable *A History of Cambodia*, Boulder, Colorado, 1983, 2nd edition, 1992. Detailed coverage of King Norodom I's reign is contained in my own study of that period, *The French Presence in Cochinchina and Cambodia: Rule and Response (1859–1905)*, Ithaca, N.Y., 1969. Sisowath's reign is examined in Alain

Forest, *Le Cambodge et la colonisation française: Histoire d'une colonisation sans heurts (1897–1920)*, Paris, 1980. The critical description of Norodom's court on p. 15 was made by the governor of Cochinchina, Le Myre de Vilers, in 1882 in a dispatch to the minister of the Colonies.

Sihanouk's most detailed account of his childhood is contained in *L'Indochine vue de Pékin: entretiens avec Jean Lacouture*, Paris, 1972 and in his later *Souvenirs amers et doux*, Paris, 1981. There is also interesting material provided in Charles Meyer, *Derrière le sourire khmer*, Paris, 1971; Meyer worked for Sihanouk for fifteen years and his book provides many useful if sometimes bitter insights. The labyrinthine course of shifting French positions on who should succeed Sisowath and then Monivong is traced in my article 'King-making in Cambodia: From Sisowath to Sihanouk', *Journal of Southeast Asian Studies*, IV, 2, September 1973. The 1916 Affair is examined in my article, 'Peasant politics in Cambodia: The 1916 Affair', *Modern Asian Studies*, 12, 2, April 1978. The assassination of *Résident* Bardez is discussed in David Chandler, 'The assassination of *Résident* Bardez (1925): A premonition of revolt in colonial Cambodia', *Journal of the Siam Society*, 70 (1982). For a sympathetic French account of Cambodia in the early decades of the twentieth century, see A. Pannetier, *Notes cambodgiennes: au coeur du pays Khmer*, Paris, 1921. Admiral Decoux's account of his period as governor-general of Indochina, *A la barre de l'Indochine*, was published in Paris in 1949. Sihanouk gives his own account of his succession in *Souvenirs*, pp. 69–72.

For information about the inner world of the Cambodian royal family, and in particular about Sihanouk's early life, I remain indebted to four informants, all now dead: Prince Sisowath Entaravong, who vanished after being driven out of Phnom Penh by the Khmer Rouge in 1975; Bishop Paulus Tep Im Sotha, who was executed by the Khmer Rouge in May 1975; Donald Lancaster, who served as Sihanouk's English-language secretary during the 1960s; and Bernard-Philippe Groslier, the longtime *conservateur* of the Angkor temple complex and the fourth generation member of his family to work in Indochina.

3

Maréchal, nous voilà

In his highly personalised account of the early years of his reign, Sihanouk tells of the evil omen that marked his coronation. The great candle of victory made of precious beeswax that had been lit by the court brahmins as part of the coronation ritual was blown out by the November winds two days later. Terrified for the implications, the priests tried to hide this disturbing news from all but the young king's mother, but the story of what had happened quickly spread, arousing popular concern for the future course of Sihanouk's reign. Whatever the supposed link between omens and the actual course of events, there were enough undisputed facts to make the small politically aware Cambodian elite apprehensive about the future when Sihanouk mounted the throne. France had been defeated in Europe and Japan was, by the time of Sihanouk's coronation in November 1941, the ultimate power throughout Indochina, despite the French administration's remaining in place. Yet more potentially threatening to Sihanouk's position, in the longer term, was the presence in Phnom Penh of a small but influential group of young Cambodians who can justly be described as the country's first modern nationalists.

The most prominent of these young and then essentially moderate men was Son Ngoc Thanh, who has been the object of some of Sihanouk's most bitter commentary over the decades in his various accounts of his life. As is so often the case with Sihanouk's versions of the past, closer examination of the historical record indicates a more complex picture than his own self-interested record of events. Without question, Son Ngoc Thanh and his close associates, Pach Chhoeun and Sim Var, represented the first stirrings of modern nationalism in Cambodia. They had come together at the Buddhist Institute in Phnom Penh. This institution had been founded by the French in 1930 with the patronage of the Cambodian and Laotian kings in an effort to counter what was seen as the excessive influence of the Thai Buddhist establishment over its much smaller neighbours. Thanh came to the institute in 1933. Born in southern Vietnam (Cochinchina), Son Ngoc Thanh was one of several individuals from Kampuchea Krom, or lower Cambodia, who were to play prominent roles throughout Sihanouk's tenure of power. Thanh's father was an ethnic Cambodian; his mother has been variously described as Vietnamese or Sino-Vietnamese. Since his parents were moderately prosperous, Thanh had the rare advantage for an ethnic Cambodian in the 1920s and '30s of experiencing education in France. Employed as a librarian at the Buddhist Institute, Thanh was in a position to be aware of both the degree of Buddhist alienation from French educational programs, which sought to limit the traditionally important role of the monastery schools, and the extent to which a small but growing number of his compatriots felt aggrieved at being subjected to French rule. To publicise his views and those of the men with whom he was now associated, Thanh in 1936 founded a Cambodian-language newspaper called *Nagaravatta* (Angkor Wat).

The publication of this newspaper involved one of the historical ironies that are such a frequent part of Sihanouk's life, for the member of the royal family who agreed to become the paper's patron was his father, Prince Suramarit. The editors had first turned to Sihanouk's bluff, no-nonsense uncle, Prince Monireth, for patronage, but he, in a manner strikingly reminiscent of the Duke of Wellington's views on railways, refused, since he thought improving the education of Cambodians would 'make them more difficult to govern'. Suramarit had no such hesitation and Sihanouk says that, as a teenager, he often saw Thanh and his associates in his father's company. But, he adds in speaking of this time, he was himself barely 'politicised'.

Just how 'politicised' Sihanouk's father was at this time is also an open question. An intelligent if rather lazy man, he seems to have sympathised with the basically moderate views that were explored in *Nagaravatta*. While the editors of the newspaper argued for 'Cambodia for the Cambodians' and called on their countrymen to 'awake' to the challenge posed by the Chinese and Vietnamese domination of commerce in the country, they did not

29

advocate violence to achieve their aims. Not until after Sihanouk's accession to the throne in 1941 and the clear indication by 1942 that Japan was the ultimate power in Indochina did the tone of *Nagaravatta* change and its editors come to contemplate more militant ways to advance their cause. By that time, Sihanouk, in his own words, had resigned himself to 'acting the role of "playboy" '.

From the time he was named king in September 1941 until the Japanese *coup de force* in 1945 that temporarily eliminated French control over Indochina, the essential feature of Sihanouk's life was his readiness to play the part the French planned for him. For more than three years he was subservient to the French in all the public issues that counted. His unreadiness to accept French control over his private life was another matter. So it is necessary to treat with some scepticism Sihanouk's retrospective account of the political significance of some of his experiences between late 1941 and early 1945 when, he argues, he came to know his country and its people well and, finally, became ready to confront both the French and the Japanese on behalf of his compatriots. There is, indeed, a sharp contrast, in Sihanouk's own fairly lengthy description of these years given to Jean Lacouture in 1971, between his barely suppressed relish at having devoted his time to the pursuits of 'horse riding, the cinema, the theatre, water skiing, basket ball, without speaking of my amorous adventures', and his account of his political awakening. While the truth may well lie somewhere in between, one of the most evocative images Sihanouk has given of the war years is of his attending Sunday football matches in the Phnom Penh stadium. Before the match began, the Cambodian crowd was required to chant the Pétainist slogan, '*Maréchal, nous voilà,*' (Marshal, we are with you). Sihanouk was excused from actually shouting the slogan himself, he tells us, but he had to stand to attention with the rest of the spectators as the ceremony took place.

A measured assessment of Sihanouk's life during the war years needs to balance his subservience to the French against the opportunities they gave him to have more contact with his countrymen than any other Cambodian ruler had ever enjoyed. The motives of the French in encouraging Sihanouk's exposure to the Cambodian population were self-serving, but in pursuit of their own interests they further reinforced the symbolic importance of the Cambodian monarchy, a fact that Sihanouk used to his great advantage in his subsequent political career. The French efforts to bolster their position in Cambodia through association with the young king reflected their increasingly desperate need to disguise their own weakness. They knew they were dependent on the Japanese and this became more and more evident as the war dragged on. What was true throughout the French colonial possessions in Indochina was given particular point in Cambodia by the events of 20 July 1942.

In the months that had followed Governor-General Decoux's September 1941 decision to allow the Japanese to maintain a military presence in Indochina, Son Ngoc Thanh and his associates had taken note of the changed political circumstances in which they were living. How far they were encouraged to contemplate action against continuing French rule by the Japanese secret police, the *Kempe Tai*, is unresolved. Certainly Sihanouk, who has consistently chosen to minimise the importance of what took place in July 1942, has sought to emphasise a link between Thanh and the Japanese military. Son Ngoc Thanh, he has claimed, was to be seen wearing a Japanese military uniform as early as 1941 and when a major demonstration against the French took place in Phnom Penh on 20 July Thanh, Sihanouk asserts, was hiding in the *Kempe Tai* headquarters.

The catalyst of this demonstration was the arrest earlier in July by the French authorities of two Cambodian monks who had attacked French rule in their sermons and distributed anti-French pamphlets among the laity. The French had acted firmly but clumsily, since to arrest the monks while they were still members of the Buddhist clergy was an act of sacrilege in the eyes of all Cambodians, and most particularly in the eyes of their fellow monks. Son Ngoc Thanh and Pach Chhoeun saw the arrests as an opportunity to rouse the population against the French. If previously their aim had been to reduce French political control in favour of some ill-defined greater degree of Cambodian participation in the administration of the country, they now appeared to believe that they could dictate how the French should behave. On 20 July Pach Chhoeun led a crowd of some thousand Cambodians, roughly half monks and half laity, to the French administrative headquarters in Phnom Penh. Watched by thousands along the route of their demonstration and at the *résidence supérieure*, Pach Chhoeun and those accompanying him presented a petition calling for the immediate release of the two arrested monks. When the French officials they were confronting refused, the demonstrators led by Pach Chhoen broke into the *résidence supérieure*, attacking French officials and smashing furniture.

Although no-one was killed in the demonstration, the French saw it as a savage affront to their dignity. They arrested Pach Chhoen and exiled him to the prison island of Poulo Condore (modern Con Son) off the southern Vietnamese coast. Interestingly, Son Ngoc Thanh did not take part in the demonstration, although it is not certain, as Sihanouk has claimed, that he was waiting in the safety of the *Kempe Tai* headquarters. Whatever the degree of his involvement—and he later protested forcefully that he was not associated with the events—he found it desirable to go into hiding, first in Phnom Penh and then in Battambang in northwestern Cambodia, at that time a region administered by Thailand. From there he sought Japanese agreement to his living in Tokyo. After spending some months in the Japanese embassy in Bangkok he was given permission to travel to Japan, where he remained for the next two and half years.

Controversy still surrounds the July 1942 demonstration, and many who have described the events have done so in ideological terms. Of all the approaches taken to the affair, Prince Sihanouk's readiness to gloss over its importance is probably the most interesting. Since Son Ngoc Thanh was to become the prince's most bitterly denounced enemy, it is perhaps not surprising that Sihanouk has chosen to emphasise his own role during 1945, when he proclaimed Cambodia's short-lived independence, rather than to give any credit to those who agitated against the French in 1942. Yet while it may still be distasteful for Sihanouk to contemplate, the July 1942 demonstration *was* important, the first major demonstration of popular discontent with French rule in Cambodia since the 1916 affair. Not only did the event represent the emergence of modern Cambodian nationalism, it set the tone for an element within that nationalism that was to dog Sihanouk for the rest of his political life. For Son Ngoc Thanh and Pach Chhoen came to be seen by many Cambodians as representing not only nationalism, but just as importantly an alternative, non-royal focus for nationalist leadership. This strain in Cambodian politics was often submerged in the years that followed and as Sihanouk rose to political dominance, but its survival, still involving Son Ngoc Thanh, was to bring the Prince down nearly 30 years later.

With Pach Chhoen incarcerated in Poulo Condore and Son Ngoc Thanh in exile in Japan, an uneasy calm returned to Cambodia. It was now that the French administration embarked on a determined campaign to gain the maximum advantage by associating itself with the young King Sihanouk. To this end French officials arranged for Sihanouk to travel widely throughout Cambodia, including, as Sihanouk proudly recounts, 'on elephant back from the Tonle Sap to Koh Kong'. Although characterising himself as a 'miserable orator' at the time, Sihanouk made dozens of speeches to the French-sponsored Cambodian Youth Corps, an organisation modelled on similar youth groups in Vichy France. The benefit to the French was obvious: they were able to identify their administration with the monarch for whom the bulk of the Cambodian population still had the deepest reverence. Should we believe Sihanouk when he states that his travels gave him an understanding of his people's needs and interests, including their resentment of the demands placed on them by the Vichy-dominated colonial regime? The best answer is probably a heavily qualified 'yes'. Sihanouk heard what the peasants told him and on at least two occasions, by his own account, he took their complaints to the formidable *Résident Supérieur* Gautier.

Among the demands placed on Cambodia's rural population by the French administration during the war was the requirement that, beyond conserving an absolute minimum for their own use, the peasantry had to sell all of the fish oil they produced to the government. Equally, they had to sell their entire production of kapok to the administration so it could be exported to Japan. Sihanouk's protests against these measures were of no avail. Equally unavailing were his protests against continuing efforts by the French to promote the romanisation of the Cambodian writing system and the substitution of the Gregorian calendar for the traditional Cambodian calendar, in which the New Year begins in April.

In many ways the French attempts to make these cultural changes represented a more serious issue of dispute than the requirements for forced delivery of fish oil and kapok, for in both cases their aims struck at two of the deepest elements of traditional Cambodian culture. Gautier's wish to see the romanisation of the Cambodian writing system was not a new French goal. It had been suggested before as part of a planned revamp of the traditional education system, in which most education at the primary level was provided in monastery schools. The monks deeply resented any suggestion that they should lose their privileged position as the guardians of education. Equally strongly resisted was the suggestion that Cambodia's calendar should be changed, for the calendar determined when the kingdom's festivals, both great and small, should take place.

Sihanouk's account of his protests against these proposed changes are quite believable, including his claim that, in relation to the romanisation issue, he thought seriously of abdicating. He was dissuaded from doing so by his parents, who reminded him of past French readiness to exile fractious members of the royal family who had opposed the colonial power. Moreover, his father argued, he would have opportunities later in his reign to impose his will on the government of the country. Nevertheless, it is hard to believe that his concerns over these issues of state were a dominant part of his life any more than that his visits to meet the other sovereigns of Indochina—Bao Dai in Hue and King Sisavang Vong in Luang Prabang—were more than a necessary task to be undertaken before returning to his real preoccupation, the pursuit of pleasure.

Ranking first among Sihanouk's pleasures were women. Rejecting the urgings of the French that he follow Bao Dai's example and marry a solid *bourgeoise*, he readily found distraction within his own court. He has described himself in the early years of his reign as a *chaud lapin*, French slang that is probably best rendered in English as 'randy as a rabbit'. Charles Meyer, Sihanouk's longtime French adviser, provides a catalogue of the women who have borne Sihanouk's acknowledged children. The first was a commoner, Moneang Kanhol, who was mother to Princess Bopha Devi (born 1943) and then Prince Ranariddh (1944). Bopha Devi later became the star of the royal classical ballet. Ranariddh studied law in France and taught at the university in Aix-en-Provence before reluctantly joining the anti-Vietnamese resistance in the 1980s. Next was Princess Monikessan, who as a member of the frequently intermarried Cambodian royal family was Sihanouk's aunt. She became the mother of Naradipo (1946), whom Sihanouk was later to name as his successor. Another princess and aunt, Pongsanmoni, became the mother of four of Sihanouk's sons, Yuvanath (1943), Ravivong (1944), Chakrapong (1945) and Khemnurakh (1949). Their daughters were Soriyaraingsey (1947) and Botum Bopha (1951). A Laotian woman, Mam Manivann, was mother to another two daughters, Sucheatvateya (1953) and Arunrasmey (1955). But the most enduring of Sihanouk's relationships has been the one with Monique Izzi, the Eurasian beauty who bore him two sons, Sihamoni (1953) and Narindarapong (1954). None of these women ranked as official consorts under traditional Cambodian law. This title was reserved for Princess Thavet Norleak, a cousin of Sihanouk who was largely hidden from public view throughout his years in power and who bore him no children.

This catalogue of consorts and children is far from complete. The important point once again is that Sihanouk's rabbit-like behaviour was not in itself a cause for criticism by his compatriots, most certainly not in his early years on the Cambodian throne. His own comment that it was better to have had a private life marked by a degree of 'excess' than to have been 'a pederast or impotent' seems curiously defensive and pitched towards a Western audience. By the standards of his royal predecessors, Sihanouk's enthusiasm for women has been restrained. His great-grandfather, Norodom I, maintained a female establishment that numbered in the hundreds, though not all of these women shared his bed. Monivong, Sihanouk's immediate predecessor, was said to have had 60 wives. The fact of royal polygamy has never troubled Cambodians. As the source of all power within the kingdom, the king was expected to ensure his succession and to demonstrate his virility as a metaphor for the mystic forces which ensured the power and prosperity of the kingdom and which he alone controlled. Only when Sihanouk's amatory life became entangled with politics, as happened many years later, would whom he took to his bed become important.

Given his own professed lack of interest in affairs of state and his commitment to pursuing a life of personal indulgence, it is somewhat surprising that Sihanouk early placed his stamp on the management of the internal world of the royal palace. It is unclear to what extent this reflected his own wishes or was urged upon him by the French advisers who now clustered about him as he hesitantly began to perform his duties as king. But whatever the cause, the young king set about clearing the palace of the seemingly innumerable members of the royal family and their servants and retainers who had turned its buildings and grounds into something resembling a vast transit camp. On his orders the provision of opium to members of the royal family and to some senior officials was terminated, so ending a practice which the French had encouraged from the time of Norodom I onwards. Even if Sihanouk acted in part in response to advice, a concern with overseeing the functioning of the palaces in which he lived, and in particular the services provided for the guests who stayed in them, remained an almost obsessional aspect of his character throughout his later career.

Sihanouk's readiness to cooperate with the French administration while playing his part in the cycle of ceremonies prescribed for a Cambodian monarch partially disguised the extent to which resentment of the French continued to simmer among elements of the Cambodian population. Putting a number on those who felt this resentment is impossible, and the degree of resentment and its causes varied from group to group. Most clearly, members of the Buddhist *sangha* continued to harbour bitter feelings against the French for the arrests that had taken place in 1942. And this bitterness was made sharper when one of the first two monks arrested, named Chieu, died in captivity. Additionally, ignoring Sihanouk's protests and well aware of the opposition from the Buddhist clergy, *Résident Supérieur* Gautier in 1943 and 1944 proclaimed regulations that required the use of romanised script to render the Cambodian language in official documents and the introduction of the Gregorian calendar.

Other groups chafing at the nature of French rule are less easy to identify. The French requirement for forced deliveries of fish oil and kapok would have left a generalised resentment in much of the countryside. But, most importantly, by the time Sihanouk came to the throne there was a growing pool of Cambodians whose education, in a range of institutions, left them unready to contemplate an unchanging relationship with the colonial power. While the level of formal education achieved in Cambodia before the Second World War was extraordinarily low—an often quoted and telling statistic is that by 1939 only four Cambodians had completed their education to *baccalauréat* level within Cambodia—some had gone on to higher education in France and a larger number had attended technical and professional courses in Hanoi.

In addition, there was, by the early 1940s, a group of Cambodians working for the French or in the Cambodian administration who had trained at the School of Administration in Phnom Penh. Established by an ordinance in 1917, the school did not function properly until 1922. Those who passed through its courses were far from radicals but their training and their experience, even given the limited responsibility the French allowed them, made them an important source from which new political parties could draw members when the end of the war transformed the relationship between the French and the Cambodians they administered. In the years immediately before that change, these middle-level civil servants formed yet another group that was slowly coming to question the colonial status quo.

Pretending that such a status quo existed became increasingly difficult for the French in Indochina as the Pacific War entered its final year. The Allied reconquest of Europe, with the liberation of France in August–September 1944, meant that Governor-General Decoux and those in the French administration throughout Indochina who shared his outlook could no longer justify their support of the Vichy regime.

Even more important, by the end of 1944 the tide of the war in the Pacific was inexorably turning in the Allies' favour. As a result of General MacArthur's strategy of 'island hopping' and leaving land attacks on the Japanese in much of mainland Southeast Asia for the final phases of his planned campaign, Allied air forces were able to carry out bombing raids against Japan and occupied Southeast Asia by early 1945. Phnom Penh sustained such a raid in February 1945. The Allied air campaign also contributed to a growing natural disaster that further undermined the tattered 'legitimacy' of the French administration in Indochina. Because of the Allied blockade of shipping leaving southern Vietnam at the end of 1944, a terrible famine began to grip the northern areas of that country as a combination of crop failure and grievous flooding led to the death of many thousands of peasants.

Amid this combination of prospective defeat of the Japanese and General de Gaulle's proclaimed intention to join the Allied campaign in the Pacific, some French civil and military officials in Indochina began to reassess their position. So too did the Japanese military command in Indochina. Aware of the changing mood of some in the French community and imbued with a determination to maintain their grip on Indochina, despite the signs that the war was being lost, the Japanese struck on 9 March 1945. In a brief and largely bloodless *coup de force* they disarmed the French military and interned them and the French civilian officials. Four days later Sihanouk, acting under Japanese tutelage, proclaimed the emergence of his country from French 'protection' as the independent state of Kampuchea.

How prepared was Sihanouk for the role he was now required to play as ruler of a country no longer linked to France, and who were the other actors who emerged into prominence following the dramatic change in Cambodia's fortunes that has been aptly described by Philippe Preschez as an 'electric shock'?

The short answer is that Sihanouk was ill-prepared indeed. The nearly four years that had passed since he was designated king had brought no notable development of political maturity and the knowledgeable, if critical, long-time adviser Charles Meyer is not alone in arguing that some years were still to pass before Sihanouk seriously engaged himself in affairs of state rather than making the pursuit of pleasure his dominant concern. Certainly, the evidence is overwhelming that after the Japanese *coup de force* Sihanouk was content to rely on the largely conservative advice of men such as his uncle Prince Monireth or Khim Tit, a provincial governor who was to join the cast of politicians whose names repeatedly featured in the revolving door cabinets of the 1940s and '50s.

Yet if he was ill-prepared to participate in the critical political decisions that now had to be made by Cambodians, Sihanouk's four years as king had already had an important and lasting effect on his personality. Unless account is taken of this, any study of the prince will fail to understand adequately the ebb and flow of Sihanouk's emotions and his almost pathological inability to accept criticism. The point is simple but frequently overlooked. Whatever restraints the French were able to exercise over Sihanouk during the early years of his reign, he was nevertheless the King of Cambodia and within the palace his word was law. Custom and practice might qualify his theoretically absolutist position, but in terms of the deference he was afforded and the efforts made to satisfy his whims Sihanouk enjoyed privilege and position far removed from the experience of any other person in the kingdom. His kingly status carried with it an assumption that he should not be gainsaid and that, at least in theory, he would know what was best for his country in all matters great and small.

For the moment, however, presumptions about kingly rights were subordinated to the political necessity of deciding how to act in the radically different circumstances that now applied in Cambodia. Sihanouk was content to leave the day-to-day running of the kingdom in the hands of a largely undistinguished group of officials who were constituted as a cabinet and who reported to the Japanese. Apparently attracted to the idea of Cambodia's regaining its independence at the time of the *coup de force,* Sihanouk's most significant political decision was to ask the Japanese to permit Son Ngoc Thanh to return to Cambodia from his exile in Japan. Given the later bitter enmity between Sihanouk and Thanh, the irony of his request needs no emphasis, not least since Sihanouk and Thanh were at odds before the end of 1945. David Chandler could well be right in suggesting that Sihanouk may have acted as he did because of urgings from his father, Suramarit, who had been on friendly terms with Thanh during the 1930s. Whatever the explanation, Thanh returned to Cambodia in May 1945 and in doing so began his long career of opposition to Sihanouk.

Throughout these momentous developments no part was played by the man who was to become the embodiment of all that was evil and tragic in Cambodia's modern history. In 1945 Saloth Sar, who later became known by his revolutionary name of Pol Pot, was a seventeen-year-old high school student in Kompong Cham, a major provincial town northeast of Phnom Penh on the banks of the Mekong River. It is scarcely likely that Sihanouk knew him, but ironically, not at all impossible that he should have seen the future Khmer Rouge leader in his early childhood. For, as important research by Ben Kiernan and others has shown, unlikely though it may seem in terms of his later career, Saloth Sar had a range of royal connections and had lived close to the palace in Phnom Penh.

The future Pol Pot came from a family of relatively prosperous peasants who farmed land near the central Cambodian town of Kompong Thom, a major stopping place on the road linking Phnom Penh to the provincial centre of Siemreap, near the Angkor ruins. Sar's connection with the royal family stemmed from an older female cousin's recruitment into the royal ballet in the 1920s, a move that was followed by her becoming one of Prince, later King Monivong's secondary wives. The connections became closer when Sar's elder brother went to work in the palace; he was followed by Sar's sister, who, like their cousin, first joined the royal ballet and then became another of Monivong's many minor wives.

At the age of six Saloth Sar was sent to join his relatives in Phnom Penh. Shortly after arriving in the capital he spent a year as a novice in a Buddhist pagoda, but he then returned to live with his sister, brother and cousin in a house close to the palace. During the day he attended a Catholic-run primary school, the Ecole Miche. David Chandler, his biographer, has painted a convincing portrait of the young Sar watching in the wings as his sister and cousin played their part in the slow, stylised movements that are the essence of classical Cambodian ballet. He asks whether this experience might have shaped the young child's mind, with the grace of the dancers becoming a metaphor for the image of smooth, unruffled competence that the later Pol Pot sought to present to his followers.

There can be no answer to such an intriguing suggestion. What we do know is that in 1942 Sar moved to Kompong Cham to enter a newly established high school, the Collège Norodom Sihanouk. He was still there, along with three other prominent radical leftists

of the 1960s and '70s—Hu Nim, Hou Youn and Khieu Samphan—
when the Japanese carried out their coup.

Notes

For surveys covering this period, see Chandler, *Tragedy* and *Brother Number
One*; Kiernan, *How Pol Pot Came to Power: A History of Communism in Kampuchea,
1930–1975*; V.M. Reddi, *A History of the Cambodian Independence Movement*,
Tripurti, 1971; Meyer, *Derrière;* and Osborne, *Politics and Power.* Other useful
material may be found in Philippe Preschez, *Essai sur la démocratie au
Cambodge*, Paris 1961, and R.M. Smith, 'Cambodia' in G.McT. Kahin, ed.,
Governments and Politics in Southeast Asia, Ithaca, N.Y., 1964, and *Cambodia's
Foreign Policy*, Ithaca, N.Y., 1965.

Sihanouk's own commentaries on the events early in his reign are
contained in *L'Indochine vue de Pékin* and his later autobiographical work,
Souvenirs doux et amers. Sihanouk's articles originally published in the weekly
semi-official newspaper, *Réalités Cambodgiennes* from 13 September 1958 to
3 January 1959 and later republished as *L'Action de S.M. Norodom Sihanouk
pour l'indépendance du Cambodge 1941–1955*, Phnom Penh, 1959, also deal with
this period.

My own understanding of the events discussed in this chapter reflect
interviews with a number of Cambodian and French informants over a period
of years, in particular during my residence in Cambodia in 1966.

On Son Ngoc Thanh, in addition to valuable material contained in
Kiernan, *How Pol Pot* and Chandler, *Tragedy*, which draw on Thanh's private
papers, there is a dated and brief biography by P. Christian, 'Son Ngoc
Thanh', in *Indochine Sud-Est Asiatique*, October, 1952, pp. 48–9. I also benefited from information given to me by Thanh's brother, Son Thai Nguyen,
when I interviewed him in Saigon in January 1971.

The quote from Prince Monireth is drawn from Chandler, *Brother Number
One*, p. 16.

Sihanouk's quote on his role as a 'playboy' comes from *L'Indochine vue
de Pékin*, p. 33. His list of diversions is given in the same book on pp. 33–4;
his account of standing for the chant of loyalty to Pétain is on p. 33.

Sihanouk glosses over the events of July 1942 in *L'Indochine vue de Pékin*
and does not mention them in *L'Action de S.M. Norodom Sihanouk.* Most
western accounts are in general agreement about the events on that day if
not about their appropriate interpretation. See C. Fillieux, *Merveilleux
Cambodge*, Paris, 1962, and Wilfred Burchett, *Mekong Upstream*, Hanoi, 1957,
for contrasting treatment. Sihanouk describes his travels through Cambodia
and his confrontations with Gautier in *L'Indochine vue de Pékin, passim.* His
characterisation of himself as a *chaud lapin* occurs in *L'Indochine vue de Pékin*,
p. 34. On this period of his life, see also his pamphlet *Jeunesse cambodgienne*,
Phnom Penh, 1944, and his article, 'La Monarchie khmère', in *Le Sangkum*,
Phnom Penh, no. 9, April 1966.

The listing of Sihanouk's consorts and children is given by Meyer in
Derrière, pp. 117–18. Sihanouk's comment on 'excess' occurs in *L'Indochine*

vue de Pékin, p. 34. Sihanouk provided a revealing account of his amatory interests in a speech delivered in Kampot on 9 October 1963. Sihanouk comments on his various alliances in *Souvenirs, passim,* and in particular Chapter XI, pp. 77–83.

On the School of Administration, see Osborne, *Politics and Power*, p. 27.

A valuable account of the famine in northern Vietnam is given by Ngo Vinh Long in his *Before the Revolution: The Vietnamese Peasants Under the French*, Cambridge, Mass., 1973, Chapter 6.

This account of Pol Pot's early life relies on Kiernan, *How Pol Pot* and Chandler, *Brother Number One*, Chapter Two.

4

The return of the French

The months following the Japanese *coup de force* were profoundly important for the future course of Cambodia's political history, but despite his later self-justificatory accounts, there is real difficulty in assessing Sihanouk's role during this period. When all the evidence is reviewed, a strong impression remains that he was swept along by events rather than helping to shape them. This is scarcely surprising. The circumstances were extraordinary and Sihanouk was still in his early twenties. His French advisers had been interned and he had now to rely on his countrymen for guidance. Above all, he and those of his compatriots who began to test the political waters had to contend with the fact that the Japanese were still very much in charge. Nevertheless, the period between March and October 1945, the month the French reasserted their control over Cambodia, represented a vital break with the colonial past. As was the case elsewhere in Southeast Asia, the humiliation of the colonial power ensured there could never be a return to the prewar status quo.

After the Japanese coup, Sihanouk assumed the title of prime minister in addition to continuing his role as the monarch. As prime minister he presided over a cabinet of largely undistinguished ministers, men who had held senior posts in the Cambodian administration that operated under French control. One of

Sihanouk's first acts in the new order was to match action to his earlier complaints about Gautier's romanisation of the Khmer alphabet and introduction of the Gregorian calendar. On 14 March, Sihanouk revoked these measures. Discussing this decision shortly afterwards, Sihanouk prefigured a theme that was to recur time and again in his speeches and writings. 'We are,' he said, 'a people deeply attached to the traditions bequeathed us by our illustrious ancestors.'

Sihanouk was undoubtedly sincere in making this observation and correct in pointing to the reverence accorded tradition in Cambodian society. But these facts should not disguise the paradox that marks his appeals and those made by others, not least Pol Pot in later years, to a glorious and powerful Cambodian past. For, until the arrival of the French in the second half of the nineteenth century, Cambodians whether royalty or commoners knew virtually nothing of the distant past. Angkor, it is true, had remained a site for Buddhist pilgrimage and the distinctive towers of its most famous temple, Angkor Wat, had appeared on a coin struck during King Ang Duang's reign in the middle of the nineteenth century. But no-one in the kingdom had known why the temples of Angkor had been built nor who had ruled there. So for Sihanouk, as for others, the past was a recently discovered talisman which offered an assurance that Cambodia and its population might have a more glorious future than seemed possible in the uncertain and troubled present.

Amid the uncertainty following the 9 March coup, Son Ngoc Thanh's return to Cambodia in May 1945 quickly made clear the extent of his continuing support among those Cambodians who took an interest in politics. This group now included the growing number of students who had had some secondary education as well as the monks who still resented the arrest of their fellows by the French in 1942. Shortly after his return, Thanh was appointed foreign minister in the Cambodian government at the behest of the Japanese military command, who saw advantage in having in the cabinet a man they believed shared their interests. What role Thanh was supposed to play in his new post is unclear, since Cambodia's 'independence' had not even been recognised by Tokyo, though he did travel to Saigon in June to press Cambodia's claim to long-lost territory in southern Vietnam. In any case, Thanh's principal interest was in gaining domestic political power. Some recognition of this fact probably lay behind the appointment of Sihanouk's conservatively oriented uncle, Prince Monireth, as a councillor of the government almost immediately after Son Ngoc

Thanh's appointment. If this was, as seems likely, a sop to conservative opinion, it did little to inhibit Son Ngoc Thanh's drive to achieve a dominant domestic position. When a ceremony was held to mark the 20 July 1942 demonstration, Son Ngoc Thanh, now reunited with Pach Chhoeun, who had been released from prison, joined King Sihanouk in presiding over the commemoration. From then until his arrest by the French in October 1945, Thanh was engaged in feverish activity to bolster his position and prepare for the return of the former colonial power to Indochina, a return that Charles de Gaulle had vowed would take place.

With Sihanouk largely a spectator through the summer of 1945, the Japanese military authorities in Cambodia made their own preparations for what they expected would be an Allied advance into Southeast Asia. Against this possibility, the Japanese had begun training a paramilitary youth corps that was intended to fight as a militia beside Japanese troops in a land battle with the Allies. Such a battle did not come to pass, as the Japanese surrendered after the second atomic bomb was dropped on Nagasaki. But before the surrender on 15 August, a series of events occurred that have been given only limited attention in most surveys of modern Cambodian history. Much of the detail of what took place remains obscure and the roles played by some of the participants are still a matter of controversy.

On 6 August, a major demonstration took place outside the royal palace. Possibly as many as 30 000 people were involved, a very large number considering that the total population of Phnom Penh at the time was little more than 100 000. Members of the paramilitary youth corps paraded past the palace as part of the demonstration, but exactly what those who participated in this affair intended remains unresolved. Bringing complaints to the attention of the Cambodian monarch was a tradition in Cambodian society, but we do not have enough evidence to know whether the demonstration represented support for the monarchy or the beginnings of a more public campaign to back Son Ngoc Thanh's increasingly open desire to become Cambodia's political leader. It is tempting to see the latter motive behind the presence of at least some of the demonstrators, particularly in the light of what occurred three days later. After nightfall on 9 August a group of young men rounded up all the members of the Cambodian cabinet, with the exception of Son Ngoc Thanh and Prince Monireth. Although the ministers were soon released as the result of intervention by both Thanh and Monireth, members of the group, in an act of *lèse majesté*, broke into the palace with the aim of confronting the king and calling on him to dismiss the cabinet. But Sihanouk was not in the palace, for his mother, forewarned, had sent him to hide in a nearby monastery. Although they slightly wounded Sihanouk's private secretary, the intruders were eventually disarmed and arrested. Four days later, Sihanouk dismissed the cabinet and named Son Ngoc Thanh prime minister.

While he was alive Son Ngoc Thanh consistently denied that he was behind the events of 9 August, a position backed by Japanese officials in Phnom Penh at the time the intruders broke into the palace. Other rumours suggested that Thanh's longtime associate Pach Chhoeun might have masterminded the seizure of the cabinet members and the attempt to confront Sihanouk in the palace. Still other explanations were founded on the possibility of the royal family's involvement, since questions were raised as to why Monireth was not seized by the plotters. The fact that Sihanouk's mother, Kossamak, apparently had advance warning fuelled this line of speculation. The argument for the involvement of Sihanouk's relatives rests on the improbable assumption that the real intention of those who seized cabinet members and broke into the palace was to strengthen the position of the young king. Wherever the truth may lie, the events of 9 August 1945 were of great importance: they led to Sihanouk's naming Thanh as prime minister five days later, and also to his lifetime distrust of and enmity towards Thanh, whom he saw as posing a direct challenge to his position. Beyond these personal considerations, the failed 9 August plot gave added emphasis—despite the small number of active participants—to the fact that Cambodian politics now involved people who did not accept the absolutist assumptions inherent in the traditional monarchical system. Tension between those who clung to the old ideas and the increasing number—of various political persuasions—who did not, runs as a constant thread through the political fabric of Cambodia's history in the years following the Second World War.

The period between the end of the war in mid-August and Sihanouk's formal acceptance of the return of French power on 23 October was marked by confusion and uncertainty. For two months there is little evidence that Sihanouk had any real impact on the course of developments, though a case can be made for his astuteness in having avoided making any irrevocable decisions during this troubled time. Indeed, in later commentary on this period he has stated that he considered abdicating in order to retreat from the demands of public life. He was dissuaded from doing so by the unlikely combined advice of Monireth and Son Ngoc Thanh. But if Sihanouk was depressed and inactive at this time, Thanh threw himself into the task of establishing a government that could in some fashion cope with what was now seen as the inevitable return of the French.

Controversy surrounds discussion of how much support Thanh had as he sought to place his stamp on politics within Cambodia and to develop links with foreign regimes. Sihanouk in his writings has spared no effort to denigrate Thanh and those who supported him, and some of Thanh's own actions raise doubts about his grip on reality. A fair-minded assessment would have to conclude that for several weeks after his assumption of office Thanh did command the support of a substantial number of politically conscious Cambodians.

Many of these men later worked with Sihanouk, but in August and September 1945 Thanh was the dominant figure in Cambodia. Indeed, when Thanh's policies provoked a conservative decision to seek his ouster, the plotters turned to the French to achieve their goal, clearly not confident of local support for their action.

Little that Son Ngoc Thanh did within Cambodia survived his subsequent overthrow and, strikingly, his domestic program was not marked by any dramatic measures aimed against the monarchy. Although he clearly believed that as prime minister he had the right to determine the political course of Cambodia, he showed no intention of converting Cambodia to a republic and, as already noted, he urged Sihanouk not to abdicate. But in preparing to oppose France's return to Indochina Thanh placed himself in sharp opposition to the many members of the Cambodian elite who felt strongly that their interests and those of Cambodia as a whole would be better served by cooperation with France. Men such as Monireth, who had held a commission in the French army, and Khim Tit, Son Ngoc Thanh's minister for defence and an unquestioned francophile, became increasingly concerned as Thanh sought to establish links with the emerging communist-dominated regime in Vietnam. The suggestion that Cambodians might join with Vietnamese to oppose the French return by force was anathema to conservative forces in Phnom Penh. Of equal concern to these forces was the extent to which Thanh appeared ready to rely on the support of Vietnamese resident in Phnom Penh. The fact that Thanh was reputed to be half Vietnamese himself added to the growing sense of unease his actions generated.

In what seems to have been a last desperate throw of the dice, Thanh organised what he called a referendum seeking support for his policies. Although styled a referendum, it was not conducted on a basis that could genuinely reflect popular opinion throughout Cambodia. Thanh sent a series of questions to a restricted number of provincial officials, who were required to report back on the views of the male population for which they were responsible. The wildly improbable result of this 'referendum' was a tally of more than 500 000 ballots embracing Thanh's policies and only two dissenting; one of these recorded a negative vote, the other was returned blank. This 'vote of confidence' did not sway the small but determined group of opponents who had decided Thanh had to be removed. Even before Thanh announced the results of his referendum on 3 October, the first returning French had reached Phnom Penh. They bore letters addressed to Sihanouk calling for Cambodian participation in a conference to determine the future status of what had been French Indochina. Their presence made even clearer the fact that only a short time remained before a confrontation between Thanh and the French was likely to occur.

Sihanouk has denied that he was instrumental in the plot that was now hatched to remove Thanh from power, placing all responsibility on Khim Tit. Khim Tit's own version of the events surrounding Thanh's removal from office is self-serving and unsatisfactory. Some facts seem beyond dispute, even if a question mark ultimately hangs over how much more Sihanouk knew than he has admitted. While Son Ngoc Thanh seemed prepared to risk armed conflict with the French, Sihanouk heeded the advice of his conservative advisers, responding in cautious and polite terms to a call from Admiral d'Argenlieu, whom de Gaulle had sent to Indochina as high commissioner, to dispatch representatives to the planned meeting in India that would discuss Cambodia's future relations with France. Writing to the French representative in Phnom Penh, Major Gallois, Sihanouk indicated that he was ready to have Cambodians present at such discussions but insisted that Cambodia was already independent. Despite this assertion, the king's cautious tone took account of the realities of power and of the fact that not even imperial Japan had recognised the independence he had proclaimed in March. The contrast between the king's behaviour and the risky path on which Son Ngoc Thanh had embarked convinced Monireth, Khim Tit and other senior members of the royal family that the time had come to act against the prime minister. On 8 October, Khim Tit suddenly left for Saigon with Gallois. Once there he held discussions with the head of the French military mission, General Leclerc. A week later Leclerc flew from Saigon to Phnom Penh, personally arrested Thanh, and took him back to Saigon. Tried as a 'traitor' in 1947, Thanh was sentenced to twenty years imprisonment, a sentence that was soon commuted to exile in France. For the next four years Thanh lived comfortably in France, completing the law studies he had begun many years before.

Should we believe Sihanouk when he asserts that he did not send Khim Tit to Saigon to arrange for Son Ngoc Thanh's removal? The terms in which Sihanouk makes this assertion are interesting, for he does not deny *knowledge* of why Khim Tit went to Saigon, only that he did not send him. Moreover, it is disingenuous of Sihanouk to speak, as he has in ironic terms, of Khim Tit's disappointment that, once the French had ousted Son Ngoc Thanh, it was Monireth rather than he who reaped the reward of becoming prime minister. That was so, but as Charles Meyer acidly observes, referring to Tit's later career, 'One simply notes that Sihanouk gave Khim Tit very important responsibilities despite knowing his unpopularity.'

At first glance, the period after Son Ngoc Thanh's arrest appears an anticlimax, a time of calm following the febrile excitement that had been aroused by the Japanese coup in March 1945 and reached its height in the two months after the end of the Second World War. Within Cambodia, the balance of power had clearly moved back in favour of the conservatives epitomised by King Sihanouk's uncle, Prince Monireth, who favoured cooperation with the French rather than confrontation. Monireth assumed office as prime minister in Thanh's place on 17 October, certainly with French backing and, as best can be determined, without opposition from Sihanouk, who seems to have played an essentially passive role at this critical time.

The French now began discussions with Monireth on Cambodia's future status. Their clear goal was to restore the pre-1941 relationship between Cambodia and France with as few modifications as possible. After all, the French who spearheaded their country's return to Indochina were partisans of Charles de Gaulle, a leader who had only recently asked rhetorically to whom Indochina could belong if it did not belong to France. But the freedom of manoeuvre of the French who now began negotiations with Monireth and his supporters was not unlimited, for if the prospect of armed resistance to a French return to Cambodia raised few fears, the problems France faced in reasserting its presence in neighbouring Vietnam were of an altogether different order. Ho Chi Minh and his followers were already a force to be reckoned with by the time the French started to filter back into Vietnam in the last months of 1945. Politically well organised and with a slowly growing military arm, the Vietminh already posed a major challenge to French plans to re-establish themselves as masters of the whole of Indochina. This need for the French to behave in Cambodia with constant concern for the course of events in Vietnam became an ever more vital factor once the First Indochina War began in 1946. France, despite its potential to deploy greater material power in Cambodia, could ill afford to let events there distract it from its increasingly bloody battles against the communist-led Vietnamese fighting for independence.

By January 1946, the French and Monireth had agreed to a *modus vivendi*. Writing of this agreement, Sihanouk has been at pains to distance himself from it, describing his uncle as 'having taken it upon himself' to sign the document in company with General Leclerc. He had wanted more, Sihanouk has said, than what was, in principle at least, a return to the former protectorate regime. This is a retrospective claim and difficult to verify. Nonetheless, two observations can be made. First, even if Sihanouk was unhappy with the terms to which Monireth agreed, he was not able to sway his uncle from the course on which he had embarked. Second, it is extremely doubtful that the French negotiators would have been ready to agree to more generous terms than those contained in the *modus vivendi.*

Nothing in the historical record suggests that Sihanouk felt a need to try to accelerate the pace of negotiations with France for a greater degree of independence once the *modus vivendi* was concluded. Barely six months after the agreement was signed he accepted an invitation to visit France at the time of the Fontainebleau negotiations between the French government and Ho Chi Minh's Vietminh, in July 1946. The high point of that visit, he makes clear in his memoirs, was his 'private' visit to Charles de Gaulle at Colombey-les-Deux-Eglises, when Madame de Gaulle herself served the afternoon tea. De Gaulle, recounts Sihanouk, 'scarcely spoke of Cambodia's independence', but rather of the need for leaders to assure that national unity was achieved in their countries. Emphasising his long-term admiration for de Gaulle, Sihanouk records, without critical comment, the general's assurance that France had returned to Cambodia to 'ensure its emancipation'.

As it was, there was enough in the *modus vivendi* to give temporary satisfaction to both the negotiating sides, if not to those who rejected the basis on which discussions had been joined. Under the terms of the agreement, France was to return to a Cambodia that was no longer styled a protectorate, but rather an autonomous kingdom within the French Union. Although France was to control the key areas of defence and foreign affairs, the *modus vivendi* document recognised that the king had authority in internal affairs. Importantly, the agreement stipulated that further negotiations needed to take place. To this end a Franco-Cambodian commission was to be set up to draft a constitution and seek the restitution to Cambodia of the western provinces seized by Thailand in 1941.

The second of these tasks was achieved before the end of 1946, largely thanks to pressure by the United States on a Thai government anxious to show its repentance for having sided with Japan through much of the war. Establishing a satisfactory constitution was another matter altogether, and a review of the manoeuvring that accompanied its formulation makes dusty reading. Yet the detail of what took place cannot be disregarded, for it holds clues to the failure of Sihanouk and his supporters and opponents to find a political system that could accommodate their conflicting interests.

For the moment the issue of Cambodia's independence became less important in the world of Phnom Penh politics than the problem of reaching agreement on the kind of political system Cambodia should have. Reflecting the still strong position France occupied within Cambodia, the initial draft of a constitution was prepared by French experts, though Sihanouk is probably correct in claiming that it also was, in its conservative cast, highly acceptable to Monireth and his associates. Among key features of the initial draft were provisions for a limited male suffrage; this would elect an advisory assembly whose powers would be subordinate to those of the king.

If the conservatives were ready to accept a constitution cast in these terms, the same was not true of a number of young, energetic Cambodians who now began to exercise an influence on the developing political process. Chief among them were a member of the Sisowath branch of the royal family, Prince Youthevong, and a young school teacher, Chheam Van. Both held French university degrees, Youthevong a doctorate in science and Van a bachelor's degree in liberal arts, and as the result of long residence in France they were better acquainted than most of their fellow Cambodians with the theory and practice of democratic government. For Youthevong and those who now grouped about him, the proposed constitution was unacceptable because of the power it left in the hands of the king. The system to which Cambodia should aspire, they argued, was a constitutional monarchy with real power vested in an elected parliament. It was in this atmosphere of increasing politicisation, with early moves towards the formation of the first Cambodian political parties, that King Sihanouk entered the fray. In April 1946 he promulgated two key amendments to the draft constitution. With the aim of introducing a form of constitutional democracy into Cambodia, Sihanouk called for a future parliament to be elected on the basis of universal male suffrage. Freedom of association, previously denied, was now to be granted, as was freedom of the press, in principle. A consultative assembly was to be elected to finalise the details of the future constitution.

In later years Sihanouk has claimed and been accorded credit for these decisions. This judgment needs qualification. Beyond the intense discussion taking place in Phnom Penh, real power over how much freedom of action was to be allowed Cambodia's aspiring politicians still remained firmly in the hands of the French. The young king would certainly not have been able to make his proclamations without the agreement of the French, who clearly estimated that consent would not undermine their grip on the kingdom. Indeed, while Sihanouk may well have had a genuine sympathy for the measures he proclaimed, it is probable that he was guided in what he did by French advisers. Additionally, there is no reason to believe that Sihanouk saw his intervention as opening the way to fully fledged democracy in Cambodia. Moreover, the proclamations of April 1946 also owed much to the agitation and arguments of men such as Youthevong who were calling for a parliamentary system of government both in public and in private discussions with Sihanouk. They and their supporters were seen by many as the inheritors of the modern nationalist values first seriously advocated by Son Ngoc Thanh; as testimony to this, the party Youthevong was to found, the Democrats, drew much of its support from former followers of Thanh.

So far this chapter has dealt with the groups and individuals who pursued their political goals openly, chiefly in Phnom Penh. These men, Sihanouk, other members of the royal family, and the emerging politically conscious elite formed by the official and educated classes, were ready to try and work within the constraints of legality, even if they wished to change the existing political arrangements. There were others who did not share this view, men of various political allegiances who opted for armed dissidence.

Much that has been written about those who went into the *maquis* either during or shortly after the Second World War has been flavoured as much by ideological commitment as by sober assessment of fact. But research carried out over the past fifteen years, in part spurred by efforts to understand the apparently inexplicable actions of the Pol Pot regime, has added greatly to our knowledge of radical revolutionary politics in Cambodia from the end of the Second World War. Although they involve a degree of simplification, the following broad points may be made in relation to those who chose the extra-legal path as Cambodia slowly began its search for an appropriate constitutional system.

In 1946 the number of dissidents was small. This was true both of those dedicated to opposing arrangements that allowed the French to return and of those who combined opposition to the French with adherence to left-wing policies. For the latter, the transformation of Cambodia's social system was an essential plank in their political program. Dissidents of both right and left laid claim to the title of Khmer Issaraks (free Cambodians). Initially, just as their numbers were small, so was their influence. And whether of the left or right, they depended for their existence on support from foreigners. In the case of Prince Norodom Chantaraingsey, the best known of those who opposed France's return to a controlling position in Cambodia but a man who had no vision of a Cambodia transformed by radical social ideas, early support from Thailand was important.

For those on the left, linkage with the much stronger Vietnamese communist movement was of great importance and among those who emerged as leaders of left-wing bands part-Vietnamese parentage was common. This association with Vietnamese communists and the presence of men of mixed Cambodian and Vietnamese ancestry were to have profound consequences as the Cambodian left developed over the ensuing decades, but in the immediate postwar years links with Vietnam played a vital part in sustaining the embryonic Cambodian communist movement.

The extent to which nationalist and leftist groups joined in common cause to oppose the return of the French is still a matter for argument. Certainly there were some alliances, but many of these seem to have been tactical rather than strategic, and essentially of limited duration. Moreover, what passed for political dissidence was often little more than banditry cloaked in political justification. In the unsettled conditions immediately after the war the long tradition of rural banditry received a considerable impetus. Still, whether of the left or the right or simply outlaws who refused to live a life of grindingly hard labour for little reward and the prospect of ending in debt to the local Chinese rice merchant, these men were yet to have a significant effect on Cambodian politics. In later chapters we will see how Sihanouk, once he emerged as the dominant figure in Cambodia, seemed successful in gathering most of his right-wing opponents into the political organisation that he himself headed. For most observers, he appeared to have done the same with the left. Both these judgments were to prove wrong, as the right came to plot his overthrow from within the existing political system and as, increasingly, Sihanouk's leftist opponents saw no other choice than to pursue revolution clandestinely. Not only was all of this still far off in 1946, but not even the most farsighted observer could have predicted the awesome events that were being set in train by developments at that time. And as his biographer has pointed out, we know nothing of what Saloth Sar, the future Pol Pot, who was still in his teens, did throughout 1946.

What can be said of Sihanouk's view of all these developments? Should we accept his denial of suggestions that it was not until 1952–1953 that he underwent his transformation from pleasure-loving king to wily and determined politician? In his review of the early postwar years, Charles Meyer characterises Sihanouk as temporarily moved by 'youthful ardour' in his search for ways to apply a democratic system to his country, but as devoting 'the greatest part of his time to worthless activities and above all his affairs of the heart'. The evidence for the latter assertion is hard to ignore. By 1946, still only 24 years old, Sihanouk had fathered six acknowledged children.

We are not greatly helped by Sihanouk himself to judge his degree of serious commitment to political issues during 1945 and 1946, for his own accounts of those years are heavily informed by self-justification and denigration of anyone who then or later questioned the wisdom of his actions or lack of them. In a very real sense, Sihanouk has created his own problem so far as criticism is concerned. The perfectionist within him aspires to have matched impossibly high ideals. But side by side with this trait is an intolerance bred of unrestrained adulation from the population and the unreadiness of all but a few of his advisers to question his judgment. It was not he who asked to be known as the 'Father of Independence', he has argued disingenuously; rather, this was a title given him by his compatriots. But of course it was and is a title that Sihanouk cherishes, and it was he who proclaimed the title. He has seen any qualification of his absolute right to claim it as grossly affronting personal criticism—nothing short of *lèse majesté*. Herein lies, in large part, the basis for his long and bitter feud with Son Ngoc Thanh. This is the attitude that has led him to denounce foreign commentators who suggest that he came only slowly to the conviction that full independence from France was a goal worth working towards.

Yet while a reasonable observer will suspect that Sihanouk protests too much, that same observer is likely to conclude that Sihanouk's behaviour in 1945 and 1946 was broadly understandable, if less unquestionably heroic than he has wished to suggest. Despite the efforts of the French administration to expose the young king to his countrymen during the war years, Sihanouk, from the time he was named king, lived an extraordinarily circumscribed life. Locked into participation in a cycle of ceremonies and ritual appearances, he spent most of his time behind the high, crenellated walls of the Phnom Penh palace. Almost without exception, his advisers were of a more or less conservative cast of mind. The interest shown by his father, Suramarit, in arguing that Son Ngoc Thanh should be allowed to return to Cambodia in 1945 does not qualify this judgment. If Suramarit hoped for some measure of liberalisation of the protectorate regime, there is no indication that he advocated a total rupture with France, let alone the republicanism that Thanh was later to embrace. Moreover, Thanh himself at this period publicly supported a continuing important role for the monarchy.

Once the French were firmly re-established in Phnom Penh, Sihanouk again found himself surrounded by French officials who, while they couched their advice in exquisitely polite terms, were nevertheless a constant reminder of France's continuing greater material power. That power and the benefits it could still provide to Cambodia were recognised by senior figures in the kingdom whose views Sihanouk could not ignore. Most prominently, his uncle Monireth firmly opposed any effort to achieve a sudden break with France. Like many of his generation, he did indeed see

France as capable of playing a protector's role, most particularly against the ambitions of Vietnamese revolutionaries, but also against Thailand. Other, non-royal advisers, of whom Penn Nouth was to emerge as one of the most important, were equally cautious and conservative.

Added to the overwhelmingly conservative advice that he received, and which in total inclined Sihanouk to caution rather than hasty action, was an aspect of his character that became increasingly apparent in later years. Facing problems for which there was no immediate solution, Sihanouk time and again has withdrawn from confrontation. Frequently he has done so expecting that those opposing him would come to their senses and bend to his will. On other occasions his withdrawal has represented a psychological retreat. This seems to have been very much the case for the first few years after France regained a position in Cambodia. There were times when Sihanouk displayed bursts of energy; the proclamations of April 1946 were an example. But for long periods he was content to turn his back on the world of politics and to find solace in women, sport and the cinema. The attraction of the last, dating as it did from early childhood, suggests a personality deeply attracted to idealised solutions, with right triumphing over wrong and the hero over the villain, and with everything ending happily.

The real world was a more complex, troublesome place. And the forces that had been unleashed since the Japanese *coup de force* now began to take concrete form in the emergence of Cambodian political parties and the alternative of dissidence. For a period, these were twin if opposing forces over which King Sihanouk could exercise little control. His later protestations to the contrary, his achievement of political maturity was still some years away.

Notes

In addition to the works by Sihanouk, Kiernan, Preschez, Chandler, R.M. Smith, Reddi, Meyer and Osborne listed in the Notes to the previous chapter, useful surveys that deal in part with the return of the French to Cambodia in 1945–46 are: Donald Lancaster, *The Emancipation of French Indochina*, London, 1961, and R.B. Smith, *International History of the Vietnam War*, 2 vols, London, 1983–85.

In addition to the published material on Son Ngoc Thanh, I am indebted to his brother Son Thai Nguyen for discussion of Thanh's political career (interview, Saigon, January 1971).

Full details of the 1945 'referendum' organised by Son Ngoc Thanh are found in Preschez, *Essai*.

Sihanouk's denial that he sent Khim Tit to Saigon is contained in *L'Indochine vue de Pékin*, p. 43. Khim Tit provided his own critical commentary on Son Ngoc Thanh's role during this period in *Réalités*, 9 June and 16 June 1967. Meyer's comment on Sihanouk and Khim Tit is from *Derrière*, p. 116. See, also, Sihanouk's *Souvenirs*, pp. 108–14.

For Sihanouk's later newspaper commentaries on the evolution of the Cambodian political system, see *Réalités*, 8 and 15 February 1958; 'How democracy was born in Cambodia,' a series of articles published in *Réalités* between 24 May and 20 September 1958 and later republished as *La Monarchie cambodgienne et la croisade royale pour l'indépendance*, Phnom Penh, 1961; *La Monarchie Khmère: L'Action de S.M. Norodom Sihanouk pour l'Indépendance du Cambodge 1941–1955* (*Réalités* 13 September 1958–3 January 1959), and 'Will Cambodia become a republic?' *Réalités* 22 August to 23 October 1959.

Kiernan, *How Pol Pot*, provides invaluable detail on the growth of dissidence in Cambodia at this time.

Sihanouk's rejection of the charge that he came to political maturity in the early 1950s is to be found in *La Monarchie Khmère*, in the section headed 'How one does not write history', pp. 18–26. Meyer's comment is from *Derrière*, p. 117.

5

From the chrysalis, slowly

Until quite recently, surveys of Cambodia's history in the years immediately after the Second World War have focused on Sihanouk's emergence as a major actor on his country's political stage. Notwithstanding the prince's contrary assertions, he has been accurately portrayed as only slowly seizing his opportunities to shape the course of politics in Cambodia and to pursue negotiations with France for independence. At the same time, attention has been paid to the failure of the constitution developed in 1946 and 1947 and largely based on a European (French) model, to meet Cambodia's political needs. These issues remain important in charting Sihanouk's transformation into the dominant figure in his country's political life. But to these twin themes must now be added a sharper awareness of the development of radical leftist dissent in the years after the Second World War. For the subterranean growth of the radical left was the counterpoint to the dominant theme of Cambodia's modern history: the failure of open politics to provide stable government, which led, ultimately, to the terrible years of the Pol Pot tyranny.

Just how ill-prepared Sihanouk's fellow countrymen were for the parliamentary game was apparent in the campaigning that preceded the first election for a consultative assembly in September 1946. Of the three parties that contested that election, only one, the Democrats, could lay claim to anything like party organisation and a party platform. That it could do so was due in large part to the energy and the intellect of Prince Sisowath Youthevong, but his abilities were supported by those of a few other able men, particularly Sim Var and Ieu Koeuss, a scholarly and energetic figure originally from the northwestern province of Battambang. Youthevong is one of the major 'might-have-beens' of modern Cambodian history, a fact that has not endeared him to Sihanouk. More than 30 years after Youthevong's untimely death in 1947, Sihanouk chose to disparage him when he looked back at this period in his memoirs, apparently unable to abide the thought that there was a richly talented man who proved able to garner support at a time when he, as king, spent much of his time on the political sidelines. Curiously mean-spirited in his views of any of his compatriots who might be seen as more talented than himself, Sihanouk has been consistently resentful of this long-dead member of the royal family—a Sisowath, to add further offence—whose formal academic achievements were substantial and whose talents had been recognised by the French government.

Youthevong quickly demonstrated his appeal to many of the politically conscious in Cambodia. Arguing for a greater role for Cambodians in the administration of their own country, he attracted the support of younger elements in the civil service. Youthevong and those about him were viewed as embodying many of the policies that Son Ngoc Thanh had espoused. Despite's Thanh's forced political eclipse, the goals that he was thought to stand for—genuine independence and firm support for Cambodia's Buddhist heritage—led many in the *sangha* to support the Democrats, while former monks and school teachers were also active in promoting the Democrats' cause.

The contrast between the social breadth of the support given the Democrats and that given the other two parties contesting the September 1946 election was sharp. Like the Democrats, the Democratic Progressive Party and the Liberal Party were also led by princes, but princes of a very different stripe from Youthevong. The Democratic Progressive Party was led by Prince Norodom Montana, while Prince Norodom Norindeth headed the Liberal Party. Despite their names, both these parties were essentially conservative in outlook and there was little in their policy programs to separate them. Both called for the eventual introduction of a constitutional monarchy. In the case of Norindeth's Liberals, this was accompanied by a call for the maintenance of links with France—not surprisingly, since the French were secretly giving

Norindeth financial support. To some extent Montana's party could be regarded as linked with, if not actually representing, the commercially important Sino-Cambodian families in Phnom Penh. The Liberal Party was a larger grouping, drawing its supporters from a rather wider base. If the Democratic Progressives spoke for the urban bourgeoisie, the Liberals depended principally on the support of men with property interests in the provinces, where Norindeth himself was a substantial landholder. The Liberals also had the support of an older generation of Cambodian civil servants who had worked happily in harness with the French throughout their adult lives and saw little reason to turn their backs on what, for them, had been a perfectly acceptable relationship.

The much greater appeal of the Democrats in comparison to the other parties was strikingly illustrated in the 1946 election. With universal adult male suffrage and with 60 per cent of the electorate voting, the Democrats won 50 of the 69 positions in the contest. The Liberals won sixteen seats, and the remaining places were gained by independents. Despite instances of electoral irregularity and some doubts about the extent to which those voting in the elections fully understood the process in which they were participating, the landslide result seemed to assure the Democrats of a key role in determining how Cambodia would be governed in the years ahead. More immediately, Youthevong and his followers seemed poised to dominate the continuing discussion about the form of Cambodia's constitution with the goal of reducing the king's power. Yet none of this was to be. Within six years hopes for a parliamentary system had faded as political power passed firmly into Sihanouk's hands. How did this happen?

Viewed with the hindsight of nearly 50 years, and with the salutary record of the rejection of Western constitutional models by other former colonial states, the failure of the 1946–47 Cambodian constitution to provide a basis for stable government is not surprising. Most fundamentally, the constitution assumed that a population that had never experienced anything remotely like democracy could quickly adopt the attitudes and practices of a largely alien system. Complicating this fundamental problem were the inherent weaknesses of some of the constitution's key provisions. On the model of the French Fourth Republic, power was divided between the executive and the legislature, but the legislature retained the right to bring down the executive should there be disagreements on policy. This arrangement resulted in protracted instability in France, an instability that was to be matched in Cambodia.

Further undermining the possibility of Cambodia's experiencing a smooth transition to electoral politics were those provisions of the constitution relating to the appointment of ministers. With France once again as the model, the king was to designate the prime minister, and the prime minister to choose his ministers. None of these ministers needed to be members of the legislature, yet the cabinet so formed had to be approved, and even more importantly could be voted out of office, by the legislature. Put baldly but accurately, the system could only work if the king, his ministers and the legislature were all of one mind on any major issue.

Sihanouk has written dismissively of the politicians who later contested office under this flawed constitution, but such scant evidence as exists suggests that he did little to oppose its general form or that he himself held strong views in favour of alternative systems for governing Cambodia. But his conservative advisers *were* concerned by what they saw as inherent risks in the kind of constitutional monarchy advocated by Prince Youthevong. With an eye to preserving their own influence, and attached to the ideal of a powerful monarch, they successfully called for provisions in the constitution that allowed the king to dissolve parliament on the advice of his prime minister. They were also able to ensure that the constitution proclaimed that 'All powers emanate from the king' (Article 21). These provisions were to become powerful tools in Sihanouk's hands once he became determined to impose his will on Cambodia's political life. For although Cambodia was ill-prepared for parliamentary democracy, Sihanouk was later astute in using the flawed constitution to his own advantage.

One final section of the constitution deserves attention, since it was to be of considerable importance in 1960, when Sihanouk's father died. (Suramarit had become king in 1955 after Sihanouk's abdication.) This was the section dealing with succession to the throne. Articles 25, 26 and 27 dealt with the issue of succession, largely codifying provisions already in force. Importantly, a new provision was added giving all male descendants of King Ang Duang (died 1860) the theoretical right of succession to the throne. Although the Cambodian monarchy had been elective in the past, in practice the succession was limited to close relatives of the dead king. The effect of this new provision was to greatly increase the number of princes who could, in the future, aspire to the throne. Given the philoprogenitive character of the Cambodian royal family, this new provision meant that even in 1946 more than 100 princes were theoretically eligible to succeed. The number was much greater in 1960.

When elections for Cambodia's first National Assembly under the new constitution took place in December 1947, Prince Youthevong was no longer the head of the Democrats. He had died suddenly the preceding July. His death, from a range of causes including tuberculosis and malaria, was a blow to those who hoped that Cambodia could develop into a democratic state. At the time of Youthevong's death, and long afterwards, his family and supporters harboured suspicions that he had either been murdered by the French security services for being far too able, and therefore inconvenient to their plans to retain real power in Cambodia, or allowed to die through medical neglect. The best evidence suggests these suspicions were groundless. But there is no doubt that Youthevong's death benefited those who wished to hasten slowly in curbing the power of the monarchy and seeking real independence from France.

The December 1947 election once again proved the Democrats' electoral appeal, as they won 55 of the 75 seats contested. But their victory did nothing to ensure that Cambodia would enjoy parliamentary stability. Despite the fact that the first two Cambodian ministries formed under the new constitution drew their members from men favourably disposed to the Democrats, clashes developed between the ministry and the assembly, and in each case the ministry had to resign, in August 1948 and January 1949 respectively. After these two ministries led by Chheam Van and Penn Nouth had fallen, the frailty of the new political system was further demonstrated by the failure of three successive attempts to form a new ministry.

Throughout this period of increasingly futile political manoeuvring, with real power still firmly in French hands, Sihanouk was a largely silent figure. Even his own memoirs, with their undisguised intent of justifying his actions, skate swiftly over the period between 1946 and 1949. For only in 1949 did he become more active, both in relation to domestic politics and in his efforts to obtain concessions from the French on the issue of independence. Until then he still lived a largely self-indulgent life within the palace. His devotion to the cinema continued and his interest now turned to the making of amateur film dramas, foreshadowing the consuming passion of the late 1960s. Horse-riding was another interest and he practised over jumps set up within the palace grounds. In mid-1948 he spent some weeks attending courses on equitation and military tactics at the famous French cavalry school at Saumur. His participation as a trainee officer (*officier stagiaire*) is an interesting testimony to Sihanouk's lack of commitment at this time to any forceful confrontation with the French. It was also, it should be admitted, a recognition that—as the war against Communist-led forces in Vietnam grew bloodier and as insecurity increased in the Cambodian countryside—neither Sihanouk nor any other Cambodian was in a position to sway the French from their determination to maintain a tight grip over Cambodia. While Sihanouk exercised his mounts in the lush valley of the Loire, Chheam Van, now prime minister of Cambodia, was in Paris endeavouring, without any success, to advance the cause of his country's independence.

No single event explains why Sihanouk increasingly involved himself in Cambodia's political life from early 1949 onwards. Nor should it be imagined that his involvement was unwavering. Several factors played their part. Most importantly he came to recognise that the unproductive character of domestic politics, the lack of any real progress on the issue of independence, and the growing insecurity throughout the country posed a danger to his own position. Once again, attention also needs to be given to the continuing influence upon him of his conservatively inclined royal relatives, who, though they saw no need to move quickly on the independence issue, worried about the endless bickering of the parliamentary system and the threats to security coming from both left and right. Against this background a new figure came to prominence: Yem Sambaur.

Although he was, like so many others, later to have a falling-out with Sihanouk, Yem Sambaur in 1949 offered action and policies that appealed to the king and his advisers. Open in manner, frequently smiling, but exuding a peasant toughness, Sambaur made no secret of his humble origins, nor of the fact that these had not prevented his rising to the senior ranks of the police. As much for reasons of personal interest as of concern with issues of policy, Yem Sambaur, backed by other members of the Democratic Party, turned on his colleagues, bringing down first Chheam Van's government in August 1948 and then Penn Nouth's in January 1949. King Sihanouk did nothing to help Penn Nouth on this occasion, a fact that did not prevent Penn Nouth from later becoming perhaps the most trusted of Sihanouk's non-royal advisers. When various names were put to Sihanouk as successors to Penn Nouth, he rejected them all, insisting that Yem Sambaur should become prime minister. Evidently he welcomed Sambaur's no-nonsense approach to solving problems. But the new prime minister's 'steer for the sound of the guns' political style brought its own difficulties and a familiar clash between the executive and the assembly, and in September 1949 Sihanouk dissolved parliament.

Before this, Sambaur's government took two decisions that deserve note. First, to cope with his government's financial demands, Sambaur authorised the opening of a casino in Phnom Penh. It was, in financial terms, a stunning success and may well have persuaded Sihanouk that casinos were an answer to Cambodia's revenue needs, for he remained attached to the idea of raising money through casinos for many years. More fundamentally important, Sambaur's government offered an amnesty to the dissidents in the *maquis*, who opposed the continued French presence in Cambodia and were a serious threat to security in large areas of the country.

The intermingling of domestic politics and the search for greater independence from France now became increasingly complex. Temporarily seeing their interests in common, Sihanouk and Yem Sambaur turned their backs on the parliamentary system. Having dissolved the National Assembly in September 1949, Sihanouk over the next two years appointed a series of ministries, including one he led himself for a month in May 1950, that governed without reference to parliament. He and his advisers justified this approach on the basis of the constitutional provision that all power emanated from the king. Nevertheless, the difficulties associated with this period were sufficient, at one stage, for Sihanouk again to contemplate abdication. But once again he was dissuaded from doing so.

As the war in Vietnam dragged on, France slowly responded to Cambodian overtures for a greater degree of independence. Sihanouk's involvement in the negotiations that led to these changes was real, but by no means dominant. What he proclaimed in late 1949 to be true independence he later described, in discussions with Jean Lacouture, as no more than '50 per cent independence'. Under agreements that he signed in 1949, Cambodia still did not have control of its finances or defence. But it did receive the right to establish its own diplomatic relations under patronising French constraints. Meanwhile, as part of the slow ceding of authority from France to Cambodia within the country itself, the Cambodian government gained authority over the northern and northwestern military sectors of Siemreap and Kompong Thom. This decision led to the surrender of one of the most powerful dissidents who had been opposing the French military presence in Cambodia. After long negotiations with Sihanouk's cousin Prince Sirik Matak, Dap Chhuon rallied to King Sihanouk in October 1949. As a reward he was given virtual unlimited control of the northwest of the kingdom. Ten years later he was to be at the heart of the 'Bangkok plot', a dramatic but unsuccessful attempt to topple Sihanouk.

A comprehensive history of the various groups who opposed the return of the French to Cambodia by force of arms after the Second World War has only recently been written and further research may add to the complex picture that has now emerged. Certainly, what is now known severely qualifies the rather simple picture Sihanouk has presented over the years which portrayed left wing opposition as inherently un-Cambodian—not least because the left were *his* opponents—and indissolubly linked with Vietnamese ambitions to dominate Indochina. And for Sihanouk, if the charge of leftist treason could not be sustained, then he simply dismissed the dissidents as bandits.

Certainly, by comparison with the Vietnamese communist movement, radical left-wing politics was slow to emerge in Cambodia, not least because throughout the 1930s Vietnamese communists did not believe there was any place for a separate Cambodian communist party. Moreover, as has already been noted, there was a strong Vietnamese input into the radical left that slowly developed after 1945. Some of the radical leaders had mixed Cambodian–Vietnamese ancestry. Others, more importantly, accepted the leadership of the Vietnamese-dominated Indochinese Communist Party (ICP) as representing the only truly revolutionary organisation dedicated to ending French rule over all the countries of Indochina. Even those who clearly did not embrace the ideology of the left, men such as Prince Chantaraingsey and Dap Chhuon, worked in uneasy and shifting alliances with the radicals to oppose the French. This fact and the subsequent history of deep division within the left itself has made understanding the radical element in Cambodian politics difficult.

Just as important as recognising the complex character of the forces opposing the French presence in Cambodia until the early

1950s is the need to understand how substantial was their capability to complicate France's war aims in Indochina. That capability was to become even more of a hindrance in 1951–52, but by 1949 the dissidents were active throughout wide areas of Cambodia, placing a costly strain on French resources.

The Cambodian communist movement gained its own identity, separate from the ICP, when the latter, Vietnamese-dominated grouping dissolved itself in 1951. From this point on there were three national communist movements in each of the Indochinese states, Vietnam, Laos and Cambodia. The new party in Cambodia called itself the Khmer People's Revolutionary Party (KPRP) when it was founded in September 1951. Estimates of the size of its membership at this stage vary. It may have had as many as a thousand in its ranks, but many of these were ethnic Vietnamese rather than Cambodians. Importantly, too, the influence of the Vietnamese Worker's Party (the successor in Vietnam to the ICP) was very strong; some scholars argue that the KPRP's statutes were first drawn up in Vietnamese before being translated into Cambodian.

The names of the radicals from this period have barely been remembered outside Cambodia. Chief among them was the pseudonymous Son Ngoc Minh, a former monk who had changed his name from Achar Mean with the aim of gaining some reflected glory from the better-known Son Ngoc Thanh. Two other important leaders on the left were Sieu Heng and Tou Samouth. The latter subsequently became Saloth Sar's patron within the Cambodian communist movement and then was executed as one of the leftist victims of Sihanouk's security police.

The future Pol Pot and his best-known associates, Ieng Sary and Khieu Samphan, were still not part of the Cambodian political scene. Indeed, during the early 1950s they were not even in Cambodia. Recipients of French-funded scholarships, they had gone to Paris to embark on a variety of post-secondary courses, some at university level. Saloth Sar started an electrical trade course, which he never completed. Although Cambodian students in Paris were later to become a frequent target of Sihanouk's ire, he knew little of the group which, in the early 1950s, was coming to view Communism and its disciplined party structure as the answer to Cambodia's problems, dismissing their importance and their numbers. As Saloth Sar and his fellow future revolutionaries underwent their political conversion in Paris, Sihanouk was coming to terms with the fact that the Cambodian voters were still ready to endorse the views of politicians with views inimical to his own.

Sihanouk's suspension of the National Assembly in September did not end political manoeuvring in Phnom Penh. This was made brutally apparent in January 1950 when the prominent Democratic Party politician Ieu Koeuss was fatally wounded by a grenade thrown into his party's headquarters. His death brought an extraordinary reaction: an estimated 50 000 mourners attended his funeral procession. Rumours abounded as to who might have hired the assassin, who had been quickly apprehended and who clearly had not acted on his own behalf. Some blamed the French, others Prince Norindeth's Liberal Party. Yem Sambaur and even Sihanouk himself were the targets of other rumours suggesting that they, at least, knew that the assassination was going to take place. Whoever was really responsible has never been established. But it is clear that with Ieu Koeuss's death the Democrats had lost yet another outstanding leader and, as shown by the huge attendance at his funeral, the party still retained a wide backing despite being prevented from participating in parliamentary government.

In the months that followed Ieu Koeuss's assassination little happened in Cambodia that was reassuring to the conservatives, Sihanouk included. Insecurity continued to grow in the countryside, and in Phnom Penh the Democrats persisted in their demands for new elections. These Sihanouk finally permitted in September 1951 when, once again, the Democrats were returned as the largest party in the assembly. Well before the elections were held Sihanouk had been pressing the French to allow Son Ngoc Thanh to return to Cambodia. In doing so he clearly had no inkling of the consequences.

Why did Sihanouk act as he did, given the firm evidence that he already regarded Thanh as his political enemy in 1946? His own explanation is that Thanh was a 'friend of the family'. This, indeed, was true. As already noted, Thanh and Sihanouk's father, Suramarit, had been on friendly terms in the 1930s. Suramarit probably influenced his son when Sihanouk asked the Japanese to allow Thanh to return to Cambodia in 1945. Were other calculations involved? As David Chandler speculates, Sihanouk may have thought that he could use Thanh both to strengthen his hand in negotiations with the French and to weaken the domestic political appeal of the Democrats. But given Sihanouk's known tendency to hold grudges for a lifetime, there is no fully satisfactory explanation for his action, which according to one account even involved Sihanouk's paying Thanh's fare home. Perhaps, in the final analysis, Sihanouk's action reflected an overwhelming confidence that his appeal was now sufficient to eclipse whatever residual support Thanh could muster.

Whatever the case, the French government finally responded positively to Sihanouk's intervention, allowing Thanh to return to Cambodia in October 1951. His arrival in Phnom Penh on 30 October was dramatic: more than 100 000 people cheered his motorcade as it travelled from Pochentong airport into the city. Sihanouk was angered by this public display of admiration and unmollified by the protestation of loyalty Thanh offered in a letter he sent the king on the day of his return. Thanh wanted, he wrote to Sihanouk, to be given an audience so that he 'could offer to Your Majesty the expression of my loyalty, my gratitude and my complete devotion to the fatherland'. Thanh's proffered loyalty was a charade, and lasted little more than four months. Although he refused the offer of a ministerial appointment in the latest Democratic Party–dominated government, Thanh soon showed that he had not abandoned his taste for politics. He travelled widely to attend Democratic Party rallies and, even more disturbingly for the French, turned again to the press to advance his political views. This time the newspaper's title was more aggressive: *Khmer Krauk* (Cambodians Awake!). Its message was one the embattled French could not tolerate—a call for Cambodia's immediate independence. Within a month the newspaper was closed, in February 1952. On 9 March, Son Ngoc Thanh left Phnom Penh, supposedly to accompany a customs official on an inspection tour to the Thai border. In fact, Thanh had chosen to join the *maquis*. This had apparently been his plan even before he returned to Cambodia. Once ensconced in the northwestern region of Siemreap, he again declared his commitment to immediate independence and called for the establishment of a republican government in Cambodia. From this point until his association with the coup that ousted Sihanouk in 1970, Thanh remained in permanent dissidence. Denounced first as a 'communist' and then as a 'fascist' by Sihanouk, Thanh was to survive on the margins of Cambodian politics in the late 1950s and through the 1960s. In 1952 his decision to oppose Sihanouk's Fabian approach to the goal of independence sent a shock wave through Cambodian politics.

Indeed, if one seeks a single factor that above all others contributed to Sihanouk's transformation from dilettante politician to a ruler committed both to gaining independence and to ensuring that he alone held the reins of power within Cambodia, Thanh's affront would be that factor. Not only had Sihanouk been made to look foolish by having pressed the French government to allow Thanh to return, but that image of foolishness was now compounded by Thanh's act of *lèse majesté* in calling for an end to the monarchy. Moreover, while the number of those who actually rallied to join Son Ngoc Thanh in his northern guerrilla base was small—perhaps 300 in all—the goals he was advocating were supported by students in demonstrations that took place in May and June in Phnom Penh and in major provincial cities.

In this crisis-ridden atmosphere the French fumed against both Sihanouk and his opponents. Sihanouk alternately sulked and raged. And the Democrats, probably misreading the king's mood, made no effort to apprehend Son Ngoc Thanh, a man many of them continued to admire, nor to take any decisive action against dissidents more generally. The threat of confrontation grew greater through the first two weeks of June as Sihanouk took ever sharper exception to what he saw as efforts by the Democrats to diminish his authority.

At a party congress in early June the Democrats professed loyalty to the king, but this sentiment seemed denied shortly afterward, when Thanh's old associate, Pach Chhoeun, delayed the publication of an address by Sihanouk which had been implicitly critical of the Democratic Party. When tension was further heightened by Democrat prime minister Huy Kanthol's arresting political opponents, including Yem Sambaur, who retained Sihanouk's affection at this stage, Sihanouk concluded that he must act. In collusion with the French authorities, he dismissed the Huy Kanthol government on 15 June 1952 and assumed all powers, citing the provision of the constitution that all power emanated from the king. Naming himself prime minister, he formed a new cabinet in which trusted allies held the key portfolios.

Sihanouk was now about to embark on his self-styled 'royal crusade' for independence. Justifying his action in dismissing Huy Kanthol's government, he promised his compatriots that he would achieve independence within three years, a promise that caused considerable confusion in the ranks of dissidents in the *maquis*. And he vowed that once he had accomplished his mission he would submit himself to popular judgment. Whatever his hesitations in the past, the king at this point seems finally to have realised that factious internal politics could not be ended so long as Cambodia did not enjoy true independence. And without that independence, Sihanouk's own position could be undermined. For, while still recognising the desirability of maintaining an amicable relationship with France, Sihanouk saw that continuing French control over many of the vital components of the state's machinery strengthened the hands of those politicians who opposed him. Whether at this time he had come to the conclusion that the system of party politics had to be abolished is not certain. For the moment he felt able to disregard that issue as he threw himself into the task of neutralising his political opponents and extracting concessions from the French.

In pursuing these two goals, Sihanouk began to reap the full benefit of his kingly position. The importance of his symbolic role within the state had been limited so long as he did not seek to take advantage of it. Now his opponents had to weigh their opposition to his policies not only in political terms but also in the light of the extent to which they would be opposing the king's majesty. Sihanouk was able to profit from the efforts the French had made to enhance the role of the Cambodian monarch as the key focus of national identify, even as they had curtailed his temporal power. And as a further direct result of policies pursued by the French, no other member of the royal family could claim the same symbolic importance and thus boost his political ambitions. Whatever opposition King Sihanouk had encountered from urban-oriented politicians between 1946 and 1952, he was now ready to tap the support of the predominantly rural population of Cambodia, aware that among them he was viewed as semi-divine, the essential intermediary between men and the gods.

Sihanouk's growth to full political maturity was still not complete as he contemplated the future in triumphant mood in mid-1952. But a new, more assured and determined Sihanouk had begun to emerge. Son Ngoc Thanh's defection into dissidence should not be given too much emphasis. Other less politically tinged factors played their part. By 1952 Sihanouk had begun his liaison with Monique Izzi, the beautiful daughter of a Franco-Italian father who had lived with, but never married, a Madame Pomme, in the 1930s. Although some Phnom Penh gossips claimed that Monique's mother was of Sino-Vietnamese ancestry, and others that her father was Cambodian but her mother was of mixed race, she was, in fact, Khmer. The female offspring of the Izzi–Pomme relationship were strikingly attractive and when Sihanouk first saw Monique in a beauty contest he had her brought to the palace, some reports say against her will. The same reports suggest that Monique's first reaction to King Sihanouk's offer of royal favour was to run back to her mother, who promptly ordered her to return to the palace. Whether or not these accounts are apocryphal, she soon became a fixed part of Sihanouk's life—not a sole interest, but a comforting presence. In the light of later events, there is particular irony in the fact that Prince Sirik Matak had acted as Monique's protector during her childhood.

Finally, the death in 1952 of a much-loved daughter is widely credited with having had a deep emotional effect on Sihanouk. Quite why Kantha Bopha's death from leukaemia at the age of four should have caused Sihanouk such grief is not clear, other than that his daughters, rather than his sons, were the recipients of whatever degree of affection he bestowed on his children. For years afterward, Sihanouk carried the urn containing Kantha Bopha's ashes with him when he travelled abroad. While all the details of this personal tragedy are not known, there is no doubt that it played its part in promoting Sihanouk's now more sober and vigorous approach to the conduct of affairs of state.

Notes

For the period covered in this chapter, Chandler, *Tragedy*, provides the most authoritative survey. Kiernan, *How Pol Pot*, is a ground-breaking analysis of the development of radical politics in Cambodia. A sophisticated leftist summary of Cambodian radical politics may be found in Michael Vickery, *Kampuchea, Politics, Economics and Society*, Sydney, 1986. Other valuable survey material is in Reddi, *A History*; Preschez, *Essai*; and Meyer, *Derrière*. There is also a survey of the period in my *Politics and Power*.

Sihanouk's critical comments on Prince Youthevong are to be found in his *Souvenirs*. Other comment on Youthevong's death may be found in Burchett, *Mekong Upstream*. I owe a continuing debt to Youthevong's brother, Prince Sisowath Entaravong, for his discussion of this period and of Youthevong's death, particularly during meetings in 1966.

Details of the results of the September 1946 elections may be found in Preschez, *Essai*.

For a commentary on the constitutional provisions relating to the Cambodian monarchy, see J. Imbert, *Histoire des Institutions khmères*, Tome II of the *Annales* of the *Faculté de Droit de Phnom Penh*, Phnom Penh, 1961.

My understanding of this period was assisted by discussions with Yem Sambaur in Phnom Penh in 1969 and 1970.

Sihanouk's description of the 1949 arrangements as being '50 per cent independence' is in *L'Indochine vue de Pékin*, p. 43. See also Chapter II of *La Monarchie khmère*, 'Le traité de 1949, indispensable base de départ vers l'indépendance totale', pp. 10–17.

In addition to Kiernan's *How Pol Pot*, other useful material on radical politics in Cambodia may be found in J.-C. Pomonti and S. Thion, *Des Courtisans aux partisans: Essai sur la crise cambodgienne*, Paris, 1971; Burchett, *Mekong Upstream*; and the recently published *Brother Number One*, by David Chandler. Also still important is M. Laurent, *L'Armée au Cambodge et dans les pays en voie de développement du Sud-Est Asiatique*, Paris, 1968, in particular

Annexe II, 'Deux notes de Général Séta (C.R.) for discussion of Cambodian dissidents, including Son Ngoc Thanh. See also Meyer, *Derrière*, pp. 185–9.

On Thanh's return, see Sihanouk's *Souvenirs*, pp. 170–3, and Chapter III in *La Monarchie khmère*, 'Comment on n'écrit pas l'histoire', pp. 18–26. Thanh's expression of loyalty is in a letter in this chapter, p. 24. Chandler's comment is in his *Tragedy*, p. 58. Sihanouk dates Thanh's return 30 October, but all other authorities cite the day before.

Sihanouk made allegation of Son Ngoc Thanh's complicity with the Vietminh in the Cambodian government's *Livre jaune sur les révendications de l'indépendance du Cambodge*, I, Paris, 1953, p. 17. Characterisations of Thanh as a 'fascist' were frequent in the 1960s, when he was seen as supported by the authoritarian governments in Thailand.

On Monique Izzi (now routinely described as Princess Monique, a usage not current before Sihanouk's downfall in 1970, and since Sihanouk's return to the throne in September 1993 as Queen Monique), I rely largely on private information given to me by informants in Phnom Penh, including Prince Sisowath Entaravong and Donald Lancaster. Prince Entaravong married Monique's mother's sister. In a confirmation of the interlocking nature of the various strands of Cambodian political life, David Chandler has drawn my attention to the fact that, in 1948, Ieng Sary tutored Entaravong's children. See also Sihanouk's *Souvenirs*, Chapter XXVIII, pp. 178–80.

For a comment on the importance of Kantha Bopha for Sihanouk, see the article by Donald Lancaster, 'The decline of Prince Sihanouk's Régime', in J.J. Zasloff and A.E. Goodman, eds., *Indochina in Conflict*, Lexington, Mass., 1972, p. 54.

6

A madman of genius

If Sihanouk expected that his assumption of power in June 1952—
many commentators believe his action constituted a *coup
d'état*—would show rapid results, he was disappointed. He made
much of a military operation mounted in September of that year
against dissidents in the north of the country, and led by the
former rebel Dap Chhuon. But there was no indication that the
French were much disturbed by his dramatic announcement that
he would gain Cambodia's independence within three years.
Despite the continuing bloody costs of the war in Vietnam and the
lesser but still debilitating opposition they were encountering in
Laos and Cambodia, the French military still believed they could
bring the conflict throughout Indochina to a successful conclusion.
Cambodia for them was a secondary problem and its king, on the
basis of all past evidence, scarcely likely to cause them real difficulties.

As for Sihanouk's domestic opposition, there was little sign that
the diverse groups of which it was composed were ready to abandon
their positions, whether in the world of legal politics, in the case
of the Democrats, or in the dissident ranks in the countryside.
Some dissidents came to question whether remaining in the *maquis*
made sense in the light of Sihanouk's assertion that he was now
committed to independence, but they were in a small minority, and
as 1952 drew to a close dissident activity, much of it led by men
affiliated with the KPRP, continued to grow.

When the National Assembly met in January 1953, it did so in an atmosphere of unresolved crisis. It was apparent that the Democrat majority in the assembly was prepared to confront the king despite the warning inherent in his actions and announcements six months earlier.

For his part, Sihanouk was now determined to brook no opposition, possibly believing, as his mother is said to have done, that some members of the Democratic Party were plotting to abolish the monarchy and declare Cambodia a republic. If previously he had had any doubts about the role he should play, these now vanished as Sihanouk became convinced that he, and he alone, possessed the capability and the right to determine his country's future. After cataloguing the many ills that afflicted the Cambodian state, and following the National Assembly's refusal to grant him power to rule without reference to parliament, the king acted decisively. He dissolved the assembly and proclaimed martial law.

Sihanouk's own sense of confidence and his unshakeable belief that he knew what was best for Cambodia were to be hallmarks of his rule until his hold on Cambodian politics began to slip in the late 1960s. Occasionally, tensions arose between his fundamental conviction of the necessity to impose his absolute rule and a fluctuating admiration for those politicians who were prepared to question the social and political values of his essentially conservative state. But in the end, belief in the infallibility of his own judgment and a conservatism nurtured by his own upbringing prevailed. As he was to comment in the mid-1960s, 'had I been born to an ordinary family, I would have been on the leftist side. . . . But I was born a prince and have the royal family around me. I cannot detach myself.' In January 1953 that lack of detachment led him to jail more than a dozen of his Democratic opponents without trial as he turned his mind towards an equally direct confrontation with the French.

That King Sihanouk was able to act as he did at this time reflected more than the maturing of his own personality and a hardening of his belief in his indispensability. Of great importance, too, was the fact that he could look to the support of a group of men, all older than himself, who were ready to become Cambodia's equivalent of George III's 'king's friends'. The names of these individuals recur time and again over the next seventeen years. The most senior was Penn Nouth, who, as Sihanouk's closest adviser, followed him into exile in 1970. Advising Sihanouk on financial and economic matters, though ultimately to clash with him in the late 1960s, was Son Sann, an ethnic Cambodian from southern Vietnam who had the rare distinction of having trained in commerce at a distinguished French tertiary institution, the Ecole des Hautes Etudes Commerciales. Sim Var, who had been close to Sihanouk's father from the middle 1930s, supported the king, as did Nhiek Tioulong, who, under Sihanouk's patronage, moved from being a provincial official to hold a senior post in the fledgling Cambodian armed forces. Prince Sisowath Sirik Matak was still at this stage ready to give Sihanouk his unstinted support. So too was Lon Nol, who had transferred from a senior post in the police to serve in Sihanouk's army. Although—like Sihanouk himself, Nhiek Tioulong and Sirik Matak—a former student at the Lycée Chasseloup-Laubat in Saigon, Lon Nol was already a butt of private sneers based on his appearance. Darker-skinned than most elite Cambodians, he was mocked behind his back, including by Sihanouk, as the *khmau*, the black one, a term suggesting he was of peasant origins.

Sihanouk's account of his 'royal crusade' has lost nothing in his telling. Yet for all its theatricality, and the highly favourable comments Sihanouk makes on his own endeavours, what he managed to accomplish between February and November 1953 was a remarkable achievement. Leaving the conduct of the kingdom in the hands of his trusted advisers, he left Phnom Penh for France in February 1953, announcing that he was going on holiday. The French government apparently took him at his word, complacently believing that Sihanouk's decision to take all power into his own hands and to dissolve the National Assembly was as much in their interest as in the king's. Sihanouk was soon to disabuse them of this calculation. Setting himself up in La Napoule, in the Alpes-Maritimes region of southeastern France, Sihanouk prepared to do battle.

He fired his opening salvo in a letter addressed to French President Vincent Auriol on 5 March 1953. The letter encapsulated the essence of the argument Sihanouk was to repeat over the ensuing months. He had no hesitation in testifying to his own virtues as being 'in Indochina the ruler who maintains the closest contacts with his people'. Because of this, Sihanouk argued, he was aware that the Cambodian government lacked in credibility so long as France continued to control such important instruments of the state as finance, the military and the judiciary. The solution to this situation was simple, he went on. France should transfer to the Cambodian sovereign and his government the powers it still retained. If this were done, France would not be stigmatised in the future for having failed to act in the interests of the Cambodian people. Indeed, Sihanouk's letter continued, giving an insight into his view of his compatriots' state of mind, 'I will go further, saying that if Cambodia is able to give up its position of permanently playing the role of *demandeur,* then its elite would be able to abandon their complex of inferiority resulting from the kingdom's lack of independence'. In these circumstances, Cambodia would be ready and able to turn to France for the material aid which it needed.

If to this point Sihanouk's letter was a largely straightforward statement of his negotiating stance, it is impossible to believe that his subsequent account of his personal position was other than dissimulation. He did not seek independence from France, he assured Auriol, either in a spirit of demagoguery or through personal interest. 'For, in the face of a rising generation wedded to republican, if not communist, ideas, the monarchy that I represent risks disappearing shortly after Cambodia gains its full independence.' In any event, Sihanouk concluded, he was ready to send his senior advisers to Paris to discuss the issue of independence or even to visit the president of France himself.

When two weeks had passed without a reply from the president, Sihanouk wrote again in more insistent terms on 18 March. 'It would be dangerous,' Sihanouk told Auriol, 'to take comfort in the illusion that all was happening for the best in the kingdom.' What was needed was for the king to be given command of the country with real responsibility and for the military problem to be addressed before all others. His compatriots in Cambodia did not know that he was in France to negotiate with the French because he did not want to embarrass the French government, he noted. Many might be thinking that he was simply seeking distraction on the Côte d'Azur. He regretted having to insist to the president on the need for action, but finding a way out of the current impasse was of the greatest urgency.

This second letter did elicit a reply, in the blandest terms. The French president had read the two letters with the greatest interest and had sent them to his government, which would study them with 'care and the least possible delay'. Meanwhile, he would be happy to receive the king at the Elysée Palace on 25 March—he confirmed his invitation for lunch on that day.

By now Sihanouk almost certainly realised that the French government was unwilling to meet his demands. His letter of 5 March had resulted in an invitation to a lunchtime meeting three weeks later. That meeting brought no satisfaction. Moving first to Fontainebleau and then to the luxury of the Hôtel Crillon in the heart of Paris, Sihanouk continued his offensive, but to no effect. Instead of progress as a result of further arguments submitted to the French, Sihanouk was now shown a glimpse of the mailed fist that his interlocutors had previously hidden behind the velvet glove of respectful words and courtesies. When the French commissioner for the associated states, Jean Letourneau, came to call on Sihanouk, he told the king that his actions were 'inopportune'. Since Sihanouk's compatriots obeyed him without question, all that was needed was for the king to be 'reasonable' and the problems he had raised with President Auriol would disappear.

Letourneau and his colleagues had badly misjudged Sihanouk. They still saw in him the king who only five years before had been ready to divorce himself from the politics of his country to turn to self-indulgent pleasures at home or the distraction of riding classes at Saumur while Chheam Van vainly struggled to dent French intransigence in Paris. Like many of Sihanouk's own countrymen, the French authorities did not yet recognise the changes that had occurred in his personality. Perhaps if they had, Letourneau would not have used the inflammatory language that he did when he found that Sihanouk was preparing to leave Paris to take his case for Cambodia's independence to a wider international audience. Alerted to Sihanouk's plans to visit Canada and the United States, Letourneau summoned Prince Monireth, then serving as Cambodia's high commissioner to France, to his office. Tell the king, Letourneau said to Sihanouk's uncle, to show 'prudence' in his travels in North America, for his crown could be at issue. Furious at this unveiled threat, Sihanouk left Paris, bound for Montreal, on 11 April. He was now stepping onto a different stage and, with his plans for a visit to Washington to meet Secretary of State John Foster Dulles, about to begin a relationship with the US that was seldom less than troubled and, on occasion, sharply hostile.

Arriving in Montreal on 12 April, Sihanouk soon found that the issue that preoccupied the Canadian media was communism. Interviewed for Radio Canada, he was asked to compare the threat posed by communism in Cambodia with that facing Vietnam. Shrewdly, if somewhat critically, he concluded that the only way to draw attention to Cambodia's call for independence was to argue that unless this was granted, Cambodia, and all the Indochinese countries, would not be able to defeat the communist challenge. As he travelled on to Washington he must have thought that this argument would be persuasive when he met the American secretary of state. He was, as he later wrote, to be 'deeply disappointed'.

Dulles had no quarrel with the suggestion that communism posed a major threat in Indochina. Indeed, he spoke to Sihanouk in the sombre terms that would be more and more frequently heard in the months that followed, as France's grip on Vietnam became increasingly tenuous—the same terms that later led him to contemplate the use of a nuclear weapon to relieve the besieged French garrison at Dien Bien Phu. But for Dulles, the situation in Indochina required a very different solution to the one the king envisaged. Sihanouk quotes him as saying: 'We are at the most crucial point of the war. We must win it. That is why, more than ever, we must unite, unite our forces, our capabilities and not argue among ourselves. Your dispute with France can only play into the hands of our common enemy.' Dulles continued with an assertion that deeply wounded Sihanouk, telling him that without French military aid Cambodia would be conquered by the 'Reds' and would lose its independence.

Dulles's analysis, in Sihanouk's eyes, 'put the cart before the horse'. Increasingly conscious that he had to appeal to a wider audience than France and already aware of the power of the Western press to affect governmental opinion, he arranged—possibly guided by the astute Cambodian ambassador in Washington, Nong Kimny—to give a interview to *The New York Times*. Never inclined to undervalue his own endeavours, Sihanouk has described the effect of his interview with Michael James, published on 19 April, as 'a bombshell—not just for American public opinion alone, but worldwide'. Without doubt, the article did attract widespread attention: Sihanouk spoke to the American reporter in terms that mixed sharp criticism of France with bitter irony. It was not he who risked Indochina falling to the communists, he insisted, but rather the French, through the intransigent policies they pursued. To suggest, as some in Paris were doing, that he had come to the US to try to ensure that American investments replaced those of the French was ridiculous. Cambodia was deeply sorry that its wishes displeased France, but he would not ask anything of any other country, Sihanouk said. He would simply return to Cambodia and ask his people what he should do next.

In the short term, Sihanouk's visit to Washington and the media attention he received did little to advance his campaign for Cambodia's independence. France did respond, it is true, by inviting Sihanouk's representatives in Paris, Penn Nouth and Sam Sary, to resume discussions, which were to result in only marginal changes to the Franco-Cambodian relationship. In the longer term, Sihanouk's visit to North America, followed by a three-week sojourn in Tokyo, had two very important results. The first was Sihanouk's new recognition of the extent to which he could advance his case through the foreign media. While much of the coverage of his visit was critical or dismissive in France and to a lesser extent in Britain, he had been able to advance his cause in *The New York Times* and had received editorial support in *The Washington Post*. Equally important, and complicating Cambodia's relations with the United States for years to come, was Sihanouk's belief that the American government had not shown him the respect that was his due while he was in Washington. He had expected to receive an invitation to dine with President Eisenhower, but none was forthcoming. When he had met Dulles, their discussions had been 'long and passionate' but ultimately 'negative' as the Secretary of State had lectured him on Indochinese affairs. And there was a final indignity: the State department had suggested he might seek diversion during his time in Washington by attending a circus. Sihanouk left the United States convinced, not without reason, that the American government and its officials did not take him seriously.

Despite an enthusiastic welcome when he returned to Phnom Penh, a welcome which, like all others in Sihanouk's Cambodia, owed something to stage management as well as to genuine feeling, the king still had few tangible results to show for his efforts. He now searched for a new dramatic gesture that would, he hoped, galvanise the French government into positive action. He decided to go into 'exile' in Thailand—a decision, Sihanouk has subsequently noted, that Western commentators treated as 'a ridiculous and preposterous flight, epitomising a capricious and inconsequential ruler'.

Quite what Sihanouk hoped his brief exile of seven days in Thailand would accomplish is difficult to judge. He had reached his decision after quitting his palace in Phnom Penh to establish himself in Siemreap, the northwestern provincial capital close to the Angkor ruins. Continuing to press the French for concessions, but still receiving no response, he decided to travel to Bangkok. The move foreshadowed his later readiness to withdraw temporarily from political battles in the expectation that his opponents would come to their senses and submit to his authority. As it was, Sihanouk's temporary exile in Thailand was, indeed, marked by elements of farce. If he had thought he would be welcomed by the Thai government—perhaps expecting, as Charles Meyer has written, a response similar to that accorded his distant ancestors when they turned to Siam for assistance—Sihanouk was to be sadly disappointed. Acting without any advance warning to the Thai government, at this stage headed by Marshal Pibul Songgram, Sihanouk crossed into Thailand on 14 June, reaching Bangkok two days later. On 16 June he issued a lengthy statement repeating yet again the demand for Cambodia's full independence, warning of the dangers of France's not granting this, and insisting that he had no quarrel with France as a country, only with its policies.

Thai reaction was swift and unhelpful. Sihanouk was firmly told that he was to regard himself as a 'plain political refugee' while he was in Thailand, and as such not to engage in polemics on his country's behalf. Thailand, officials made clear, intended to maintain its friendship with France. Disgruntled and with his already critical views of the Thai leadership further reinforced, Sihanouk returned to Cambodia on 21 June in an angry mood. His pique was heightened by the tone of some of the reporting in the French press, routinely telegraphed to the king whether its tone was laudatory or critical. In his own review of these events, Sihanouk singles out the Paris newspaper *L'Aurore* for its comments on his 'laughable pretensions' and its description of Cambodia as a 'country which has more *bonzes* (monks) than soldiers'.

Yet while Sihanouk's visit to Bangkok achieved little, it ushered in a period of remarkable success for the king. How much of this success was due to his efforts, and how much to the change of French policy towards Indochina as a whole, depends on the observer's perspective. This is the period that led to the characterisation of Sihanouk by the French military commander in Cambodia that the prince gleefully recorded in his own memoirs. Sihanouk was 'a madman', stated General de Langlade, who had commanded the cavalry school at Saumur when Sihanouk trained there in 1948, 'but he is a madman of genius'.

The element of genius was perhaps present in the king's decision, taken at the end of June 1953, to call into being a popular militia to oppose the dissident forces, of whatever stripe, that were ranged against the authority of the Cambodian state. Like the generals Napoleon treasured, Sihanouk was lucky in his timing. Wearied of insecurity in the countryside and critical of pointless political manoeuvring in Phnom Penh, tens of thousands rallied to his call to arms, including some Cambodian soldiers under French command who now deserted to align themselves with the king. Within weeks more than 100 000—Sihanouk himself says 400 000—men and women, young and old, had embarked on basic military training. For serious military operations, these popular forces, *chivapols* in Khmer, were of only the most limited value, armed as they were with obsolete firearms if at all. But as a political message they could not be ignored, either by France or by the dissidents. For Son Ngoc Thanh, in particular, Sihanouk's success in raising the *chivapols* was a blow. To the radicals in the *maquis*, also, Sihanouk was clearly a formidable opponent, quite unready to abandon his leadership to any alternative political group, whether on the left or the right.

Within days of Sihanouk's calling his compatriots to the colours, the French government, headed by Joseph Laniel, announced its intention of examining relations with the three states of Indochina, Cambodia, Laos and Vietnam, with the aim of granting them full independence within the French Union. The decision had little to do with Cambodia and a great deal to do with the deteriorating situation in Vietnam, where France had now been engaged in an increasingly costly war for nearly seven years. Although the military was determined to fight on, despite the fact that casualties in the officer corps alone were absorbing the entire graduating class from the military academy at St Cyr each year, the French public had lost their stomach for what had become known as *la sale guerre*, 'the dirty war'. The problem for the French government was how to extricate France from Indochina with some semblance of honour and over the opposition of its military and the entrenched and powerful interests still reaping economic benefit from the region. There was no easy answer to this dilemma, particularly so far as Vietnam was concerned, not least because the United States was pressing France to make a final effort to resist the advance of the Vietnamese communists, still seen as little more than surrogates of 'Red China'. As a result, over a year was to pass before the war in Vietnam was finally brought to a close by the Geneva Conference. But Laniel's government was ready to take a more flexible approach to the irritation that was Cambodia and its wilful ruler.

By the end of August, agreement had been reached between Cambodia and France for the transfer of authority over judicial and police matters to the Phnom Penh government. In the case of defence, the transfer took a little longer to negotiate, but this too passed to Cambodian hands before the end of October 1953. Sihanouk has written of the negotiations being 'tense', but there was never any real doubt how they would end, a fact underlined by his remaining in Siemreap while the discussions took place in

Phnom Penh, where the Cambodian delegation was led by the ever-faithful Penn Nouth. More annoying to Sihanouk than any French prevarication, and adding to the disillusionment he had felt after his visit to Washington earlier in the year, was the continuing evidence of American opposition to France's transfer of defence responsibilities to Cambodia. This opposition, and the critical tone of elements of the press in both the United States and Britain, left Sihanouk with a lasting conviction of the incapability of 'Anglo-Saxons' to understand him and his country's interests.

With agreement concluded on all matters, Sihanouk returned to Phnom Penh on 29 October, cheered along the route from Siemreap by hastily assembled crowds of his compatriots. This was his moment of triumph, a rebuff to Son Ngoc Thanh and all those who had opposed him during the years of unproductive parliamentary bickering. The formal declaration of Cambodia's independence took place on 9 November, with the transfer of sovereignty symbolised by a farewell march-past of the French forces commanded by General de Langlade. Sihanouk, accorded the title of 'National Hero' the day before, reviewed the departing troops with French High Commissioner Risterucci and de Langlade as torrential rain poured down on the parade. 'Sire, you have whipped me,' de Langlade had told Sihanouk on his final courtesy call. 'But no, General,' Sihanouk had replied. 'I have followed as best I can the excellent lessons in tactics that you gave me at Saumur. I have just behaved as a pupil worthy of General de Langlade.'

Was Cambodia indeed independent, as Sihanouk has always vigorously insisted, on 9 November? Juridically, the answer is 'yes'. The country's independence was quickly recognised by the West, even though some French control over technical matters, such as aviation issues, was not transferred until the following year. But more important than juridical judgments was the fact that Cambodia's radical dissidents denied that true independence had been achieved and remained in the countryside in opposition to the government in Phnom Penh. On the basis of a range of sources, including French intelligence reports, Ben Kiernan presents a picture of large areas of the country still out of control of the Phnom Penh authorities in the months after independence. In a classic guerrilla warfare situation, territory the government forces could claim during the daylight hours slipped rapidly out of their control once night fell. Now, more than ever, the dissidents were overwhelmingly radical in character. Those Cambodians who had conceived their opposition to the French in essentially nationalist terms—and Son Ngoc Thanh's followers were only part of this group—now had little justifcation for remaining in the *maquis*. But for the radicals, with their strong links to the Vietminh-led insurgency in Vietnam, the issues were quite different. France might have granted independence to Cambodia, but the battle continued in Vietnam. And in the radicals' eyes, what both Sihanouk and the French called independence was a highly qualified status which preserved French interests.

Moreover, from the radicals' point of view there was little that was reassuring about the government that Sihanouk headed in Phnom Penh. In their eyes it was classically 'feudal' and clearly opposed to their goal of transforming Cambodian society. This, certainly, was the view of the man destined to become the most infamous of all Cambodia's leftists, Saloth Sar, who had returned to Cambodia in early 1953. He left France without having completed his studies and so without any technical qualifications, but he had become a dedicated communist. By the end of 1953, like some thousands of other Cambodian leftists, the future Pol Pot had joined a Vietminh unit operating in eastern Cambodia. While the Khmer People's Revolutionary Party may have had 1000 ethnic Cambodian members at this time, the real challenge to Phnom Penh's authority still came from those who had joined or were associated with the Vietnamese communists. That Saloth Sar should have been one of these is another irony in Cambodian history, since his later tyrannous rule over Cambodia based much of its *raison d'être* on opposition to the Vietnamese and ended in bloody confrontation with them.

Major challenges still lay ahead of Sihanouk despite his success in wresting independence from the French. Not least, the Democrats remained unwilling to abandon their goal of developing a political system for Cambodia that would relegate the monarch to a secondary position. But both they and the extra-legal opposition had to contend with the indisputable fact that Sihanouk now dominated the political scene. Whatever problems remained to be solved, the king could confront them with a combination of personal assets that nobody else could match. The cloistered existence that he had once led in the royal palace was now a thing of the past. He had shown himself to the people and had gone out among them, and the peasantry had responded with unrestrained enthusiasm for the man whom, as their king, they considered little short of divine. If he had once been an indifferent orator, Sihanouk by now had mastered the art of extemporaneous public speaking. What appeared to Western observers to be long and rambling discourses were listened to by crowds that hung on their king's every word, regarding his speeches as royal commands on how to behave and as entertainment frequently marked by earthy and scatological passages. As a Cambodian king asserting his political role as well as benefiting from the aura of his office, Sihanouk now had a core of supporters drawn from the royal family and senior officials whose conservative outlook combined distrust for popular democracy with the conviction that a powerful ruler would best serve their own interests. Beyond their identification of personal interests with the interests of the state, these men in 1953, no less than their ancestors 100 years before, paid genuine respect to the monarch and the traditions that he enshrined.

Their active support was to be vital in the next round of political infighting, which took place during the two years after Cambodia's achievement of independence. One of the great myths of modern Cambodian history—a myth promoted by Sihanouk himself—is that the peasantry provided the essential support that sustained Sihanouk throughout his years as Cambodia's leader. That he received the support of the bulk of the peasantry—more than 80 per cent of Cambodia's population—is undeniable. But that support was essentially passive and had no real influence on Sihanouk's policy-making. Indeed, in his candid moments Sihanouk did not hide his disdain for the mass of his subjects. As David Chandler notes, he could dismiss them brutally as children who knew nothing about politics and cared less. They were there to be commanded and to follow his wishes. If some had been associated with dissident forces they had been misled. They could not be regarded as having interests separate from Sihanouk's own.

For the moment, King Sihanouk faced a future that gave him little opportunity to bask in the glow of his achievements. He and his advisers had to decide what to do with the independence they had gained. With political opposition still present in Phnom Penh and dissidents remaining active in the countryside, there was a clear need for action, but no certainty as to what that action should be. More than a year was to pass between the declaration of Cambodia's independence and Sihanouk's next act of genius: his decision to abdicate. In the meantime developments in Vietnam, at Dien Bien Phu, and in Geneva came to dominate the course of Cambodian politics.

Notes

In addition to the general works cited previously by Chandler, Kiernan, Meyer, Preschez, Raddi and Osborne, this chapter draws extensively on Sihanouk's *L'Indochine vue de Pékin*, and on *Souvenirs*. Roger Smith's article 'Cambodia', op cit., remains useful. Marie-A. Martin, *Le Mal cambodgien*, Paris 1989, offers some penetrating analysis.

On the suggestion that Sihanouk's mother, Kossamak, believed the Democrats were plotting to overthrow him, see Chandler, *Tragedy*, pp. 65–6. The statement by Sihanouk concerning his lack of detachment comes from the Foreign Broadcast Information Service (FBIS), Washington, reporting Radio Phnom Penh on 10 March 1967.

I observed all of those mentioned during the 1960s and beyond. Information on the derisive characterisation of Lon Nol comes from various private sources.

On the 'royal crusade', see *La Monarchie khmère*, containing reprints of articles in *Réalités* from 13 September 1959 to 3 January 1959; a series on the Cambodian monarchy and the 'royal crusade' published in *Réalités* between 24 May and 20 September 1958, and later republished as *La Monarchie cambodgienne et la Croisade royale pour l'indépendance*, Phnom Penh, 1961. Among the various Cambodian, and pro-Sihanouk, documents covering the period, probably the most notable is Sam Sary, *Bilan de l'oeuvre de Norodom Sihanouk pendant le mandat royal de 1953 à 1955*, Phnom Penh, 1955.

The text of Sihanouk's letters to President Auriol may be found in *La Monarchie khmère*, pp. 27–30 and 30–1.

The text of Auriol's letter to Sihanouk is contained in *La Monarchie khmère*, pp. 31–2. The same source provides Sihanouk's account of his meeting with Letourneau, and of the latter's warning conveyed through Monireth, pp. 35–6. *La Monarchie khmère* gives Sihanouk's account of his visit to Montreal and then to Washington, where he met Dulles, pp. 37–43. David Chandler, *Tragedy*, p. 68, quotes former State department official Paul Kattenburg on the circus invitation.

On the abortive 'exile' to Thailand, see *La Monarchie khmère*, pp. 44–59. On Meyer's comment, see, *Derrière*, p. 122.

Sihanouk quotes de Langlade in *L'Indochine vue de Pékin*, p. 54. For further detail see Chandler, *Tragedy*, pp. 68–9.

On the raising of the *chivapols*, see Sihanouk, *L'Indochine vue de Pékin*, 49, *La Monarchie khmère*, pp. 51–59 Meyer, *Derrière*, pp. 122–3.

Sihanouk's account of his government's negotiations with the French during 1953 is contained in *La Monarchie khmère*, pp. 60–79, where he comments on tension, p. 63. In the same work, he comments on the 'incomprehension' of Anglo-Saxons, pp. 66–7.

On Sihanouk's riposte to de Langlade, see *L'Indochine vue de Pékin*, p. 54.

On the role of the dissidents, see Kiernan, *How Pol Pot*, p. 121 *et seq.*

A madman of genius

Sihanouk's dismissive view of the Cambodian peasantry was expressed to the French military commander in Indochina, General Ely, in June 1954. See Chandler, *Tragedy*, p. 72.

7

A framework for power

There is convincing evidence that the events of the two years after Cambodia won its independence were fundamental in determining the future shape of both Sihanouk's and Cambodia's history until the *coup d'état* of 1970. Sihanouk's primacy as the leader of the country was confirmed. His opponents, both legal and clandestine, were marginalised. Relations with foreign countries were set upon bases of warmth or suspicion that altered little for over a decade. Brutality and intimidation were firmly established as instruments of state policy. And farce was occasionally present as well as tragedy. As an independent country in a rapidly changing and dangerous Southeast Asian setting, Cambodia and its ruler all too readily provided sensational material for journalists, while little attention was given to the deficiencies and inequalities of a state dominated by one man.

The achievement of independence was a triumph for Sihanouk and for his faithful senior advisers, but a daunting list of problems remained to be addressed. Foremost among these was the continuing presence in Cambodia of men committed to the communist cause, both radical ethnic Khmer leftists and Vietnamese supporting the Vietminh troops now engaged in an ever more deadly battle with the French expeditionary forces. In December 1953, amid much adulatory publicity, Sihanouk took formal command of a

Cambodian army sweep against a Vietminh base in the northwestern province of Battambang. Operation Sammaki (Solidarity) was to enter the official folklore of Sihanouk's career, and it cemented Colonel Lon Nol's position as one of Sihanouk's most trusted military advisers after he wrote an account of the affair full of lavish praise for the king. Photographs of the smiling monarch leading his troops in a freshly pressed uniform with shining combat boots appeared and reappeared over the years. During the 1960s, the boots themselves were displayed in the Norodom Sihanouk Museum in Phnom Penh. Yet the operation achieved very little, French advisers were responsible for what small success it had—ten of the enemy killed for the loss of one Cambodian soldier. More important than the operation itself, as Sihanouk later made clear when he spoke to Jean Lacouture in 1971, was his 'consternation' at the pamphlets he found left behind by the rebels. They showed Sihanouk as a cartoon figure, a puppet dangling on a string controlled by the French. This was only one of a continuing series of experiences that left the king bitterly suspicious of any who sided with the left within Cambodia.

So it was that, when Sihanouk sent Foreign Minister Tep Phan and General Nhiek Tioulong to head the Cambodian delegation to the Geneva Conference on the war in Indochina in May 1954, he was determined not to make any concessions to those who had been associated with leftist forces in Cambodia over the previous eight years. Despite the presence in the Vietminh delegation of two Cambodian leftists, and the efforts of Pham Van Dong, who led the Vietminh delegation, to argue a case for treating the Cambodian radicals in the same way as the Pathet Lao movement in Laos, the Cambodian delegation remained adamant that it alone had the right to speak for its country. Tep Phan and Tioulong kept in daily touch with Sihanouk. Their dogged resolution through long hours of debate and argument, and the forceful presence of Sihanouk's special envoy, Sam Sary, were aided by a curious combination of circumstances. As a result of broader international pressures, the Soviet Union was reluctant to back all the demands of the Vietnamese communists, not least in relation to what territory should come under the latter's control. China, possibly uncertain about United States intentions and even then disturbed by the prospect of expanding Vietnamese influence over both Laos and Cambodia, did not support the right of Cambodia's leftists to be heard. And the Western delegates saw issues associated with Cambodia as less important than those linked to Vietnam, where France suffered the humiliation of devastating defeat at Dien Bien Phu while the conference was taking place. As a result, Cambodia emerged from the conference with its territorial integrity intact, unlike either Vietnam or Laos, and with no special rights given to its leftist rebels. Moreover, no limitation was placed on Cambodia's right to seek military aid from any source should it face aggression.

For the moment the Cambodian left was in disarray, facing a setback from which it was not to recover for many years. Although Sihanouk's government had issued a proclamation shortly before independence claiming it 'did not oppose communism so long as it is not imposed from outside', there was no reason for the leftists to believe this. In the event, and with eventual terrible consequences in the Pol Pot years, more than 1000 Cambodian communists went into exile in the Democratic Republic of Vietnam (North Vietnam). A much smaller number of dedicated leftists remained behind, some to risk engaging in open politics, others, like Saloth Sar, the future Pol Pot, to hide their political affiliations while continuing to work clandestinely in pursuit of their radical goals.

In fact, in the wake of the Geneva triumph, the only real domestic political threat to Sihanouk's interests, and the interests of those aligned with him, came not from the communists but from his old antagonists, the Democrats. Even with the hindsight of nearly 40 years it is difficult to assess both the size of that threat and the motivations behind the Democrats' continuing determination to oppose the king. Some were no doubt moved by personal ambition and feared that with Sihanouk in control of Cambodia's political life they would not gain the rewards of power. Others were influenced at least to some extent by Son Ngoc Thanh's ideas—particularly on the role of the monarchy. This was despite the fact that Thanh remained in hostile exile after having failed to gain Sihanouk's approval for his return to participate in Cambodian political life. (Thanh had sought to enlist the aid of Indian Prime Minister Jawaharlal Nehru, whom he saw secretly when the latter was visiting Angkor in 1954. According to Sihanouk, Nehru urged Thanh to work with Sihanouk, but Thanh rejected this advice.) Another reason for the Democrats' continued activity was the fact that the party was now the political home of some of the more able leftists, such as Keng Vannsak and Thiounn Mumm, former students in France, who had decided to infiltrate a legal party that was, at least, already sympathetic to republican ideas and opposed to Cambodia's developing links with the United States.

Still buoyed by the results of the Geneva Conference and already receiving approving judgments on his policies from such widely respected world figures as Nehru, Sihanouk resented the fact that any within the kingdom should express doubts about the wisdom of his policies. He therefore announced in early 1955 that, consistent with the promise he had made in 1952, he would submit his 'royal crusade' to the judgment of a national referendum to be held on 7 February 1955. The result of this ballot was an overwhelming affirmation of support for Sihanouk, with the official figures showing more than 99 per cent approval of his actions (925 667 approving, 1834 against). The referendum also pointed up the difficulties associated with any transfer into Cambodian society of such a Western concept as a referendum. Propaganda from Sihanouk's supporters made clear that not to vote approval of the king would be the equivalent of *lèse majesté*. When the referendum was held, ballot secrecy was generally disregarded. Voters were handed two voting papers: one white, indicating approval of Sihanouk, and one black. Under the gaze of officials and security men they were told to destroy on the spot the ballot they did not wish to cast. Nevertheless, despite the referendum's shortcomings and Sihanouk's own later suggestion that the number of disapproving votes may have been higher than the official figures, the referendum was yet another triumph for the king. Within a month he was to capitalise on it with a totally unexpected step when, confounding friend and foe alike, he abdicated the throne.

Debate still continues over just why Sihanouk took such an unforeseen and radical step as leaving the throne. To a considerable extent, the debate is fuelled by the various explanations Sihanouk himself has given of his actions. Possibly that diversity should simply be accepted as reflecting the multiple concerns of a man who increasingly expected total support from his compatriots but who, even after the result of the referendum, found his views were still questioned both at home and abroad. A few bold editors even continued to insist that Cambodia had not gained independence in November 1953, an act that led to their being jailed on Sihanouk's orders shortly after the referendum.

In the light of the referendum's overwhelming approval, Sihanouk announced that he was proposing to introduce major constitutional change. Drafted initially by Sam Sary and Yem Sambaur, these proposals had as their central feature a series of provisions that would have made any king of Cambodia supremely powerful over his ministers and parliament but which also envisaged extending the vote to women and providing electors with the right to dismiss their parliamentary representatives. To Sihanouk's surprise, his proposals, some of which he genuinely saw as giving a greater voice to the Cambodian population at large, were opposed both by domestic critics and by sections of the international community. Although most of his closest allies favoured his proposals, Sihanouk was taken aback by Yem Sambaur's decision to distance himself from the changes the king was contemplating and for which Sambaur himself bore some responsibility. This was an important breaking of ranks, for Yem Sambaur never fully returned to favour and was to be a cautious but quietly influential critic within the legal political system over the next fifteen years. After the 1970 coup that overthrew Sihanouk he was an enthusiastic supporter of the new regime.

Others, most notably the Democrats, questioned the desirability of Sihanouk's proposals, invoking the support of the Polish representatives on the International Control Commission that had been set up to supervise the implementation of the Geneva accords in all the countries of Indochina. There was also diplomatic opposition to the suggested constitutional changes from the British government, one of the guarantors of the Geneva settlement. While Charles Meyer has raised the possibility that Sihanouk never intended that the proposed alterations to the constitution be introduced—he suggests that Sihanouk may have been using the proposals as a stalking horse to flush out local opinion—the best judgment seems to be that he was sincere in advancing his proposals and genuinely surprised at the opposition he had provoked.

To that surprise was joined anger arising from two rather contradictory sources. On the one hand Sihanouk learned that much of the adulation he was receiving from delegations praising the referendum result had not been a genuine outpouring of popular feeling but the carefully arranged stage management of his supporters. On the other hand he was deeply offended by the suggestion, still coming from the Democrats and others who had sympathy for Son Ngoc Thanh, that the proper role for the Cambodian king was that of a constitutional monarch without executive powers. For the man who had successfully gained Cambodia's independence through his royal crusade, whose envoys had achieved their goals in Geneva, and who had won a resounding vote of approval in the referendum, such a proposition could not be entertained. It was a profoundly wounding insult. Comparing himself without any hesitation to his French idol, Sihanouk was to say to Jean Lacouture years later, 'Imagine de Gaulle called upon to countersign decrees introduced by Mitterrand or Marchais'. It was for this reason, and to avoid becoming nothing more than a 'political invalid', that he decided to abdicate.

After announcing he was cancelling his proposed constitutional amendments on 27 February, Sihanouk gave no hint of what he later called the 'atomic bomb' he was to drop a week later. He has insisted that he told no-one of his intentions, not even his parents, and no evidence has emerged to contradict his assertion. While the possibility of his acting on advice from close associates cannot be dismissed entirely, there is, again, no convincing evidence for this. Nor is there more than speculation to buttress the suggestion that in abdicating Sihanouk may have sought to walk away from the political arena as he had contemplated doing before and was to do again. His robust actions after the announcement and his evident sense of having achieved triumph after triumph during the preceding twelve months make this interpretation improbable. With his inherent sense of drama he arranged for his abdication to be announced over Phnom Penh radio, sending a recording in a sealed envelope to the station with instructions for it to be opened and played at noon on 2 March. King Sihanouk was to become, he has said in one of his accounts of this period, 'citizen Sihanouk'. Under no circumstance, he vowed, would he ever return to the throne.

Plain 'citizen Sihanouk' never existed, neither in fact nor in his mind. All the evidence points the other way. Certainly, in all the prince's explanations of his actions, both at the time and later, he is to be believed when he says that he was inspired by determination to recast a political system that was bogged down in unproductive rivalries and squabbling. Equally, there is no doubt that he was sincere when, in explaining his decision to the Cambodian people less than two weeks after the abdication announcement, he spoke scathingly of the constraints which being king placed upon him. Shut up in the palace, he complained, he was prevented from knowing what went on outside. And that palace was 'stuffed full of a hierarchy of court mandarins and intriguers. They are like the blood-sucking leeches that attach themselves to the feet of elephants.' Ever emotional, Sihanouk is convincing when he states that in the period just before he abdicated he despaired of the divisions characterising Cambodian political life and was unable to sleep.

But however determined he was to shake off the kingly chains that constrained his actions and kept him from appreciating the lot of his fellow citizens, Sihanouk was far from ready for, or desirous of, shedding the trappings of royalty that were to his personal and political advantage. He had ceased to be king, but he now took a formal title that reminded his former subjects of what he had been. Prince Sihanouk was now *samdech upayuvareach* (the prince who has been king). Although Sihanouk now persuaded his father, Norodom Suramarit, to mount the throne, where he received all the deference that his new position demanded, there was no diminution in the respect that Sihanouk received from the bulk of the population. While a few brave and determined politicians took account of the prince's changed formal status, most did not. He still benefited from all the services that the palace could provide. His word was a command to the Cambodian military. So far as status and respect were concerned, he remained a king in all but name.

Politically, his abdication was a masterstroke, for while retaining all these advantages, Sihanouk now had a freedom of action that had eluded him before. With his father on the throne, Sihanouk had no need to be concerned that any other member of the royal family would seek to gain the throne with the hope of using it for political ends. Yet while his abdication solved an immediate problem, it left Sihanouk uncertain about the future role of the monarchy in Cambodia. His talk of becoming citizen Sihanouk aside, he recognised the benefit he had gained from his occupancy of the throne. From the time of his abdication onwards, Sihanouk frequently discussed in public the role of the monarch and the throne in Cambodia, as if unable to resolve his own contradictory thoughts about the institution. On the one hand he saw it as a vital unifying factor. On the other he realised that the throne could become the base for political initiatives by an ambitious man. Yet in giving so much consideration to the role of the king in the Cambodian state Sihanouk made at least a partial miscalculation. In focusing his attention on the issue of personal power and who was to exercise it, he presumed his own indefinite tenure of power. At the same time, he failed to consider the extent to which his own political position could come under threat from forces that were in some cases not greatly affected by the existence, or otherwise, of a monarchy. In brief, Sihanouk could never forget he had been king and could neither forgo royal prerogatives nor believe that his country would accept an alternative leader or policies other than those he advocated.

Such threats lay far in the future, as Sihanouk moved to the next stage of his political agenda. In early April he announced the formation of a new political movement that he would head. The Sangkum Reastr Niyum (People's Socialist Community) was Sihanouk's answer to what he saw as the sterility of 'conventional' Cambodian politics. The Sangkum, the prince insisted repeatedly, should not be regarded as a political party. To the contrary, it was to be a national organisation flexible enough to accommodate a wide range of political opinion. Loyalty to the throne and to the political policies that Sihanouk now advocated were the essential requirements for membership. To what extent was the idea that such a movement could provide an answer to Cambodia's political woes Sihanouk's alone? Probably not entirely, for politicians sympathetic to Sihanouk had held tentative discussions touching on party mergers shortly before he announced his abdication. But just as his abdication was a brilliant stroke at the time, so was the decision to try and submerge party differences within a mass national movement both unexpected and politically successful in the short to medium term.

The broad basis of membership provided the movement's immediate strength, just as it was the major reason for its later weakness. At the time of its formation men of widely differing outlook could unite in support of limited, if important, political principles. But precisely because of its extremely broad character as a political movement, the Sangkum, after its initial success, lacked cohesion and was shot through with the perennial Cambodian problem of political factionalism. Nevertheless, it served Sihanouk's immediate needs well. As he embarked on a program of overseas travel that was important in shaping the outlines of Cambodia's foreign policy for over a decade to come, his closest supporters worked energetically to ensure that the supposedly apolitical Sangkum would become Cambodia's predominant political force. As they pursued this goal, they were acutely conscious of the next hurdle in the political calendar: a National Assembly election to be held before the end of 1955.

Amid the frenetic domestic political activity which had absorbed so much of Sihanouk's attention during 1954, the question of what foreign policy an independent Cambodia would pursue remained to be settled. The position the Cambodian delegation had adopted at the Geneva Conference suggested that Cambodia under Sihanouk's guidance would show little sympathy to international communism. But, at the same time, Sihanouk had made very clear

his irritation with the unsubtle efforts of the United States to have
Cambodia join the Western camp of nations. The king's visit to
Washington in 1953 left him with a jaundiced view of American
diplomacy and, in the personal terms so important to him, of
Secretary of State Dulles in particular.

With the Geneva Conference concluded, the United States had
set about promoting a regional organisation to contain what it saw
as the threat from China. While Cambodia was not eligible to join
the Southeast Asia Treaty Organisation (SEATO), inaugurated in late
1954, the United States was anxious for Cambodia to place itself
under the treaty's protection. Despite the markedly pro-American
sympathies of some of his closest associates, notably Sam Sary and
Lon Nol, Sihanouk refused to do this. The reasons for his reluctance were mixed. His experience in Washington in 1953 still
rankled. Clumsy efforts by senior conservative American politicians,
notably California's Senator William Knowland, to sway Cambodia
towards the Western camp were resented. France, as the former
colonial power in Cambodia whose counsels were still given weight
in Phnom Penh, cautioned against acceding to American blandishments. And the American ambassador to Phnom Penh, Robert
McClintock, displayed an uncanny ability to offend Sihanouk.

When John Foster Dulles came to Phnom Penh to see Sihanouk
on 28 February 1955 he found the king in no mood to compromise.
Still smarting from the opposition he had encountered to his
proposals for constitutional change, Sihanouk was unprepared to
be lectured by Dulles. As Dulles persisted in arguing for Cambodia's
accepting SEATO's protection, the king, as he still was, grew furious.
Dulles's mission was a failure. Nevertheless Sihanouk was still not
fixed in his views, so far as foreign relations were concerned. The
next few months were to influence him decisively.

Shortly after Dulles's visit Sihanouk travelled to India, where
he renewed his friendly relations with Prime Minister Nehru, afterwards making a brief visit to Burma. Then, as later, Sihanouk
regarded the Indian leader with a mixture of respect and affection,
a combination of attitudes he has accorded to few others apart
from General de Gaulle of France and Prime Minister Zhou Enlai
of China. Nehru was, Sihanouk has said, his guru, convincing him
of the virtues of neutrality in international affairs and of the validity
of the Five Principles of Peaceful Co-Existence that Nehru and
Zhou Enlai had endorsed a year earlier. The picture that emerges
of this meeting in March 1955 is of Nehru instructing Sihanouk
from a familiar position of self-righteous conviction while flattering
the prince with praise for the latter's 'act of glory' in abdicating

the Cambodian throne. In a revealing comment, Sihanouk later noted his reservations about Nehru's insistence on non-violence, the Gandhian precept to which India's political leaders proclaimed their adherence. His own 'Buddhist neutrality' was not without some 'little bits' of violence, Sihanouk has observed. So that when Nehru's army invaded Portuguese Goa in 1961 he was happy, he has said, to see that his guru, too, could on occasion resort to force.

The prince's visit to India and Burma was followed by his participation in April 1955 in the Afro-Asian Conference in Bandung. The conference reinforced Sihanouk's belief in his own importance and further inclined him to a position of neutrality in the then-intense confrontation between the West, led by the United States, and the Soviet Union and its communist allies. Feted and flattered by the leaders of nations vastly larger than his own, Sihanouk revelled in the attention he received from President Sukarno, from Nehru, and from Zhou Enlai. Seldom given to questioning the sincerity of those who spoke approvingly of his actions, Sihanouk felt at ease in an ambience that mixed self-congratulation with routine denunciation of the United States. For, added to the resentment he felt over his reception in Washington in 1953, he was now convinced that the United States, in the support it lent to his neighbours in Thailand and South Vietnam, was at least tacitly signalling its disapproval of Sihanouk and his policies.

There was, indeed, more than a little reason for Sihanouk to hold such a view. After Son Ngoc Thanh had fled into dissidence in 1952 he received support from the Thai government. That support continued after Cambodia gained independence, as successive Thai governments pursued a traditional policy of giving aid to groups that could destabilise their smaller eastern neighbour. In the 1950s and into the '60s this policy was given a sharper edge through the existence of East–West rivalry, with Thailand firmly in the Western camp, backed by the United States. To what extent American intelligence services were involved with Thanh, and which services were involved, is not always clear. But there was some justification for Sihanouk's view that without US support, Thailand's sponsorship of Thanh would have been less important.

A similar logic informed Sihanouk's view of the Republic of Vietnam (South Vietnam). Even before there was clear evidence of that country's readiness to involve itself in efforts to bring down Sihanouk's regime, American backing for Ngo Dinh Diem's new government disturbed Sihanouk. Once the prince had made clear his readiness to opt for a policy of friendship with China, South Vietnamese denunciations of his position confirmed him in the view that another American-backed regime was seeking to undermine him.

In contrast to the reserve, at best, shown to him by his two immediate neighbours, the leaders Sihanouk met at Bandung offered friendship and, most importantly in the cases of Zhou Enlai and Pham Van Dong, assurances of non-interference in Cambodia's affairs. And the further contrast between the heavy-handed diplomacy of Secretary of State Dulles during his visit to Phnom Penh in February and the blandishments of Zhou and Dong, courtly mandarins in their behaviour if not in their politics, reinforced Sihanouk's belief that he had been right to resist the arguments put to him by the Americans.

One other reason for Sihanouk's embrace of a neutral foreign policy should be noted in the context of the Bandung Conference. Acutely conscious of Cambodia's small size as a nation and of its lack of material power, the prince found both personal and national satisfaction in adopting neutrality as a framework for his foreign policy, seeing it as an act of defiance. Asserting Cambodia's neutrality in the face of American pressure gave him a measure of satisfaction that went beyond the policy implications of his stance. Not only was the policy right, in his eyes, but the fact that it offended America added spice to the experience of adopting it. To tweak the giant's nose and then enjoy the spectacle of his having to contain his anger was exhilarating.

Yet Sihanouk still showed a measure of caution in his relations with the United States that infuriated his leftist critics in Cambodia. Although he was not ready to place his country under SEATO's protection, he did accept a US offer to establish a Military Aid and Assistance Group (MAAG) in Cambodia that would finance and equip his army. But, seeking to cover his bets and accepting the advice of Zhou Enlai during the Bandung meeting, Sihanouk refused to have his army trained by the United States. Instead he entrusted training responsibilities to the French. At the same time, he made it clear that he was ready to accept American civil aid on a large scale. For the moment Sihanouk and his supporters were able to have their neutral foreign policy cake while happily eating the benefits of generous American aid.

When Sihanouk returned home from Bandung, recruitment to the

Sangkum was in full swing. With the National Assembly elections planned for September, Sihanouk and his supporters still faced substantial opposition from the Democrats and, to a lesser degree, from the Pracheachon (People's) party, a leftist front party linked to those who had fought under the communist banner during the First Indochina War. The prince made clear his determination to see his supporters in power by appointing Dap Chhuon, the former rebel now administering Siemreap as his personal fiefdom, to take charge of security for the elections. Barely literate and known for his brutality towards his enemies, Dap Chhuon was assisted by Lon Nol, Sam Sary and Kou Roun, a man who was to earn a deservedly sinister reputation as the head of Sihanouk's secret police during the 1960s.

The campaign for the September 1955 elections has been better documented than any other that took place while Sihanouk was in power. It was marked by widespread corruption and substantial violence. Terror was used as a weapon against candidates and their supporters by all sides, but most particularly by those backing the Sangkum. Just how many died is not certain. What is beyond dispute is that Dap Chhuon's agents systematically intimidated their opponents, disrupting rallies, assaulting vote canvassers, and ensuring that only Sangkum posters were left untouched. To think that Sihanouk was unaware of what was happening is to do more than strain credulity; it is to misunderstand the nature of Sihanouk's rule until his overthrow in 1970. He knew that his supporters resorted to violence to maintain him in power. He sanctioned that violence since he could not conceive that his opponents could be other than foolish, at best, or more likely motivated by evil intent towards him personally, at worst. If the latter, they had forfeited their right to freedom and possibly to life. One of Sihanouk's most fundamental failings, clearly demonstrated in 1955, has been his insistence on claiming credit for his many achievements while being unready, certainly in public terms, to accept blame for the less savoury aspects of his regime. Some recognition of his responsibility for the latter might have tempered the excesses that occurred.

In the event, and contrary to many observers' expectations until quite close to the day of the vote, the elections were a triumph for Sihanouk and the Sangkum. According to the official results, 83 per cent of the votes cast went to Sangkum candidates, the Democrats received 12 per cent, and the Pracheachon received 4 per cent. The result meant that the membership of the National Assembly would be made up entirely of Sangkum candidates.

How valid was this result, and what did it mean? Most commentators agree that the combined effect of Sihanouk's appeal at the head of the Sangkum and the intimidatory tactics used by his supporters ensured that the Sangkum would have won a majority of seats in the election. Not least was this so because of Sihanouk's own contribution to the campaign. Capitalising on his newly discovered oratorical skills, he made full use of the freedom from kingly restraints to carry his arguments to the people. His message was simple—a vote for the Sangkum was a vote for his policies. The appeal of 'the prince who had been king' was immense. But the overwhelming result suggests that allegations of ballot box stuffing and of voting papers disappearing before being counted were valid. And David Chandler has now published convincing new evidence that Sangkum candidates were, in fact, defeated in five constituencies. As with the February 1955 referendum, voting took place under the eyes of Sihanouk's supporters, who noted how votes were cast. And the ballots themselves encouraged a pro-Sangkum result, since Sihanouk's portrait distinguished the voting paper that was to be cast for the Sangkum. Finally, but far from exhaustively, the inhabitants of Phnom Penh would have been acutely aware of the dangers that faced opponents of the Sangkum. Only days before the election, a band of Sangkum supporters led by Sam Sary disrupted a Democrat rally being addressed by one of their leaders, the left-inclined teacher Keng Vannsak. In the melee that followed a Democrat worker was killed and Vannsak was thrown into prison. The cost of opposition was made very clear.

The elections of September 1955 capped the list of triumphs to which Sihanouk could point as he addressed the initial national congress of the Sangkum. Conceived of by Sihanouk as an exercise in popular democracy, these congresses were to be held every six months so long as he remained in power. Attended by thousands, many of whom had been bused in from distant provinces, these congresses were presented by Sihanouk as an opportunity for free discussion of political and economic issues. Initially held within the palace grounds and later on the Men ground, the site of royal cremations just outside the palace walls, the congresses took place in an aura of royalty and tradition. From the end of 1957 onwards the Cambodian constitution specifically required the National Assembly to address itself to matters raised by the congresses. Yet despite the publicity the congresses were given, and despite the lively discussion that many of the topics raised at them inspired, there is still reason to question the true significance of these popular meetings.

Whatever else the congresses were, they were not opportunities for the mass of the population to exercise political power. The congresses were, on occasion, an important way for Sihanouk to neutralise opposition—most notably in the early congresses when he successfully undermined the Democrats and the Pracheachon. As a forum for airing grievances and promoting particular policies, too, they were important. But, stage-managed like so much else in Sihanouk's Cambodia, the congresses were, above all else, an opportunity for Sihanouk to demonstrate his centrality in Cambodian political life. Speaking for hours at a time, castigating opponents and interrupting endlessly when others were at the rostrum, Sihanouk used the congresses to reinforce the impression, particularly among foreign observers, that Sihanouk alone determined the course of Cambodian politics.

At the first congress, held at the end of September, Sihanouk received support for the introduction of the constitutional amendments he had proposed, and then withdrawn, earlier in the year. More fundamentally important, in calling the congress into being he demonstrated that he could mobilise public opinion through a forum separate from the elected parliament. His conception of a mass political movement was later to be shown as possessing many flaws, but for the moment it was a spectacularly successful new feature of Cambodian politics. Closely associated with the civil service, the congresses also offered a political home to the urban middle classes, who felt little identification with the princes and grand court officials who had previously regarded themselves as the sole group deserving preferment under the monarch. Yet Sihanouk's triumph did not put an end to parliamentary squabbling, nor did it eliminate Sihanouk's foreign policy problems. These two themes, both separately and intertwined, remained as challenges despite the string of successes Sihanouk had achieved by the end of 1955.

Notes

Commentary and detail on the period surveyed in this chapter will again be found in Chandler, Kiernan, Meyer, Preschez, Martin and Osborne. Some of the most useful autobiographical material is found in Sihanouk's *L'Indochine vue de Pékin* and to a lesser extent *Souvenirs*. All the words of Sihanouk quoted in this chapter come from the former, with the exception of Sihanouk's description of the limitations placed on his freedom while king, which are taken from *My War with the CIA: The Memoirs of Prince Norodom Sihanouk as related to Wilfred Burchett*, New York, 1972, an interesting but often dubiously accurate account of Sihanouk's rule over Cambodia prepared by the veteran Australian leftist journalist.

On Cambodia's role at the Geneva Conference, see R.M. Smith, *Cambodia's Foreign Policy*, Chapter III, and M. Leifer, *Cambodia: The Search for Security*, New York, 1967. Also interesting on this period is François Joyaux, *La Chine et le règlement du premier conflit d'Indochine*, Paris, 1979.

A pro-Sihanouk source covering part of the period reviewed in this chapter is Sam Sary and Mau Say, *Bilan de l'oeuvre de Norodom Sihanouk pendant le mandat royal de 1952 à 1955*, Phnom Penh, 1955.

A particularly valuable source for developments in 1955 is Michael Vickery, 'Looking back at Cambodia', *Westerly*, 4 December 1976, pp. 14–28.

The figures for the voting are provided in Meyer, Chandler and Preschez. For Sihanouk's own discussion of the referendum and the period in general see 'Etude corrective de la constitution accordée par S.M. le Roi du Cambodge en 1947', *France-Asie*, XI, 108, May 1955, pp. 656–63.

The most detailed account of the Bandung Conference and of Chinese contacts with the Cambodian representatives there is found in G. McT. Kahin, *The Asian-African Conference, Bandung, Indonesia, April 1955*, Ithaca, N.Y., 1956, in particular pp. 15, 21 and 22. For Sihanouk's own commentary on the meeting, see *Le Monde*, 13 June 1956.

In addition to published material detailing Thai support for Son Ngoc Thanh, I am indebted to General Channa Samudvanija for insights into Thai policy towards Cambodia in the 1950s and 1960s in the course of discussions in Bangkok in 1980.

For the new evidence that shows election results were altered to give the Sangkum a clean sweep at the polls, see *Brother Number One*, p. 204, n. 16.

An extended but oversimplified account of a national congress of the Sangkum is contained in Wilfred Burchett's *Mekong Upstream*, pp. 179–86. For a further discussion of the congresses as an institution, see R.M. Smith 'Cambodia', p. 623. As Donald Lancaster, Sihanouk's one-time English-language secretary, points out in his article, 'The decline of Prince Sihanouk's regime', p. 48, Sihanouk 'presided over the debates with verve, skill and authority'.

In a private comment on the Sihanouk–Nehru relationship in 1966, Wilfred Burchett told me that the prince in fact disliked Nehru intensely and felt that the Indian leader patronised him. I have found no other evidence to support this view. (Diary 1 June 1966). Certainly, the pen portrait Sihanouk provides of Nehru in *Charisma and Leadership* is an admiring one.

Sihanouk in coronation regalia, November 1941
In this photograph taken at the time of his coronation, Sihanouk shows little
joy at his elevation to the Cambodian throne.

INDOCHINE (CAMBODGE)

S.M. NORODOM SIHANOUK (ROI DU CAMBODGE)

Sihanouk, the young king
During World War II,
the French sought to use
Sihanouk to bolster their
position in Cambodia. In this
instance the twenty-two-year-
old king is depicted on a
commemorative postal
envelope issued by the
French. (*Author's collection*)

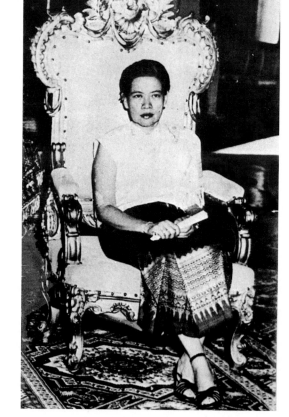

**Sihanouk's mother, Princess,
later Queen Kossamak**
Sihanouk's mother was a
powerful influence in his life
until he became chief of state
in 1960. She was critical of his
leftist advisers and opposed to
his liaison with Monique.

Sihanouk's father, Prince, later King Suramarit
Suramarit played little part in his son's upbringing. Kind but distant, he was to play a key part in Sihanouk's political strategy when the Prince abdicated in 1955. By placing his father on the throne in that year, Sihanouk ensured that there could be no challenge to his position from within the royal family.

Sihanouk at play
In his youth, Sihanouk was an accomplished horseman. Later he encouraged his compatriots to play sports such as football and basketball and led teams from the royal palace in local competitions. Sihanouk's teams always won.

The Throne Hall in the Phnom Penh palace
The throne hall of the palace is shown here illuminated for a state occasion
in 1959. Sihanouk lived in the palace until he became chief of state in 1960.
He lived there again during his period as a prisoner of the Khmer Rouge.
(*Author's photograph*)

The royal ballet
State visits to Phnom Penh were an occasion for performance by the royal
ballet. In this photograph the ballet is performing for President Sukarno of
Indonesia. The dancer on the left of the photograph is Princess Bopha Devi,
Sihanouk's favourite daughter.

Elephants in King Suramarit's funeral procession; *below* **King Suramarit's funeral pagoda**
The death of Sihanouk's father Suramarit in 1960 was an occasion for great state ceremonies. The year also saw Sihanouk consolidate his power by becoming chief of state. (*Author's photographs*)

Sihanouk carrying his father's ashes
Sihanouk's father, King Suramarit, died in April 1960 and was cremated later that year. In this photograph, Sihanouk carries an urn containing his father's ashes in the final ceremonies associated with Suramarit's funeral.

Sihanouk and President John F. Kennedy
In this photograph dating from 1961, Sihanouk greets the American president warmly. By 1963, Sihanouk was to greet Kennedy's death with equal warmth.

Sihanouk as chief of state
An official portrait photograph of Sihanouk dating from the early 1960s.

Son Sann, Sihanouk's longtime economic adviser
Throughout the 1950s and 1960s Son Sann was Sihanouk's trusted
economic adviser, before the two men fell out over policy disagreements.
After the Vietnamese invasion of Cambodia in 1978–79, Son Sann
became the leader of a resistance faction. He is seen here at the founding
of the Khmer People's National Liberation Front in December 1979.
(*Author's photograph*)

General de Gaulle in Cambodia
General de Gaulle's visit to Cambodia in 1966 provided a brief moment of
euphoria in a declining political situation. In this photograph the French
president is watching boat races on the Mekong in company with Monique
and Sihanouk.

8

Friends abroad, plots at home, 1956–59

At the beginning of 1956, Sihanouk had every reason to judge that the world was his oyster. Still only 33, he was the dominant political personality in his own country and he had found a place on the international stage that both met the interests of Cambodia, as he perceived them, and flattered his vanity. His growing conviction that neutrality was the proper path for Cambodia to follow was soon reinforced by experiences whose impact was all the sharper because they affected him personally.

At the end of January Sihanouk travelled to the Philippines on a state visit. His hosts received him with the full warmth of Filipino hospitality and Sihanouk was initially gratified. But the visit rapidly turned sour. Sihanouk remained determined that Cambodia would not seek protection under the SEATO treaty—a visit to Phnom Penh by the director of the Central Intelligence Agency, Allen Dulles, in late 1955 had, if anything, strengthened his resolve. So he was amazed when, the day after his arrival, the *Manila Chronicle* printed an editorial suggesting Sihanouk had come to the Philippines capital to announce that he would place Cambodia under SEATO's protection. Displeasure turned to anger when, after a moderate speech to the Philippines Congress, Sihanouk was approached by a shadowy figure who had travelled to Manila as part of the prince's entourage and who now offered him the draft of a speech for an engagement he was to fulfil at Camp Murphy, the Philippine Army's headquarters.

François Baroukh is one of the many bit players who drifted

in and out of Sihanouk's official life. Apparently of Lebanese origin, he had spent some months in Phnom Penh and established contact with the prince. During his time in the Cambodian capital he appeared to be that familiar figure in postcolonial Southeast Asia, a carpetbagger. In the light of events in Manila, Sihanouk has had no hesitation in labelling him an agent of the CIA. At the very least, Baroukh seems to have been working in close association with people in the American embassy in Manila when he offered Sihanouk a draft speech that called into question the stance Sihanouk had taken against associating his country with SEATO. Reacting promptly, Sihanouk circulated his own draft speech affirming his belief in the concept of peaceful coexistence. Now the *amour propre* of both sides was engaged, for the Philippine authorities saw Sihanouk's draft as an affront and the prince's visit to Camp Murphy was cancelled. Sihanouk departed, after a further tense encounter with President Magsaysay during an official dinner, convinced that his policies were right and that what he had seen in Manila showed only too clearly the dangers of close alignment with the United States. Going on the offensive shortly after returning to Phnom Penh, Sihanouk released a communique providing an account of all that had happened in Manila. Magsaysay was furious and responded sharply. In Phnom Penh Sihanouk retaliated by naming his pet dog after the Philippine president.

It was against this background that Sihanouk made his first visit to China in the middle of February. During this, the first of many visits, the prince contrasted the 'dignity and bearing of a country that stood on its own feet' with the ignominy of the Philippines, a nation 'under the domination of a foreign power'. He also reacted with awe to the welcome the Chinese provided—tall unsmiling guards of honour that dwarfed the diminutive prince as he reviewed them, sumptuous banquets in vast halls, and everywhere hundreds of thousands of people assembled by the government to greet him. Then, as on later visits and like so many Southeast Asian leaders before him, Sihanouk was almost overwhelmed by the sheer size of China and its population. He was also deeply flattered by his reception. Not only was he warmly received by Zhou Enlai, the man he had seen as a friend since their time together at the Bandung Conference, he was also welcomed by the almost legendary Mao Zedong. In a skilful gesture, Zhou offered Sihanouk economic aid without any accompanying conditions and the two leaders signed a Sino-Cambodian declaration of friendship. What is more, in addition to concluding an aid and trade agreement, Zhou appears to have provided some guarantee that China would act as Cambodia's protector against the Democratic Republic of Vietnam (North Vietnam), a state whose intentions the prince distrusted. The details of this agreement were not made public, but its existence does much to explain Sihanouk's subsequent policies and the apparent readiness of the Chinese to regard Cambodia as a special example of their readiness to seek peaceful coexistence with their Southeast Asian neighbours.

When Sihanouk returned to Phnom Penh he was further hardened in his belief that neutrality was the best policy for his country and that the United States had wilfully failed to understand this. The right-wing governments in both Bangkok and Saigon deplored his warm relations with China. South Vietnam instituted an economic blockade that briefly prevented cargo ships travelling up the Mekong River to Phnom Penh, at that stage Cambodia's only deep-water port. At the same time, Thailand closed its border with Cambodia. In Phnom Penh itself, Sihanouk was repeatedly angered and offended by the American ambassador, Robert McClintock, whose lack of sensitivity has figured in all the prince's memoirs.

Blunt-speaking and a convinced Cold War warrior, McClintock was unquestionably the wrong man in the wrong place in 1955 and 1956. Acting more as a proconsul than a diplomat, his dress and manners offended Cambodians: he strode through the capital in shorts, brandishing a baton, and even appeared with his pet dog on some official occasions. Showing his country's displeasure with Sihanouk's foreign policy at one time by ostentatiously walking away from the official dais when Sihanouk was about to address a national congress meeting, he failed to recognise that in Cambodian eyes his actions and his words were in extreme bad taste. Sihanouk has recorded a prime example of McClintock's gauche behaviour. Seeing the prince at the opening of a maternity hospital for which the American government had provided equipment, McClintock suggested that the facility would interest Sihanouk 'as a great maker of babies'. The prince replied in robust terms. There would be no more babies, Sihanouk responded sharply, for 'those that might have come have smelled the bad odour of American imperialism'.

Yet despite the clashes of policy and personalities, Sihanouk was not anxious to sever relations with the United States, which alone could provide the economic aid he knew his country needed. Although he was ready to have discussion of the desirability of accepting American aid placed on the agenda for the national congress due to be held in April 1956, Sihanouk was glad when the State department drew back from confrontation and undertook to give aid without conditions. At the same time, in actions that Sihanouk naturally saw as coordinated by America, South Vietnam lifted its economic blockade and Thailand opened its border with Cambodia.

With the congress behind him, Sihanouk embarked on a protracted journey to France, Poland, Sweden, Spain, the Soviet Union, Czechoslovakia, Yugoslavia and Austria. An essential aim of the trip was to demonstrate the reality of his country's proclaimed neutrality, particularly to the Soviet Union, which had shown a reserved attitude to Cambodia's continuing readiness to receive American economic and military aid. Overall, Sihanouk could judge his visits a success. Although, in Spain, Franco showed no interest in Cambodia whatsoever, and the visits to Warsaw and Prague were unmarked by any particular warmth, the prince had a modest success in Moscow and was greatly satisfied by his welcome in Belgrade. Tito was now added to the list of leaders Sihanouk could admire, and Yugoslavia's unique version of socialism impressed the prince as providing a guide to the kind of policies he might pursue in his own country.

A year of intensive activity in pursuit of Cambodia's foreign policy interests culminated in Sihanouk's receiving Zhou Enlai in Phnom Penh in November 1956. Sihanouk regarded the visit as a great success, not least because of Zhou's firm admonition to the overseas Chinese resident in Cambodia to respect the laws of their host country. Diplomatic relations were still not established between Cambodia and China. Indeed, the Taiwanese regime retained an official consular presence in Cambodia until 1958. But Sihanouk was convinced that in China Cambodia had a friend large enough and strong enough to provide the ultimate guarantee against the threats he perceived from his predatory neighbours. This was a comforting thought as he wrestled yet again with the domestic problems that still confronted him.

Given the electoral triumph of the Sangkum in the elections of September 1955, why was Sihanouk still not able to orchestrate domestic political harmony? In considerable part, Cambodia's political problems were systemic. The provisions of the constitution that divided power between the executive, in the form of the ministry, and the legislature, in the form of the National Assembly, remained in effect—with predictable results. Votes of no confidence passed by the assembly led to the resignation of ministries. Ministries fell because of policy disputes—or simple personal rivalries—among their members. Nine ministries came and went between September 1955 and January 1958, creating a situation that, increasingly, fed power into the hands of Sihanouk as the one apparently unassailable figure in Cambodian politics, but left a sense of drift within the kingdom.

It was a situation that Sihanouk viewed with ambivalence. He had no doubts about his centrality to Cambodia's affairs, but he deplored the expectation that he would solve all the country's problems. He had little time for politicians in general and he knew that most of them feared his displeasure. The rump of the Democrat party, now without parliamentary representation, remained an object for his anger for he was convinced, with cause, that the United States was lending financial support to his political enemies. Repeatedly threatening to resign and working eighteen-hour days, Sihanouk by the middle of 1957 was close to both physical and emotional exhaustion. Finally gaining agreement from his father, the king, for his resignation as prime minister, Sihanouk gave a fiery performance at the Sangkum's national congress before going into retreat in a monastery at Phnom Kulen near the Angkor ruins. The semi-official newspaper *Réalités Cambodgiennes* recorded this event with pictures of a sober-faced Sihanouk in a white robe with a shaven head living, the newspaper reported, 'in a humble hut'. From this bucolic retreat and shrouded in sanctity, Sihanouk announced his resignation from the Sangkum and his decision to eschew public life.

A bare two weeks later he was back in Phnom Penh, spoiling for a fight with the Democrats, his announced withdrawal from politics simply disregarded. Egged on by Sam Sary, Sihanouk demanded that Democrat leaders meet him in a public debate to sustain the charges they had made against him and his government, particularly the suggestion that he had presided over a corrupt regime. They reluctantly agreed to do so and the debate took place on 11 August. The event was a prime example of the political theatre so characteristic of the Sihanouk years. Held within the palace, the debate had been so well publicised that the crowds attending could not be accommodated in the palace grounds and spilled in their thousands outside the walls to listen to the proceedings over a public address system. Sihanouk was in his finest rhetorical form. His opponents were not: they stumbled and equivocated, hesitating even when Sihanouk called on them to join the Sangkum. When Sihanouk walked away from the rostrum some three hours after the debate had begun, he left his opponents vanquished.

This was both the actual and the highly symbolic end to the Democrats as a political force in Cambodia. But whether on Sihanouk's orders or not, the humiliation of the debate was followed immediately by violence against the Democrats who had attended it. They were attacked by soldiers of the palace guard as they left the palace. Then, over the next few days, men believed to be Democrats were savagely beaten by soldiers who clearly had been given assurances that such action was desired at the highest level and would not result in punishment. Drawing on Prince Monireth's private memoirs of this period, David Chandler notes that some of those involved in administering beatings to his Democrat opponents were subsequently honoured by the prince.

If Sihanouk believed that domestic politics would now continue on an even keel, he was soon disillusioned. As he rested on holiday in France, squabbling between the government led by Sim Var and the Assembly continued, with accusations and counter-accusations of corruption and scandal. When he returned to Cambodia Sihanouk was initially reluctant to become directly involved in solving the chronic problems besetting parliamentary politics. But after it became clear that matters were at an impasse he sanctioned the dissolution of the assembly and threw himself into the fray again. Successfully conducting a referendum that prevented the expansion of the size of the assembly as the result of extending the vote to women, he set about choosing personally each of the Sangkum candidates who would contest the elections due in March 1958. In this he was aided by a new and energetic figure on the Cambodian political scene, Chau Seng.

The results of the election were a foregone conclusion. After their humiliation the preceding August, the Democrats had no stomach for a contest. The only party to field opposing candidates was the radical leftist front party, the Pracheachon. Five of its members nominated for election in Phnom Penh, Takeo, Svay Rieng, Kampot and Battambang. Their cause was hopeless. Harassed by the police and by the Sangkum youth wing, the JSRK*, they were unable to conduct election rallies. More importantly, these leftist candidates had to contend with the fact that Sihanouk was making very clear his opposition to the communist ideal that they

---

* The full, French-language title of the youth wing was the *Jeunesse Socialiste Royale Khmère* (The Royal Khmer Socialist Youth). Almost always referred to by its initials, the rather curiously named organisation had a membership that included many in their 30s and 40s. Civil servants were expected to belong.

were hesitantly promoting. In speeches and press articles, the prince portrayed communism as a threat to Cambodia's monarchical tradition, while the Pracheachon candidates falsely portrayed him as their friend. When the elections took place, the Pracheachon candidates were eclipsed and the Sangkum swept into office with 99 per cent of the vote. The parliamentary face of the radical left in Cambodia was essentially obliterated, but among the candidates whom Sihanouk had personally selected and who now held seats in the National Assembly were men such as Hou Youn and Hu Nim who were to figure prominently in later radical politics. And only in 1962 did the Pracheachon party finally cease to exist. For the moment, dedicated communists, including the future Pol Pot, were pursuing their goals clandestinely as they led double lives as teachers and journalists. In 1958, however, Sihanouk appeared to have reason to believe that at last he had assured domestic tranquillity would reign. Less than a year was to pass before the fragility of this hope was made clear. By then, the difficulties posed by Cambodia's antagonistic neighbours, South Vietnam and Thailand, had become linked to right-wing opposition to his regime within the kingdom.

Throughout the years during which Sihanouk led Cambodia, relations with its neighbours Thailand and South Vietnam (the Republic of Vietnam) were chronically difficult. In part this reflected deep-seated historical jealousies and antipathies. Just because Cambodia and Thailand shared so many cultural values, Thai readiness to patronise Cambodia, at best, and interfere in its affairs, at worst, deeply offended Sihanouk and his supporters. In the case of South Vietnam, the sharply differing cultures of the two countries added a particularly corrosive element to contemporary problems. And in both cases, Sihanouk's readiness to perceive all issues in personal terms served to ensure that any hostile action by his neighbours was viewed as a direct attack on him. The events of late 1958 and early 1959 could only reinforce his prejudices and his fears.

During 1958 both Thailand and South Vietnam encroached on Cambodian territory. The Thais seized an Angkor-period temple, Preah Vihear, on the Dangrek escarpment forming Cambodia's northern border. Then, in June, South Vietnamese troops occupied an area of the remote northeastern Cambodian province of Stung Treng. In Sihanouk's eyes both acts bore the mark of direct involvement by the men then ruling in Thailand and South Vietnam, Marshal Sarit and President Ngo Dinh Diem. As the three governments traded ever more bitter accusations and insults, Sihanouk once again took to the road, visiting China in August and the United States in October. In Peking Sihanouk was again received with the greatest consideration, including by Mao, with whom he had several meetings. Somewhat hesitantly, Sihanouk asked Zhou Enlai to ensure that the quasi-diplomatic Chinese aid mission by then established in Cambodia would not propagandise on China's behalf among the ethnic Chinese resident in Cambodia. Zhou assured the prince that he would do so—though this did not seem to prevent Chinese officials in Phnom Penh from continuing to promote their government's policies. In the high point of the visit, the two countries announced that they would now establish full diplomatic relations.

This decision was to have far-reaching consequences, since it was seen by the fervently anti-communist leaderships in Thailand and South Vietnam as confirmation that Cambodia's neutrality was not genuine. Just as importantly, it persuaded sections of the American intelligence community that it was now appropriate to take active measures against Sihanouk. From these conclusions sprang the confusing series of events that Sihanouk has labelled the 'Bangkok plot'. Whether there was one, two or even three plots is still not clear. If, as seems most probable, there was a series of plots against Sihanouk, the evidence suggests a linkage between them—and South Vietnamese involvement in all three.

The first plot involved a man who had formerly enjoyed Sihanouk's favour, Sam Sary. A graduate in law and political science from Paris, Sary had earned the prince's gratitude in the mid-1950s by hard work and apparent devotion to the prince's interests. He had been an effective advocate for Cambodia at the Geneva Conference and had helped the prince found the Sangkum and organise the 1955 election campaign. He also found time to edit highly laudatory collections of documents extolling Sihanouk's achievements. Authoritarian by sentiment, he adopted pro-American views increasingly contrary to those of his leader. Nevertheless, Sihanouk was sufficiently grateful for his past services to appoint Sam Sary as Cambodia's ambassador to London in early 1958, thus extricating him from the embarrassment of a scandal involving the smuggling of large quantities of high-grade Cambodian pepper. (Queen Kossamak, Sihanouk's mother, may well have played a part in Sary's gaining this plum diplomatic appointment, for she had afforded him protection in the past.)

Barely six months after he arrived in London, Sam Sary was

involved in another scandal, when one of his female servants, who had been his concubine and had borne one of his children, went to the London police complaining that her employer had whipped her. Sary was immediately recalled to Phnom Penh, but not before he had put his side of the story to the eager British press. Yes, he agreed, he had whipped the woman in question, but this was entirely in accord with Cambodian custom.

Once back in Cambodia, Sary ignored Queen Kossamak's advice to abstain from political activity and began acting in a fashion that suggested he had lost the capacity for political judgment. Despite clear indications of the risks he would run if he further incurred Sihanouk's displeasure, he unsuccessfully sought to found an opposition political party and published a newspaper that was openly critical of the prince's policies. Most commentators now assume that he was, by this stage, being supported by US intelligence, probably, as David Chandler has speculated, as a consequence of contacts he made during a visit to the United States in 1956. Quite what Sam Sary next planned to do never became clear, since Sihanouk pre-empted his plans in a dramatic speech delivered in Kompong Cham on 13 January 1959. Making clear that he was speaking about Thailand, Sihanouk told his listeners that he knew of a plan to overthrow him and to change Cambodia's foreign policy to alignment with the United States. If, as he claims, Sihanouk's knowledge of such a plot came from warnings given to him by the French and Chinese embassies as well as his own security services, they had still not implicated Sam Sary. When further evidence reached Sihanouk a week later, Sary had already fled. After a shadowy existence in exile, he disappeared in 1962, probably put to death by one or another of his foreign paymasters.

Was there a plot on the lines that Sihanouk has alleged? In his account of the affair given to Wilfred Burchett, Sihanouk provides considerable detail of plans being made by Thai and South Vietnamese officials, in concert with Son Ngoc Thanh and with the knowledge of CIA agents, to overthrow him. Sam Sary's connection with these plans seems beyond doubt even if the details of his involvement remain obscure. But, with one notable exception, Sihanouk's claims are largely convincing when it comes to his account of the Dap Chhuon affair, which followed hard on the heels of Sam Sary's flight into exile.

Whatever his feelings towards the United States before the Dap Chhuon affair, after it was uncovered Sihanouk was forever to distrust America and to regard the CIA as his implacable enemy. He had visited New York and Washington during October 1958 and come away less sharply critical of his reception than before, though he later characterised President Eisenhower as having spoken to him in a 'paternalistic' fashion. The Dap Chhuon affair put paid to any hope that Sihanouk would henceforth see the United States with other than prejudiced eyes. For there was incontrovertible evidence that a CIA officer attached to the agency's station in the American embassy in Phnom Penh was involved in the events leading to the affair.

While some controversy still surrounds the details of the plot involving Dap Chhuon and the manner in which it was crushed, the essentials are clear enough. In the years since he had rallied to Sihanouk's side, Dap Chhuon had steadily increased his personal hold over the region around Siemreap, the provincial town close to the Angkor ruins. Brutal and ruthless, he was tolerated by the prince for the security his presence in Siemreap provided in this strategically important area of Cambodia. But as he dominated his fiefdom, Dap Chhuon had also become steadily more disenchanted with what he saw as Sihanouk's leftist leanings, epitomised by his warm relations with China. Making little secret of his views, Chhuon developed a clandestine association with Sihanouk's arch enemy, Son Ngoc Thanh. It was probably through Thanh that Chhuon developed further clandestine links with the Thais, Vietnamese and Americans.

Sihanouk has stated that the plots involving Sam Sary and Dap Chhuon both had their origins in a meeting in Bangkok in late 1958. But more recently presented evidence, cited by David Chandler, suggests that the catalyst for action was a decision made by President Diem of South Vietnam and his brother, the sinister Ngo Dinh Nhu. Using their representative in Phnom Penh as their intermediary, the Diems were ready to finance and assist Dap Chhuon in bringing down Sihanouk. But if the South Vietnamese leaders took the initiative in promoting the planned coup, they were quickly joined by the Thais and by the CIA. The undoubted involvement of the CIA has been seized on by Sihanouk, and others, as proof that the whole affair was masterminded by the United States. This was clearly not the case. The probable explanation for the agency's limited involvement was a hope that if the plot succeeded the US would be well placed to build on a relationship with Cambodia's new leader.

During February 1959 the pace of preparations for a coup accelerated. Weapons and ammunition were ferried in by aircraft from Thailand to Siemreap, and Ngo Hong Trieu, the Saigon regime's representative in Phnom Penh, visited Dap Chhuon, bringing with him 270 kilograms of gold to finance the planned move against Sihanouk. It was also at this time that Victor Matsui, a CIA operative of Japanese descent, visited Dap Chhuon, bringing with him a radio transmitter–receiver. Whether Dap Chhuon was aware of it or not, the unusual activity in Siemreap was being reported back to Phnom Penh, and to Sihanouk.

At some point, as these frantic preparations were taking place, Dap Chhuon had a change of heart. Apparently sensing his vulnerability, he is said to have written to Sihanouk's mother, Kossamak, and to Lon Nol revealing the details of the plot. He evidently assumed that this confession would exculpate him. He was wrong. Sihanouk was in no mood to pardon Chhuon. He ordered Lon Nol to move on Siemreap and to shoot Chhuon after seizing the gold brought from Saigon. Advancing with infinite caution up the road from Phnom Penh, Lon Nol's troops rapidly occupied Siemreap on 22 February. Lon Nol himself, accompanied by General Ngo Hou, the head of the Cambodian air force, had flown to the town earlier. Lon Nol's forces quickly disarmed Dap Chhuon's troops, but Chhuon himself, although wounded, escaped capture. When, days later, he was caught, his fate was sealed. Lon Nol obeyed the prince's instructions and Dap Chhuon was shot 'while attempting to escape'. No such swift end came for his brother, Slat Peou, who was captured and taken to Phnom Penh for questioning. It was from Slat Peou's confession that Matsui's involvement was eventually revealed—Matsui himself had by then left Cambodia in an unsuccessful attempt at damage control.

In his detailed account of the failed coup Sihanouk has claimed that Lon Nol was himself part of the plot, and that Dap Chhuon was shot to prevent him from revealing this fact. This *post factum* allegation has more to do with the prince's fury over Lon Nol's part in the coup that toppled Sihanouk in 1970 than with the events of 1959. In yet another ironic footnote to the affair, Sihanouk was later to use the plot as the basis of one of his feature films, *Shadows over Angkor*, in which he played a leading role.

The long-term repercussions of this affair cannot be exaggerated. Sihanouk's deep suspicion of the United States shaped his foreign policy thinking for the following decade and led him to give a ready ear to those Cambodians and foreigners who wished to denigrate America. At the same time, the plots associated with Sam Sary and Dap Chhuon gave Sihanouk a rallying cry that played a major part in preserving the prince's control over the country. More than ever, from the late 1950s, Sihanouk solved his domestic problems through appeals for support in his difficulties in the international sphere. In the months immediately after the Dap Chhuon plot was crushed, Sihanouk silenced criticism from both the legal left and the right by repeatedly evoking the spectre of an external threat to Cambodia.

The spectre took on a tragically substantial form in August 1959. Under orders from Ngo Dinh Nhu, South Vietnamese agents arranged for two suitcases to be delivered to the royal palace, one addressed to Sihanouk and the other to Prince Vakrivan, head of protocol in the palace and, incidentally, a former husband of one of Sihanouk's secondary wives. The suitcases were represented as containing gifts from Hong Kong and as coming from an American engineer who had worked in Cambodia. The case intended for Sihanouk was packed with explosives; that for Vakrivan was harmless. For whatever reason, Vakrivan opened both the cases and was killed instantly, along with a palace servant. To add to the drama, the explosion took place in a room next door to where Sihanouk's parents were sitting. For a brief time after the explosion the centre of Phnom Penh was like an armed camp as armoured personnel carriers and armoured cars ringed the palace and troops patrolled the streets in full battle kit. In light of events earlier in the year, Sihanouk had no hesitation in blaming Saigon for Vakrivan's death, while his propagandists hinted darkly at possible American involvement.

Sensing an opportunity to capitalise on public indignation at these examples of foreign interference in Cambodia's affairs, Sihanouk announced another referendum to let the Cambodian people pronounce on his avowed international policy of neutrality. This decision was unanimously approved by the National Assembly in October 1959. If neutrality was not the people's choice they could, as alternatives, vote for the pro-Western policies presumed to be supported by Son Ngoc Thanh and his exiled supporters, or for communism. Although the alternatives were cast in terms of international issues, the real question was obviously one of personalities. A vote for his policies, Sihanouk argued, would ensure Cambodia's stability. A vote for the kinds of policies attributed to Son Ngoc Thanh would place Cambodia in America's orbit, subordinating the country to a power now implicated in the plots against the prince himself. A vote for communism would destroy Cambodia's ancient monarchical traditions.

Well before the referendum finally took place, Sihanouk engaged in an extended discussion in speeches and in the press of the problem of leadership in the kingdom. In a series of articles in the semi-official *Réalités Cambodgiennes*, he made clear his view that the monarchy remained a vital unifying force and that should it disappear the kingdom would be a prey to contending forces that he listed as 'pro-Seatoists', communists, royalists and nationalists. In asking 'Will Cambodia become a republic?' the title of his series of articles, Sihanouk was making clear his strong belief that the issue of leadership remained vital to Cambodia's survival and that he alone was the person to preserve and nurture his country's interests. But he also raised another prospective problem, the possibility that some future successor to his father, King Suramarit, could undermine his essential leadership.

Several points emerge from Sihanouk's lengthy meditation on the nature of leadership in Cambodia. Perhaps most importantly, the articles were, by implication, largely dismissive of other domestic problems, such as economic or social issues, that existed separately from the leadership question. This dangerously short-sighted attitude was finally to play a considerable part in shifting the tide of opinion against Sihanouk from both the right and left of Cambodian politics. Next, the articles took up an issue that was to be of increasing concern to Sihanouk in subsequent years: the tendency for a large proportion of Cambodian students studying in France to adopt left-wing views. Although he expressed his worries about this trend, Sihanouk appears to have failed to understand the attraction of communist and radical left-wing ideology to those who found fault with the social and economic conditions that surrounded them in Cambodia. For the prince at this time, communism was a danger to the Cambodia he knew and believed he understood. He simply could not conceive of it, as others did, as an ideology that offered answers to the problems of a society in which there were profound inequalities.

Finally, if far from exhaustively, Sihanouk's articles provided a sharply critical commentary on the royal family. He expressed the view that too many of his relatives were conservative in their outlook and unready to give up their privileges for the good of the state. There was a need for a 'revolution' in the court and the royal palace, a reduction in the number of 'services' provided for the court, and the elimination of the 'parasites' associated with it. If the monarchy was to survive, the next occupant of the throne would have to be modern in outlook and unwilling to accept the corruption that was still a normal part of palace life. These were brave words that Sihanouk was never able to transform into action so far as his own 'court' was concerned. They were also more relevant than Sihanouk could have ever feared or realised at the time he penned them. Despite his father's poor health there was no expectation in late 1959 that Suramarit would die an early death. When this occurred, quite suddenly in April 1960, the issue of succession to the throne ceased to be a matter of theoretical discussion and led to even further personalisation of power in Sihanouk's hands.

Notes

For commentary on the period discussed in this chapter, see Chandler, *Tragedy*; Meyer, *Derrière*; Martin, *Le Mal cambodgien*; and Michael Field, *The Prevailing Wind*, London, 1964. A critical left-wing view of these and later developments is provided by J.-C. Pomonti and S. Thion, *Des Courtisans aux partisans: Essai sur la crise cambodgienne*, Paris, 1971. Smith, *Cambodia's Foreign Policy*, and Leifer, *Cambodia: The Search for Security*, address international issues.

Sihanouk provides a detailed account of his visit to Manila in *My War with the CIA*, pp. 76–81. See, also, his *Souvenirs*, pp. 231–2, and Meyer, *Derrière*, p. 230.

For contemporary commentary on Sam Sary and the Dap Chhuon affair, see *Réalités*, 20 January 1959 and 10 March 1959. The account in this chapter relies for new information on David Chandler's researches detailed in Chapter 3 of *Tragedy*, in particular pp. 99–107. See also Notes 42–66, pp. 333–5.

Controversy surrounds the suggestion that Zhou Enlai offered Sihanouk a guarantee against the DRVN when the prince visited Peking in 1956. Martin Herz in his *A Short History of Cambodia*, New York, 1958, asserts he did. I was told by Wilfred Burchett in 1966 that such an offer was indeed made (Diary 13 June 1966).

McClintock's inelegant remark about Sihanouk's philoprogenitive nature is recorded by the prince in his *My War With the CIA*.

For the account of Sihanouk's retreat near Angkor, see *Réalités*, 3 August 1957.

The results of the March 1958 election may be found in *Réalités*, 29 March 1958.

For contemporary comment on the attack that killed Prince Vakrivan, see *Radio Monitoring Service*, United States Embassy, Phnom Penh, nos. 203–10, 1–9 September 1959, and *Réalités*, 5 September 1959.

Sihanouk's series of articles 'Le Cambodge deviendra-t-il une république?' were published in *Réalités* between 22 August and 23 October 1959. The quotation is from *Réalités*, 23 October 1959.

9

The king is dead, long live the chief of state

In contrast to the hectic events of 1959, the early months of 1960 in Cambodia were marked by a general sense of calm. There was an awareness that the king's health was deteriorating, but no notion outside the palace that he might soon die. So his death on 3 April came as a shock and a surprise. It also ushered in a period of frantic manoeuvring by Sihanouk as he searched for a political formula that would meet his determination to hold all real power but would take account of his firmly held belief that Cambodia's monarchy was an essential 'glue' holding the country together.

For Sihanouk, his father's death was a personal tragedy; this was abundantly evident to those who saw him at the formal rituals performed immediately after Suramarit's death, as the prince and his shaven-headed mother presided over the pouring of the lustral water over the dead king's body. But beyond personal grief was the question of what to do about succession to the throne. In his articles published in *Réalités* the previous year, he had insisted on the vital importance of the monarchy. The corollary to this argument was an acceptance that whoever was the Cambodian monarch was potentially in a position to play a powerful political role. Sihanouk's persuading his father to mount the throne in 1955 had circumvented this problem, but could he be sure that some other member of the royal family would be as malleable?

These were not the terms in which Sihanouk discussed the issue of succession to his father on 7 April, four days after Suramarit died. Rather, he chose to dwell on divisions within the royal family, whose unity was jeopardised by 'indescribable jealousies and hatreds'; on the efforts by 'traitors' to exacerbate these divisions so that Son Ngoc Thanh might establish a republic on the ruins of the monarchy; and on the reasons why neither his mother nor any of his sons should be placed on the throne. These points, and his repeated insistence that he would never again be king, deserve to be studied in some detail, but first it is worth briefly examining events between the old king's death and Sihanouk's impassioned speech of 7 April.

The formal requirement, once Suramarit died, was for the Crown Council, composed of a senior member of the royal family, the heads of the two parliamentary houses, the prime minister and the heads of the two Buddhist orders, to meet. At the time of Suramarit's death, Sihanouk was prime minister. This formal fact was much less important that the dominance Sihanouk exercised over all other members of the council, including its chairman, his uncle Prince Monireth. Whatever views the other members of the council may have held—and there is reason to think that Monireth favoured placing his sister, Queen Kossamak, on the throne—once Sihanouk made clear his view that there should be no successor, no other view could prevail.

The decision having been made not to appoint a successor, a special bill was rushed through the compliant parliament on 4 April to establish a Regency Council. This was to have no executive powers but would 'represent' the throne. For the moment, Sihanouk had found a stopgap measure while he pondered how to proceed.

Sihanouk gave public voice to his concerns in his mammoth speech of 7 April. Just as he had done for national congress meetings, he chose the Men ground next to the palace as the venue. This was a decision full of symbolism, since his listeners knew that the prince was discussing the future of the monarchy on the ground where, in the not too distant future, his father's body would be cremated after protracted and spectacular funeral rites.

Showing every sign of emotional and physical exhaustion, Sihanouk laid out a picture of a royal family riven by internal feuds and jealousies that suggested little had changed in the world his royal relatives inhabited since the mid–nineteenth century. Their lives were marked by rivalry and greed. Different branches of the royal family conspired against each other and kept alive memories of each other's past excesses and misdeeds to be used as weapons.

In these circumstances, with unscrupulous princes ready to capitalise on their rank, and in light of the weighty responsibilities a king had to assume, Sihanouk would not countenance naming any of his sons to succeed to the throne. They were too young and lacking in experience for the task. This was not all. In a passage omitted from the official published version of his speech, Sihanouk went on to denigrate his offspring, in particular his eldest son, Rannariddh, who was only good, he said, for driving fast cars and being rude to policemen.

In light of all the problems he had outlined, Sihanouk went on, the decision to appoint a Regency Council represented the best solution while he remained to serve the people:

> . . . If I were to resume the Throne I should be far away from you. I must be a simple citizen, a politician who through your will has been made President of the Sangkum. Only in this way can I guide the Country, the People and help the Throne and Religion.

Sihanouk's speech was a mixture of shrewd political calculation and genuine distrust of the intentions of his royal relatives. It was also a manoeuvre that gave him time to consider how to solve a difficult problem. The Sangkum solution that he had so brilliantly devised in 1955 rested in large part on his knowing that his father would not be a player in Cambodia's political game. Now that Suramarit was dead, could any other prince be relied upon to behave in the same fashion?

How valid were Sihanouk's concerns? Was his picture of a venal royal family founded in fact or in his imagination? That many in the royal family were dissolute or corrupt, or both, is beyond dispute, and many of the more than 100 princes who theoretically had the right to succeed probably did harbour ambitions to be king. But in fact, Sihanouk needed to consider only three real possibilities: succession by one of his sons, by his mother, or by Monireth. Each of these choices raised problems for the prince. He was not convinced that any of his sons was capable of discharging the duties of a monarch. His concerns in relation to his mother and his uncle were of a different order. Both, in their own way, risked being too capable, too ready to act as they saw fit rather than be pliant instruments of his will. These were not concerns that Sihanouk could voice aloud, but they are fundamental to an understanding of why he could not countenance another ruler's mounting the Cambodian throne.

Sihanouk clearly recognised that the appointment of a Regency

Council was only a temporary solution to his dilemma. While senior members of the royal family and trusted officials were not prepared to act counter to his express wishes, they were, in the absence of firm policy guidance from him, prepared to make troublesome suggestions. One such was the proposal, in late April 1960, that Sihanouk's mother should indeed ascend the throne as a reigning monarch. Quite apart from his ambiguous personal relations with his mother, Sihanouk saw this possibility as threatening genuine political embarrassment. Whether or not his mother would wish to take advantage of being on the throne, there were others who might. The curious fact that a demonstration in favour of the queen's succession had taken place in Battambang city shortly after Suramarit's death gave weight to Sihanouk's suspicion that any new occupant of the throne, even his mother, would be used in the Cambodian political game. So a more permanent solution had to be found. From the middle of April until early June 1960 he first evolved a formula to solve his problem and then carefully watched over its implementation. The fact that contemporary Cambodian reports of the period speak of 'spontaneous' demonstrations and expressions of the 'nation's will' must be regarded with the utmost scepticism. No less than was the case in 1955, Sihanouk planned his moves, aided by his principal advisers, and brought his plans to fruition. If popular demonstrations were required as part of the process, these could readily be provided.

Once he had decided that it was impossible for any member of the royal family to succeed to the vacant throne, Prince Sihanouk sought to establish a new position whereby he would supplant the occupant of the throne as the constitutional head of state and at the same time retain essential political power. First he resigned the prime ministership, which he had held at the time of his father's death. Then he watched for eight days as politician after politician refused to assume the post, effectively demonstrating the difficulty of finding an alternative to the prince. When, on 19 April, a new government was finally formed, its essentially caretaker character was underlined by the appointment as prime minister of an ageing political veteran, Pho Proeung. The end of April was marked by a second visit to Cambodia by Zhou Enlai. The visit was the signal for an outbreak of incursions across Cambodia's borders by supporters of Son Ngoc Thanh, who now termed themselves Khmer Serei (Free Cambodians), and for even more vitriolic criticism of Sihanouk by the Thai and South Vietnamese press.

This external criticism provided Sihanouk with the backdrop he required for his initiatives. He now set the date for the promised referendum, foreshadowed in October of the previous year. In the campaign that he mounted in his own favour he spoke of the attacks he had sustained from his external enemies, the Thais and the South Vietnamese, as well as the threats from internal 'traitors'. Behind the Thais and the South Vietnamese, and their links with Son Ngoc Thanh, there was the enmity, Sihanouk suggested in scarcely veiled allusions, of the United States. What he described as 'imperialist circles' sought constantly to denigrate him. In diplomatic relations, the prince noted, he had 'always had difficulties with all the ambassadors who represented the United States in Cambodia'.

When the referendum was held on 5 June the voters were offered four choices. By casting a ballot bearing a photo of Sihanouk they indicated approval of his policies. Approval of Son Ngoc Thanh could be shown by a ballot with a photo of the long-exiled enemy. Approval of communism was demonstrated by a red ballot, and a blank voting paper was available for those who had no opinion. After weeks in which Sihanouk spared no energy to depict himself as the lightning rod for all the calumnies directed against Cambodia, the referendum was a resounding affirmation of his leadership—not really surprisingly, since each voter's choice was carefully observed by military and security personnel who watched as the papers were dropped into the ballot box or discarded.

According to the official figures, more than 99.98 per cent of voters cast ballots for Sihanouk. Yet even though this official result was obviously inflated and the election was anything but free and fair, it was a notable success for Sihanouk. It confirmed that he could continue to rely on mass support from the electorate in a confrontation with those he described as his enemies. In light of the result, he acted to consolidate his position.

The referendum results were announced on 8 June. On 10 June the Cambodian parliament, members of the cabinet, the armed forces and various government departments issued statements calling on Sihanouk to assume leadership of the country as chief of state. The next day well-organised demonstrations took place in Phnom Penh, echoing the earlier formal requests to Sihanouk. Massed before the National Assembly, the demonstrators asked parliament to tell Sihanouk of the people's wish that he become chief of state. Graciously, from his seaside retreat at Kep, Sihanouk agreed to accept the people's will. His father's death, he now stated, had shown that there could not for the moment be a new king on the throne and that this lack of a symbolic leader would be exploited by Cambodia's enemies. Now that the referendum had convincingly demonstrated that he had the support of the nation, he was ready to become chief of state once the parliament had amended the constitution to provide for this new office. A hurried meeting of the parliament on 13 June added the necessary article, Number 122, allowing the appointment as chief of state of an individual 'incontestably and expressly designated by the vote of the nation'. Article 122 also contained a final paragraph which in 1960 seemed to have little significance: it provided that the president of the National Assembly could assume the powers of the chief of state if the latter was temporarily absent from Cambodia or unable to exercise his powers. Here was a constitutional time bomb that was to tick slowly away until March 1970.

Before he assumed the newly created position, Sihanouk, showing his long-standing concern for the appearance of maintaining constitutional niceties, provided a commentary on what had happened in a long interview with *Réalités Cambodgiennes*. There had been no *coup d'état*, nor had the constitution been overturned, as had happened in other countries, he averred. 'Quite simply, satisfaction had been given to the wishes of the Khmer people.' As chief of state he would not be king, nor regent, nor president. He would fulfil the responsibilities of a monarch but without the benefits of that office, such as a civil list. He had responded to the wishes of the people, but if they wished he would resign from the position of chief of state forthwith. Meanwhile, he made clear that he had by no means abandoned the hope of seeing a new monarch on the Cambodian throne at some future date. Such a monarch would need to understand the interests of the people and should live as often as possible among his people, away from the intrigues of the royal palace.

On 20 June Sihanouk drove to the parliament and was sworn in as Cambodia's chief of state. Addressing the parliament after taking his oath of office, he said that he would work to reform the administration of the royal palace in preparation for the eventual appointment of a new king. Meanwhile, he would take over various duties previously the responsibility of the monarch, such as the holding of popular audiences, which gave members of the public an opportunity to bring their grievances to the ruler. While doing all this, he would remain president of the Sangkum. Finally, he asked the parliament to approve a measure by which his mother, Kossamak, would be regarded as 'symbolising' the throne. This last proposal was an ambiguous concept at best, since as chief of state he was cloaking himself in both greater practical and symbolic power. His address completed, Sihanouk withdrew, *Réalités* reported, to the applause of a 'large crowd'. The applause, in fact, was desultory, from barely 200 onlookers. Curiously, neither Queen Kossamak nor Prince Monireth was in Phnom Penh when this ceremony took place, choosing instead to spend the period 18–20 June in Battambang.

If 1960 was the year in which Sihanouk reached the apogee of his power, it was also the year in which Cambodia's radical leftists took a firm step along the path toward their awful triumph in 1975. Electorally eclipsed in 1958, they had continued to pursue their goals, some clandestinely, others in the risky world of open politics through the vehicle of newspapers or through study sessions designed to attract discontented educated youth. Whether operating clandestinely or openly, the radicals faced two main problems. The first was ideological. However much they could point to social and economic inequities under Sihanouk's rule, the prince's pursuit of a foreign policy of neutrality meant that he and his government were not easy targets for criticism. How could they attack the leader who received support from the giants of the communist world, China and the Soviet Union, and who maintained improving, if cautious, relations with North Vietnam? Their second problem was immediate and practical. Time and again Sihanouk had made clear his distrust of radical politics within Cambodia and his readiness to sanction the repressive measures used by his security services. We will never know how closely Sihanouk was involved in authorising many of the individual cases of intimidation, torture and assassination carried out by his secret police. But it is clear that he was not distressed by such incidents as the killing of the editor of the communist front newspaper *Pracheachon* in Phnom Penh in October 1959. He may well have personally approved the humiliating beating and debagging administered to Khieu Samphan, by this time the editor of a left-wing French-language newspaper, *Observateur*, in July 1960, and he clearly approved the decision to jail left-wing journalists and suppress their newspapers in August, when they criticised his educational policies.

It was against this background of increased repression that 21 leftists gathered secretly in the goods yard of the Phnom Penh railway station at the end of September 1960. Among them were Saloth Sar, the future Pol Pot, and his long-time associate Ieng

Sary. Still closely linked to the Vietnamese communist movement, this group changed its name from the Khmer People's Revolutionary Party to the Khmer Workers' Party (KWP). Over the next several years the members of the newly formed party were to face many difficulties, including severe repression by Sihanouk's forces and internal dissent. For the moment simply to survive was their main accomplishment.

Notes

I was living in Phnom Penh during the period described in this chapter and observed the events that followed Suramarit's death, including, for instance, Sihanouk's swearing in as chief of state.

The weekly issues of *Réalités Cambodgiennes*, starting with that of 9 April 1960, provide important information on the events that took place after King Suramarit's death. The English language publication *Cambodian Commentary*, published in Phnom Penh, provides, in a Special Number, April–May 1960, No. 8, the edited text of Sihanouk's 7 April 1960 speech at the Men ground.

Preschez, *Essai*, pp. 92–4, provides useful comment on the constitutional issues raised by developments leading up to Sihanouk's becoming chief of state.

On the demonstration in favour of his mother's becoming Cambodia's monarch, see *Neak Cheat Niyum* (The Nationalist), 21 May 1960.

Sihanouk's comments on his difficulties with American ambassadors were reported in *Neak Cheat Niyum* on 28 May 1960.

Réalités 10, 17 and 24 June are particularly interesting for the detail they provide on the final moves leading to Sihanouk's inauguration as chief of state. See also *Cambodian Commentary*, 9 June 1960.

As before, I am particularly indebted to Kiernan, *How Pol Pot*, for descriptions and analysis of the history of the left in Cambodia. In relation to the meeting in the Phnom Penh railway yard, I was given a brief account of this meeting by one of the participants, Ok Sakun, during an interview with him in Paris in 1973. In *Brother Number One*, pp. 61–2, David Chandler offers interesting commentary on what, in many ways, remains a mysterious meeting.

10

Sihanouk's Cambodia: People, places and political philosophy

For all his love of sentimental French popular music, *la vie en rose* never came to pass in Sihanouk's Cambodia. Barely suppressed political divisions, major inequalities of power and wealth, endemic corruption, all these were present throughout the years he was in power. But if the carefully cultivated image of an 'oasis of peace' or 'fairytale kingdom' were never realities, there was a period around 1960 that for many, both Cambodian and foreigner alike, seemed suffused with a roseate hue.

By contrast with its neighbours, Cambodia appeared to have found a political formula that met its needs as Sihanouk progressed from one triumph to another. He seemed ubiquitous and invulnerable as he presided over state occasions, delivered mammoth speeches or led his ministers, senior officials and the heads of diplomatic missions in sessions of manual labour designed to shake the traditionally elitist city dwellers from their distaste for working with their hands. Above all, once the tremors started by the 'Bangkok plot', the Dap Chhuon affair, and the September 1959 bombing in the palace had settled, Sihanouk was the leader of a country at peace.

There were many reasons why he could take pride in this fact, not least its significance to all but the poorest residents of Phnom Penh. By 1960 the city could legitimately claim to be the most charming in Southeast Asia. Its population had grown from fewer than 100 000 before the Second World War to nearly half a million. Perhaps a third of these were Cambodians, with ethnic Chinese and Vietnamese making up the bulk of the remainder in roughly equal proportions. These three main ethnic elements of Phnom Penh's population were clearly divided along occupational lines. Educated Cambodians were officials, the uneducated were coolies. Whether educated or not, it was Cambodians who donned the robe as Buddhist monks and lived and worshipped in the city's many *wats* (pagodas). There was, it is true, some blurring of lines, as intermarriage among Cambodians and Chinese was common, so that many of the most powerful business figures in Phnom Penh were Sino-Khmers. But overwhelmingly, those Cambodians who were able to complete secondary school, cherished the goal of becoming civil servants, a position seen as guaranteeing lifetime security, social prestige, and the opportunity to become part of the complex web of pervasive corruption that oiled the cogs of daily life both in Phnom Penh and in the provinces. For those who did not have the opportunities that education offered but were determined to live in the capital there were few choices. The luckiest might become drivers for wealthy fellow countrymen, foreign diplomatic missions or trading houses. More likely was the harsh life of a coolie on the docks or a *cyclopousse* (bicycle rickshaw) rider. Both jobs carried the risk of crippling injury, and the *cyclopousse pédaleurs* also risked catching tuberculosis. Like their peasant relatives, Cambodians who laboured in the capital for wages had a life expectancy of barely 45 years.

The Chinese in Phnom Penh were businessmen, first and foremost, as they were throughout the country. Business big and small was dominated by them. They were an essential link in the rice trading network that stretched from the rice mills of rural Cambodia to the great traders of Cholon, Saigon's Chinese-dominated twin city, to the outside world. Chinese merchants controlled the purchase and export of Cambodia's high-grade pepper, grown along the sea coast of the Gulf of Siam around the provincial capital of Kampot. They monopolised the production and sale of salt. They owned the hundreds of buses that ferried Cambodia's population throughout the kingdom, just as they owned the *cyclopousses* they rented out to impoverished Cambodians in Phnom Penh. They were restaurateurs, shopkeepers, traditional doctors and pharmacists, barbers and cinema owners. If there was a commercial opportunity, they seized it. Not all were successful, and there were ethnic Chinese coolies working on the Phnom Penh wharves alongside Cambodians. But with their commitment to education as a key to advancement and their embrace of an entrepreneurial work ethic shared by few Cambodians, the Chinese population of Phnom Penh provided the commercial drive for Cambodia's capital city. Only in very particular areas of business were they unable to make their mark. Banking was in the hands of French and British firms. European agency houses controlled key import commodities, such as machinery and motor vehicles. Tobacco processing, but not growing, was out of their hands as, most importantly of all, was the rubber plantation industry, which remained a French preserve.

If Phnom Penh's Chinese community made its vibrant presence felt without apology, the same was not true of the Vietnamese minority. They were seen by Cambodians as foreigners of a different kind. Although intermarriage between Cambodians and Vietnamese was not unknown, it was uncommon. A large proportion of Vietnamese were Roman Catholics, whereas the number of ethnic Cambodians who embraced this religion in the early 1960s probably did not exceed 4000, many of them the descendants of Iberian adventurers who had come to Cambodia centuries before. When Vietnamese were adherents of Buddhism, it was the Buddhism of the *Mahayana* (Greater Vehicle) form, not the *Theravada* (Lesser Vehicle) tradition to which all Cambodian Buddhists belonged. This religious difference was only one that set the Vietnamese apart from Cambodians of almost every class. For all Cambodians the memory of past Vietnamese aggression was a given that was never forgotten. Few might know the details of nineteenth-century history and the Vietnamese occupation of their country. But all had a vague awareness of that past as well as more modern memories of the fact that, under French rule, Vietnamese provided the bulk of the minor officials of the colonial administration, most of them directly concerned with the imposition of the most irritating regulations and taxes. The state executioner in colonial Cambodia was usually a Vietnamese.

In the untroubled years of Sihanouk's Cambodia, the Vietnamese occupied a minor place in the pecking order of Cambodian commerce. They were tailors, shoemakers and bookshop owners, the latter selling material sympathetic to the Vietnamese communist cause. Vietnamese were clerks in banks and foreign businesses, maintaining relationships that had been established long before independence. A few ran small import–export clearing businesses, while many more found employment as domestic servants in the households of Europeans. They were an introverted community, apprehensive that the Cambodians' ethnic hostility towards them might boil over into anti-Vietnamese violence. The end of the 1960s was to show how right they were to hold this fear.

125

There were, of course, other identifiable minority communities in Phnom Penh when Sihanouk was at the height of his power. Indian cloth traders who doubled as moneylenders worked in shops that ringed the central market. Just to the north of the capital's outskirts there was a community of Chams, the descendants of the men and women who had fled from the once-mighty state of Champa on the central coast of Vietnam many centuries before. Converts to Islam, they had intermarried with the small community of Malays which had long maintained an unobtrusive presence along the banks of the Mekong and the Tonle Sap rivers where these converge at Phnom Penh.

Most visible of all the foreigners in the heyday of Sihanouk's Cambodia were the French. At the beginning of the 1960s they may have numbered almost 6000, though their participation in almost every facet of Cambodian life made their community seem even larger. At the official level the French were still accorded special status, with the French ambassador taking precedence over the dean of the diplomatic corps at state functions. Relations between Sihanouk and his close advisers and the French embassy were eased by the fact that most of the embassy's personnel had served in Cambodia before independence, some as members of his staff when he was king. They were acutely alert to the prince's likes and dislikes and how to cater to them. They knew that Sihanouk was an unashamed francophile, delighting in serving French food and wine, and ready to draw on his French education in Saigon to quote Molière or Racine in his speeches. In Phnom Penh, Sihanouk's personal physician was a French army doctor, Colonel Armand Riche. When the prince went abroad for 'the cure' it was to Dr Pathé's clinic in Grasse, in southeastern France.

The French seemed to be everywhere. French officers trained Cambodian troops, even though the funds to pay those troops came from the United States. French teachers staffed the Lycée Descartes, the preferred choice of the Cambodian elite for their children' secondary education. At the Lycée Sisowath, in contrast, the children of less elevated members of Cambodian society were taught by Cambodian teachers. The Banque de l'Indochine; Denis Frères, the French agency house that was Indochina's equivalent of Jardine Matheson; the Compagnie du Cambodge, the firm controlling the largest rubber plantations in Cambodia—these were the leaders of what was, in 1960, still a major French commercial presence in Cambodia. By no means all French business was at such an elevated level. French men and women owned and managed shops, bars and restaurants that were far from grand. And

French mechanics supervised the servicing of the Peugeots and Citroëns that were the most widely used vehicles on Cambodian roads. It was French pilots, too, who flew the aircraft that linked Phnom Penh's airport at Pochentong to the provincial capitals— and to the isolated landing grounds that were part of the growing Indochinese drug smuggling network, in which expatriate Corsicans had a prominent role.

In 1960 a few French people still worked within the Cambodian administration. But many more were in the capital as 'experts', advisers to the administration, and teachers, both in secondary schools and in the fledgling tertiary institutions. Some, like Madeleine Giteau, the head of the National Museum, were long-time residents of the kingdom and regarded it with a deep affection. Others were in Cambodia for no better reason than that it offered a more comfortable style of life than they might enjoy in metropolitan France. Then there were the *anciens de l'Indochine*, the old-timers who had lived in Cambodia and Vietnam when colonial mores still applied and who strove, in their own ways, to live as they had done before. Perhaps the best known was Dr Paul Grauwin, who had gained deserved fame as the 'doctor of Dien Bien Phu', the soldier-surgeon who had gone on working in appalling conditions until that ill-fated French garrison was overwhelmed by the Vietminh in May 1954. He distrusted French governments of whatever stripe and had chosen to end his working days in Phnom Penh, where he was much in demand for his expertise in treating venereal disease. Jean, of the eponymous Bar Jean, would surely have been at home on the waterfront of Marseille. As it was, he chose to operate on the banks of the Tonle Sap river. He had once worked in Vietnam, but the 'new' Saigon that Ngo Dinh Diem and his brother Nhu ruled after 1954 no longer attracted him. So he and his formidable Vietnamese wife had moved to Phnom Penh, bringing with them a shrewd ability to choose girls who could serve the bar's customers in a range of ways. Monsieur Mignon, who presided over La Taverne, the quintessentially French restaurant in what had once been the Place de la Poste, was yet another old-timer. When quizzed by his clients about the desirability of, say, eating seafood brought from the coast in April or May, when temperatures soared above 40°C, he would fling wide his arms and scold them for their anxiety. As long as the taste was pleasing, what matter the consequences?

There was yet another identifiable group of Frenchmen, those who worked directly for Prince Sihanouk. Chiefly speechwriters and journalists, they were a special group, and will warrant separate attention later in this book when the prince's own 'court' comes under examination. With some exceptions, the large complement of Americans in Phnom Penh was not nearly as visible as might have been expected. Cosseted by the facilities offered in their commissaries, and in many cases handicapped by their inability to speak any language other than English, most American foreign service officers, aid workers and military personnel kept to themselves. There were exceptions, and some American diplomats were as well or better informed than their foreign colleagues. Nevertheless, coming from a country so often pilloried by Prince Sihanouk, many felt more comfortable in the company of their fellows, and it was rare indeed to see an American in the seedy Zig Zag bar, run by a lugubrious former *légionnaire,* or at the Quoc Men restaurant, which served some of the best Chinese food in town.

Given Cambodia's actual international importance, an extraordinarily large number of foreign representatives made up the distinctly motley diplomatic corps in Phnom Penh at the beginning of the 1960s. Mao-suited Chinese stood in classically inscrutable groups at receptions. Russians from the Soviet embassy sweated miserably in the humid heat, quaffing vodka and proposing extravagant toasts. Indians and Indonesians viewed Cambodia with ill-disguised condescension. All—Australians, Burmese, British or Czechs—were seen by Sihanouk as an audience, to be commanded or dismissed at will along with the Cambodian members of his court. Clad, as custom required, in white sharkskin suits, on official occasions the Caucasian members of the diplomatic corps looked more than a little like a phalanx of seedy Italian icecream salesmen.

Just as Phnom Penh's population could be divided, broadly, into three main sections, so too could the city itself. Developed as much by the French and Chinese as by Cambodians, the older parts of the city fell into three distinct quarters, with the Phnom, the small hill from which the city takes its name, and the royal palace providing essential points of demarcation. To the north of the Phnom was the former French residential quarter, still in 1960 the location of many French homes, but increasingly sought-after by members of the Cambodian elite as well as other foreigners. Here were villas which echoed the architecture of southern France, solidly bourgeois dwellings with only a hint of frivolity in decorative cast iron along the roof line or over the porch. Here, too, was the convent where French nuns still taught the Buddhist daughters of privileged Cambodians. Reflecting the symbiotic relationship that had existed between the Vietnamese employed by the French and their colonial masters, much of Phnom Penh's Vietnamese population lived to the north of the old French quarter, close to their Catholic churches near the Tonle Sap river.

Near the Phnom, to the north and south as well as a little to the west, were many of the offices of the former French administration, now transformed into Cambodia's ministries but still painted to a pattern that had been laid down in Paris decades before. Running back from the Tonle Sap river, and set between the area near the Phnom and the open spaces that flanked the royal palace was the Chinese quarter, a place of constant noise and bustle. It often seemed to a foreign observer that the Chinese of Phnom Penh not only were immune to noise but positively welcomed it. Any big event was a cause for noise of one kind or another—Chinese New Year, most famously, but funerals too. Chroniclers of English village life in the early twentieth century, such as Laurie Lee, have written of how old people curled up and died during the harsh winter months, succumbing to the cold. In Phnom Penh it was in the hottest months—March, April and May—that funerals became almost a daily affair. Among the Chinese, the richer the departed the greater the noise, as gong bands competed with out-of-tune renditions of Schubert's *Funeral March* on saxophones and cornets; the number of lacquered pigs carried in front of the coffin provided the final earthly measure of the dead person's material wealth.

There was little architecture of distinction in the Chinese quarter, though the oldest sections, with their rows of uniform shophouses, possessed a degree of visual charm. But real charm was to be found as one moved into the area around the royal palace. This was the truly Cambodian part of Phnom Penh. No matter that the buildings of the palace, the National Museum and the Buddhist Institute were of relatively recent construction. With their shining multicoloured tiled roofs and their soaring finials, they captured the essence of traditional Cambodian architecture and provided a backdrop for the colour and movement of both daily life and great state ceremonies and festivals. Some ceremonies and royal occasions took place behind the palace walls, but others drew crowds into the open spaces that flanked the palace compound. The ancient ritual of 'Ploughing the Sacred Furrow' was enacted on the Men ground. The Water Festival, which celebrated the end of the rainy season with canoe races and ribaldry, took place on and by the river that the palace overlooked.

Close to the palace was the Buddhist University. From here hundreds of monks would emerge at the end of their morning's study, their orange-yellow robes providing a stunning display of colour. Sheltering their shaven heads beneath saffron umbrellas, they walked through the patches of sunlight and shadow along the tree-lined streets by the palace. In this part of Phnom Penh one could see the royal elephants led out to take their morning exercise; the French sign in their stables warning '*Attention, éléphant méchant*' was delightfully rendered into English as 'Attention the naughty elephant.'

A few members of the Cambodian elite, such as Sihanouk's uncle Prince Monireth, maintained large villas along the city's main thoroughfare, the Boulevard Norodom, but many more lived in these quiet streets not far from the palace, streets that had an almost rural character. In the palace quarter, too, were many of the *wats* that were an integral part of Cambodian life. Their exotic architecture was, for a foreigner, often best viewed from a distance, for too often closer examination revealed decoration that seemed tawdry when compared to the great artistic achievement of the Angkor period.

By no means all of Phnom Penh was marked by charm. There was little that was beguiling or exotic about the shanty towns that had grown up on the city's western outskirts. Beginning with forced relocations during the First Indochina War, rural dwellers had flocked to Phnom Penh. This trend had continued through the 1950s as individuals and whole families sought their fortunes in the capital. Few found more than labouring jobs. But these were enough to sustain them provided they were prepared to live in the crudely constructed wooden huts that were set along unpaved tracks and had neither running water nor sewerage.

Few foreigners, and few privileged Cambodians, saw the shanties of the poor. Most members of these groups had little interest in the poorest backwaters of Cambodia's capital. A foreign journalist who stumbled on them and reported on their existence would almost certainly have been barred from re-entering Cambodia, since Prince Sihanouk was hostile to any suggestion in the international press that all was not well in the kingdom. He later sought to translate his vision of contented peasants and a prosperous elite to the cinema screen. For many in that elite, indeed, the period around 1960 was prosperous. A Cambodian with the right connections would be courted by foreign embassies and firms anxious to gain entrée to a society that combined the exotic with a healthy appetite for material wealth. Elite male Cambodians, particularly those who had tasted the pleasures that could be found in Europe or the United States, were ready to accept foreign hospitality in the endless round of diplomatic entertaining that was such a feature of Phnom Penh life. By themselves, they patronised the 'dancings' and drank cognac or expensive brands of Scotch whisky; Johnny Walker Black Label was a particular favourite. For more intimate pleasures they would repair to the houseboats moored near Takhmau on the southern outskirts of Phnom Penh, where they could enjoy an evening of drinking and sex discreetly distant from their wives and families.

Such indulgences were the preserve of a few. Nevertheless, for Cambodians who were less privileged yet not condemned to daily wage labour, the early 1960s were also a period to remember with gratitude. For the teachers and the minor civil servants who typified this group, there was modest prosperity to be wrung from the wake of the foreign funds that washed over Cambodia and particularly Phnom Penh. Work was not too demanding, and there were opportunities for second and even third jobs. Most held Sihanouk in genuine affection and were untroubled by being required to demonstrate their loyalty through the rituals of membership of the JSRK, haphazardly supervised participation in a few weeks of manual labour each year, and occasional appearances as part of the crowds assembled to applaud Sihanouk on state occasions. Few were efficient in their jobs. Many—perhaps the majority—possessed the habit of mind so aptly conveyed by the French term *fonctionnairisme*: the myopic tendency of civil servants to value unimportant detail such as the correct completion of forms, over the productive pursuit of worthwhile goals. They strove to avoid being noticed and to evade responsibility. Nothing in Cambodia's pre-independence history had prepared them to act in any other way.

At the beginning of the 1960s, few observers, Cambodian or foreign, took much account of one element in Phnom Penh society that we now know was a breeding-ground for dissent of the most radical kind. Sihanouk had frequently spoken of his concern that Cambodian students studying in France were exposed to left-wing propaganda. But while his security officials waged a continuing campaign against outspoken critics of his policies, neither they nor the prince seem to have been aware of the quiet proselytising being undertaken in the high schools of Phnom Penh by the later leaders of Democratic Kampuchea, including Saloth Sar. In seminars and study sessions these dedicated communists preached a Marxist doctrine that condemned the 'feudal' nature of the state and the corruption it engendered. As students in their late teens contemplated their already restricted employment opportunities and had their attention drawn to the glaring inequities that existed in the country, many responded positively to the suggestion that only a total transformation of society could cure Cambodia's ills. In the early '60s, however, a commitment to taking action to achieve this was still some way off.

Away from Phnom Penh was the world of provincial towns, of rural villages and, even more distantly, of peasants and hill peoples living on the fringe of lowland society. The provincial capitals owed their existence and their characters to the clearly identifiable economic or political roles they fulfilled, either historically or in more contemporary terms. Battambang, Cambodia's second city, had grown from being an outpost of Thai power in the nineteenth century to being the hub of the expanding rice industry in Cambodia's northwest. Kompong Cham was essentially a French creation. Its public gardens, *cercle sportif* and carefully aligned streets were all reminders of the rubber and tobacco industries that had flourished in the surrounding countryside during the years of French control. Kampot, on the southern seacoast, had been Cambodia's principal port in the nineteenth century. Now it was a centre for the pepper growing industry. Life in provincial towns was slower than in Phnom Penh, so slow that a visitor to the remote northeastern town of Stung Treng might wonder how even the commercial skills of a Chinese merchant would be able to turn a profit in what seemed such unpromising surroundings. But it was a measure of Sihanouk's achievements that the inhabitants of these towns, or certainly the Cambodian inhabitants, felt themselves to be part of his state. Not only did provincial Cambodians embrace a national readiness to travel, cramming into the precariously overloaded buses or onto crowded ferries to make their way to Phnom Penh to visit relatives or attend great occasions; the prince also came to visit them.

Sihanouk's energy was phenomenal. Working at a pace that exhausted his associates, he travelled widely through the kingdom, opening schools and clinics, inaugurating factories or irrigation schemes. He exhorted, chided and congratulated his 'children'. That some who came to hear him did so because local officials told them to is undoubtedly true. It is true, also, that there was a Potemkin village element to some, at least, of what took place on these princely visitations. Water flowed from a lavatory cistern when Sihanouk pulled the chain because, unseen by the prince, a labourer outside was hastily pouring water from a bucket into a pipe to feed the cistern. At other times, subsequent neglect undermined or destroyed projects that the prince promoted. Such was the case with a much-vaunted tree planting program in the countryside not too far distant from Phnom Penh over which Sihanouk had presided. Following Sihanouk's example, officials and diplomats sweated in the sun to plant seedlings destined to restore forest cover to a denuded area. A few weeks later all of the seedlings were dead. No provision had been made to water them once they had been planted.

But the fact that there were achievements, that schools were built and clinics opened, depended overwhelmingly on Sihanouk and his energy. Just as he came to the provincial centres, so did he travel into rural areas to make his presence felt among the peasantry. It was from these visits, captured in endless official photographs of toothless old peasant women crouched before him or of Sihanouk distributing bolts of cloth, that the prince and his propagandists sought to create the legend which they tirelessly promoted. The legend tells of the 'papa prince' bringing largesse to his 'children', who in return rendered him their undying loyalty. As with many legends, this is a mixture of fact and fantasy.

Like no other Cambodian ruler before him, Sihanouk was ready to go out among his people. And as with no previous ruler, this readiness earned him an affection that went beyond the traditional awe and devotion felt by rural Cambodians towards their monarch as the ultimate embodiment of the state and Cambodia's identity. The peasantry were genuine in their warm reaction to Sihanouk, a ruler whom they still saw as possessing semi-divine qualities and who now appeared in their humble villages, arriving dramatically in a flurry of dust and wind as his helicopter sank to the ground. But their warmth of welcome did not mean that the peasants' affection for Sihanouk was unconditional nor that their passive support for his governance could necessarily be transformed into action to prop him up once his position was threatened. During the good times, as the years around 1960 can now be seen to have been, Sihanouk would point with pride to a devoted rural population as his fundamental base of support. When times were no longer good, Sihanouk found, to his dismay, that some of his 'children' were all too ready to disobey their 'papa'.

Even in these good years there were those who did not feel part of Sihanouk's state. Just how many is not certain, but Michael Vickery provides a vivid series of illustrations of the gulf that separated those peasants who saw themselves as part of a world linked to Phnom Penh and those whose world was strictly circumscribed by their immediate surroundings and who had no wish for it to be otherwise. A common feature of such groups, he says, was a deep distrust of cities and of those who lived in them. To the extent that peasants came into contact with the wider world, it was almost always in circumstances that led them to feel despised and exploited. Officials from Phnom Penh or linked to it treated these fringe dwellers with disdain whenever they encountered them.

Possibly even greater disdain was shown towards the hill peoples, some of whom lived along the foothills of the Cardamon mountains and a larger number in the mountainous northeastern provinces. Spoken of officially as Khmer Loeu (Highland Cambodians), they were more commonly referred to as *phnong*, a word connoting 'savage' or 'barbarian'. During French colonial times these hill peoples were grouped under the single term *montagnards*, a term that does not take account of their differing ethnic identities. In the early '60s they were little touched by developments in lowland Cambodia. They bartered forest products for a few prized commodities, coming shyly to the edge of provincial towns before slipping back into the forests. Theirs was a life of privation and exposure to endemic disease, particularly malaria, which had been brought under control throughout much of lowland Cambodia but still ravaged the people living in the hills and mountains. This did not disturb a lowland Cambodian official whom I questioned about the Por or Pear people, who lived at the base of the Cardamon mountains in western Pursat province. Why, I asked, did they remain in such an unhealthy location? His answer encapsulated the generally held view of such groups: 'What else could they do?'

With independence there was greater contact between the government of Phnom Penh and the hill people, particularly those in the northeast of the kingdom. That region had been strategically important during the Franco-Vietminh war and remained so after it. Slowly but surely, the government in Phnom Penh sought to exert a measure of control over these distant regions. Groups that had previously moved their villages frequently to follow a pattern of slash and burn agriculture were now urged to remain in fixed localities. Rudimentary censuses were taken. There was even an effort to institute basic education. Little of this was welcomed by people who had always lived 'free in the forest'. Although their resistance to government intrusion was little reported in the

Phnom Penh media, there were occasionally indications of clashes between hill people and Phnom Penh's soldiers. There was no sympathy in the capital for the problems which forced changes caused for the hill people. When, in 1960, I asked Sihanouk's minister for Security, Kou Roun, what the government's policy was towards these people, his answer was blunt: 'We khmerise them'.

What was Sihanouk's message to those he addressed throughout Cambodia, and what were the policies which for a time seemed to have succeeded, broadly at least, in answering the country's problems? Perusing the records of his speeches, whether in the officially edited and bowdlerised French language versions or in the earthier Cambodian originals, and reading his books and articles, leaves an impression of a politician much more concerned with achieving a limited number of practical goals than with developing a coherent political philosophy. His preoccupations throughout his long public life, or at least from the early 1950s, have been twofold: to ensure that he was at the centre of power and that Cambodia retained its independence. He had no commitment to bringing about a basic reordering of Cambodian society.

All of his actions, his speeches and his writings have reflected his view of his own indispensability. Like any skilful politician, he did, of course, tailor his words to his audience. His addresses to gatherings of peasants in rural Cambodia were couched in different terms from those used in his lengthy articles in *Réalités Cambodgiennes*. But at heart the message was the same. Beset as Cambodia was by contending clans within the royal family and by squabbling political parties, and threatened by predatory neighbours, he alone could provide the leadership the country needed. In proclaiming this message, Sihanouk, in the years around 1960, was aided both by the clear record of his own achievements and by circumstances over which he had no control. However dilatory he may have been in joining in a full-blooded fight for independence from France, he had every reason to claim the lion's share of credit for the peaceful outcome achieved in 1953. Since then he had navigated astutely through the shoals of international affairs, using neutrality as his lodestar.

In embracing a stated policy of neutrality, tinged as it was with frequent criticism of the United States and less frequent critical comments on the Soviet Union, Sihanouk does not appear to have reflected on the extent to which Cambodia during these years of success was as much a beneficiary as a victim of international circumstances. Although he had to face endemic hostility from his immediate neighbours, South Vietnam and Thailand, on the broader international scene Cold War ideological rivalries redounded to Cambodia's success. Despite nagging difficulties in his relations with the United States, that country continued to believe that it was in its own best interest to act as Cambodia's largest foreign aid donor. The CIA's flirting with Dap Chhuon and the clashes Sihanouk had with individuals aside, the United States did much to prop up the prince's regime until the early '60s. France, ever conscious of its former colonial role, could not match the extent of American aid, but could still maintain an effective presence through its military advisers, experts and teachers. For their own reasons, too, both China and the Soviet Union competed for influence in Cambodia through the provision of substantial aid. It was a game at which the Chinese, for a number of years, excelled and one in which the Soviets never really understood the rules.

In short, Sihanouk had been astute in choosing a foreign policy that was in tune with the times, but he could not ensure that those times would last. His policy of neutrality depended on there being no sudden change in the external balance of forces. When that change did occur and Sihanouk became convinced that he had to accommodate the future victory of the Vietnamese communists, he set in train a series of events over which he lost control. For the moment, around 1960, such a possibility seemed remote.

What vision did Sihanouk hold for the people of Cambodia beyond his continuing to be their leader? He has spoken and written of his commitment to 'Buddhist socialism' without ever making clear just what this term meant. Indeed, despite a thorough grounding in French classical literature, he has readily, even glee-fully, admitted to his lack of acquaintance with political theory. For, as he was to say in 1967, he did not care 'a rap about political economy, political science or other subjects. I have not read any of these books.' What he had done, Sihanouk continued, was to study 'the veins of our nation. I know those veins well.' In a later, somewhat chastened comment on his policies, Sihanouk has observed that like other Third World leaders such as Nasser and Sukarno, he was attracted to 'socialism' as the fashionable answer to the problems faced by newly independent states: 'We felt, in a more or less confused fashion, that it was an instrument for national development and a weapon against imperialism.' But, with more than usual candour, Sihanouk went on to note, 'Our attitude

. . . was not always very coherent and our internal policy did not always adapt itself very well to our eloquence and diplomacy'.

Without doubt, Sihanouk wanted nothing but good for his people, but it was to be on his terms. Those terms were far from revolutionary. He wanted more children to go to high school and then to university, but he did not want those children to use their education to question the way in which he and his supporters ran the state. He proclaimed his attachment to Buddhist principles, not least those of justice and equality, but he sanctioned a system that involved glaring denials of such principles. Above all, he appears to have seen no contradiction between his espousal of socialism and his unreadiness to tackle the disease of corruption. The metaphor may be hackneyed, but the cancer of corruption was abundantly present in the Cambodian body politic in the good years and slowly spreading. For a while it did not threaten the state's existence and Sihanouk's position at its head. In the longer term, it was terminal.

The benefit of hindsight makes clear the extent to which Sihanouk's father's death marked one of the turning-points in Cambodian's post-independence history. This was not because of any particularly positive role played by King Suramarit, but because so long as the old man was on the throne, Sihanouk knew he could associate himself with all the prestige of the monarchy while relying on the king not to act contrary to his interests. With Suramarit gone, the good years were to continue for a little while longer. But the roseate hue of those years was fading as the prince no longer felt able to share symbolic leadership with a ruling king and as new and more difficult challenges had to be faced both at home and abroad.

Notes

Much of the material in this chapter reflects my personal observation of Sihanouk's rule during extended periods of residence in Cambodia in 1959–61 and 1966 and during visits in 1968, 1969, 1970 and 1971.

The nature of the Cambodian civil service and its officials was well described by J. Cheverney, long before Sihanouk's overthrow, in his *Eloge du Colonialisme: Essais sur les révolutions d'Asie*, Paris, 1961, pp. 36–54.

Sihanouk expressed his concern that Cambodian students in France were falling victim to Marxist propaganda on many occasions. As an example, see *Réalités*, 26 September 1959, in his sixth article in the series 'Will Cambodia become a republic?'.

I owe the account of the water being poured into the cistern to the late Donald Lancaster, who witnessed the event in Stung Treng in 1966. The account of the tree planting and its aftermath is from my own experience in 1959.

The account of the 'outsiders' in Cambodia provided by Michael Vickery is to be found in his *Cambodia 1975–1982*, Sydney, 1984, Chapter 1. My conversation with a Cambodian provincial official in relation to the Por people took place in Pursat in 1966. I have borrowed the phrase 'free in the forest' from the title of Gerald Hickey's magisterial study of hill peoples in Vietnam, *Free in the Forest: Ethnohistory of the Vietnamese Central Highlands 1954–1976*, New Haven, 1982.

I base my judgment on the content of Sihanouk's speeches and writings on perusal of a wide range of both the officially sanctioned versions and verbatim transcripts as found, for instance, in FBIS material. The remark relating to the prince's lack of interest in political theory was made on Radio Phnom Penh on 10 March 1967. For his comments on the attraction of 'socialism' see *L'Indochine vue de Pékin*, p. 34. A penetrating analysis of the 'socialism' of the Sangkum Reastr Niyum may be found in Saul Rose, *Socialism in Southern Asia*, London, 1959, pp. 189–90.

11

Sihanouk's Cambodia:
Courts and courtiers

There is nothing new in the depiction of Sihanouk as directing Cambodia from a 'court'. The term seems immediately appropriate as a way of describing those who were closely associated with a former king and who acted in the classic role of courtiers: deeply subservient to the ruler's whims, ever anxious to carry out his wishes. Yet describing Sihanouk's court and the manner in which it functioned is no easy task. To begin with, there were several courts. Most intimate and important was the true inner court, which, over the years, increasingly centred on his wife Monique and her relatives, particularly her mother and her half-brother, Oum Mannorine. This inner court was sometimes expanded to include a wider grouping of close associates drawn from such trusted advisers such as Penn Nouth and Nhiek Tioulong, men who had served the prince through thick and thin, often with little thanks. Some of this second group were companions whom Sihanouk included in his periods of relaxation away from the cares of office. General Ngo Hou, the head of Cambodia's air force, was one, as was Nhiek Tioulong. Others, such as the very different Son Sann and General Lon Nol, remained closely associated with Sihanouk over many years thanks to the advice they offered or their readiness to act on his orders.

A much larger court was that composed of the senior ranks of the Cambodian civil service, the foreign diplomatic corps and representatives of the major non-Cambodian communities in Phnom Penh. This extended court was summoned to provide the backdrop and audience for Sihanouk's public activities. It seldom, if ever, had a more positive role to play, though some foreign diplomats failed to recognise this fact.

Finally there was a court of a different kind—that of Sihanouk's personal staff, some Cambodian, some foreign, the latter mostly French. These were the men who oversaw arrangements for his engagements and his foreign travel. Most importantly, they were the men who wrote his speeches, edited his various newspapers and magazines and supplied the constant stream of letters to which Sihanouk signed his name in response to foreign criticism or praise. Each of these courts deserves some attention.

Not surprisingly, the inner court was both the most interesting and the least open to external scrutiny. Some of its character, particularly the important role played by women, was reminiscent of the world Sihanouk's great-grandfather, Norodom I, inhabited in the nineteenth century. The inner court was made up of Sihanouk's consort and her relatives, a few close advisers, and officials, such as Sihanouk's long-serving aide de camp, Colonel Meas Huol, who were ready to be the butt of the prince's frequently cruel sense of humour. It was a far from stable grouping. Although by 1960 Monique Izzi was Sihanouk's clear favourite, she was not the only woman in his life, so that on occasion the more or less permanent members of the inner court were left abandoned as the prince sought his pleasure elsewhere.

Sihanouk's mother, Queen Kossamak, was not part of this inner court, though she had earlier been a powerful influence in her son's life. From the time of his abdication, Sihanouk's relations with his 'venerated mama' had become increasingly ambiguous. He held her in deep affection and had good reason to be grateful to her for warnings she had given him of danger and opposition at various times in the early years of his public career. He took account of her insistence on the importance of heeding the predictions of astrologers and soothsayers, since he had, and has, a firm belief in the influence of the supernatural. But he was conscious both of her racially motivated dislike of Monique and of her more general criticism of his readiness to risk alienating those, both within Cambodia and outside it, whom she believed should be regarded as the country's friends. Her son's penchant for employing young leftists such as Chau Seng, who made a career out of vehement criticism of the United States, reinforced the gap that developed between them. When, after assuming the office of chief of state in 1960, Sihanouk established his residence at Chamcar Mon on the southern outskirts of Phnom Penh, leaving his mother a lonely figure in the royal palace, Kossamak's influence over him was sharply reduced.

Although official publicity was frequently given to the 'working sessions' of the various cabinets over which Sihanouk presided, much more fundamental policy decisions emerged from the informal gatherings that he assembled in his residence. These were only rarely reported or hinted at, though ironically, given the date on which it occurred, one of the few reports that did surface was the account of Sihanouk and his inner court reviewing affairs of state in France in February 1970, one month before he fell from power.

The picture that emerges from such brief published material and from the few outsiders who were privileged to observe even part of this private princely world, is of policy being discussed amid a jumble of meals and film showings, and of sudden moves, such as to one of Sihanouk's many country villas. There was no fixed agenda and the prince might call his closest advisers at any hour of the day. Often beset by insomnia, he did not hesitate to work through the night or to decide at 2 a.m. that the moment had come to review an issue. But whatever the time or place, and whomever he had convoked, the final decision rested with him and, in the days when success appeared to attend his every action, few dared to argue with him once he had made up his mind.

Monique played a key role in this inner court in which hard decision-making mingled with something approaching personal chaos. Still not the sole object of Sihanouk's affections, she was able to provide a sense of calm that he found nowhere else. While not a woman of great intelligence, she matched charm and notable physical beauty to determined ambition. Conscious of the risks of instability that were never far from the surface of Cambodian political life, she accepted her family's urgings that she and they should seize any opportunity to benefit financially from her relationship with the prince. Her willingness to exploit her position in this fashion was eventually to cost her dearly, since her passing across the ill-defined but widely understood line that separated grand corruption from corruption at an 'acceptable' level played an important part in weakening support for Sihanouk among the Cambodian elite. She was still distant from that crossover point in the early 1960s, when her chief efforts seemed more concerned with trying to ensure that one of her children by Sihanouk should inherit the Cambodian throne. In denying her this wish, Sihanouk made one of the few decisions that ran directly counter to what she wanted.

Was there an even more intimate influence on Sihanouk's decisions, namely his belief in the supernatural? Did he determine policy after of consulting mediums and listening to astrologers? There is no convincing evidence that the prince was swayed one way or another on matters of real importance through such mystical means. Like many Cambodians he believes in the power of spiritual forces, and while he was in power he certainly paid attention to soothsayers and the omens they interpreted in relation to matters of personal conduct—whether it was desirable to travel on one day or another; whether it was better to spend the night in Phnom Penh or in the provinces. He did, it is true, pay special honour to the memory of a distant royal female ancestor, Princess Nucheat Khatr Vorpheak. Through a medium, he was able to reach her spirit and, according to Phnom Penh gossip, discuss foreign affairs issues with her. But even this otherworldly link has never been credited with determining his decisions one way or another.

If much of the activity of Sihanouk's inner court took place beyond the gaze of Cambodian and foreigner alike, the functioning of the larger court, that which formed the human backdrop to his roles as prime minister, chief of state and president of the Sangkum, was easily observed. State occasions occurred frequently in Sihanouk's Cambodia, whether traditional observances like the fertility rite of the 'Ploughing of the Sacred Furrow', or the pomp and ceremony provided when a foreign dignitary was welcomed to the kingdom. It was from these events—glittering affairs given a special character by their Asian exoticism—that many of the images of Cambodia and its ruler were drawn.

A visit by a foreign head of state would almost always include a routine visit to the Angkor ruins, and addresses to the Cambodian parliament and possibly to an assembly of the JSRK. But it was at the state dinner and the mandatory performance of the royal ballet afterwards that the larger court played its part. Senior Cambodian officials and the heads of diplomatic missions attended the dinner. When this ended, perhaps at 10 p.m., they moved to the open pavilion by the palace walls, where the royal ballet gave its performances. Here they were joined by less elevated officials, Cambodian and foreign. All would watch the traditional classical Cambodian dances performed to the music of the *pinpeat* orchestra, a mix of drums, gongs, traditional clarinets and strings. Seen for the first time, this was a truly exotic scene as dancers, richly clad in silks shot through with gold thread, played out stories drawn from ancient Indian legends. At times the dancing was slow and measured, full of abstract grace. At other times it was marked by buffoonery, as dancers playing the parts of monkeys in a version of the Ramayana scratched for fleas beneath their armpits. Adding a special touch of glamour to these performances was the fact that the principal female dancer was Sihanouk's beautiful daughter Bopha Devi. Well after midnight the show would end and the assembled court would wearily depart.

This was an earlier departure hour than could be expected by those invited to attend one of the prince's *soirées dansantes* in the royal palace. To be present at such an occasion was to see the most ebullient and exhausting sides of Sihanouk's character. He was a more than merely competent musician. Playing the saxophone and clarinet, he led a dance band most of whose members were also princes and whose repertoire included 1930s swing, French 'pop' and the prince's own compositions. As he acted as his own master of ceremonies, his audience strained to make sure they applauded when he announced '*Et maintenant, un petit numéro que j'ai composé moi-même. Il s'appelle 'Brise de Novembre.*'

Here was the Sihanouk and the Cambodia so beloved of magazines such as *Paris Match*. Cambodians and foreigners danced under the stars to the music of a former king while vintage champagne flowed. It was a world away from the everyday life of the country. At about 3 a.m., Sihanouk would announce that he would understand if his guests wished to leave, but he planned to go on playing until dawn. Few of his guests would dare to be the first to go. Cold War rivalries were carried into dancefloor brinkmanship as American and Soviet diplomats strove to outlast each other while their Chinese colleagues looked on impassively. On more than one occasion, the evening's proceedings acquired the tinge of farce that never seemed too far off in Sihanouk's Cambodia. In the early hours of the morning the cisterns servicing the lavatories would run out of water and the Phnom Penh fire brigade would have to be summoned to replenish them. The fire trucks' arrival seemed only to add to the evening's fantastical quality.

Ceremonies and other state occasions at which foreign representatives are required to be present are not, of course, unique to Cambodia. What was so distinctive about Cambodia while Sihanouk was at the height of his powers was his personal involvement at so many levels. When the diplomatic corps was called to attend the opening of the national congresses of the Sangkum, they saw Sihanouk presiding as president of that movement. At the 'Ploughing of the Sacred Furrow' ceremony, which marked the beginning of the rice planting season and also involved casting the kingdom's horoscope for the coming year, Sihanouk exercised a dual function. He attended as chief of state, but just as importantly, most Cambodians saw his presence as reflecting the fact that he had been king and that he had power over the spirits that determined whether the harvest would be good or bad. Later, as his popularity began to slip, he sought to capitalise further on the traditions associated with this ceremony by ploughing the furrow himself. In his period of enthusiasm for manual labour, Sihanouk expected that foreign diplomats would wield a hoe or a shovel alongside him. In the same way, he expected that they would attend hastily convened meetings to hear his denunciations of those who had in some fashion injured Cambodia or his personal pride—the two were not really separate in his mind.

When Sihanouk's pride had been injured, his hurt was given the widest publicity. Even before the predictable *mises au point* and editorials appeared in the official news bulletins and in the semi-official press, the foreign representatives in Phnom Penh would be summoned to hear his side of the particular story. This could mean receiving a 'very urgent' diplomatic note from the Ministry of Foreign Affairs, delivered after midnight and summoning them to hear the chief of state at 7 a.m. This is what occurred in May 1961, when Sihanouk's efforts to act as a mediator in the troubles that had engulfed Laos provoked a strong response from the Laotian king, Savang Vattana. The bluff old man had told Sihanouk, when he visited Vientiane, that his help was not needed. Whether Sihanouk's account of the stormy meeting was accurate, and the king had indeed called him Laos's 'public enemy number one', this was what the bleary-eyed diplomats heard as they listened to his voice rising higher and higher in anger and sipped their early morning champagne.

Not only senior Cambodian officials and resident diplomats were appropriated to Sihanouk's larger court. This privilege was extended to figures from the worlds of journalism and of arts and letters who had praised the prince. French reporters, such as Jean Lacouture who wrote sympathetically about Cambodia and its problems, readily gained access to Sihanouk. By 1960 he had become a fashionable object of admiration for supporters of left-wing causes, principally because of his outspoken criticism of the United States. He found no praise excessive and delighted in the enthusiasm for his regime expressed by such figures as the novelist Han Suyin and the Australian left-wing writer, Wilfred Burchett. They, and others like them, were assured of the warmest of receptions when they visited Cambodia and a place of honour at whichever state occasions might take place during their visit. The irony of such a state of affairs was extreme. Here were supporters of left-wing positions accepting the lavish hospitality of a man whose security police worked tirelessly to ensure that the domestic left in Cambodia was neutralised—by torture and assassination if necessary.

Then there was the very particular court of those who worked in the prince's own secretariat. Well before Cambodia won independence, Sihanouk had recognised his need to have men of energy next to him to carry out his decisions and to offer suggestions on the endless range of issues that engaged his attention. Just as he was all too ready to ignore the excesses of Monique and those who gathered around her, so did his choice of close collaborators often reflect a lack of judgment. This is not a comment about the many tried and true associates who stood beside him for twenty years, though even here he made a monumental error of judgment in believing that Lon Nol would never betray him. Rather, the reference is to men such as Sam Sary and then Chau Seng. Both were men of great energy, and both fell out with Sihanouk as the result of very different ideological commitments.

It was their energy that earned them Sihanouk's approbation. Sam Sary had served Sihanouk well at Geneva in 1954 and in the events leading up to the formation of the Sangkum the following year. Sary's energy, not least reflected in his publishing material extolling the prince's virtues, induced the prince to overlook Sary's increasing involvement in large-scale corruption. Yet even when Sary's actions were becoming a matter of public scandal, Sihanouk had been ready to send him to London as ambassador, only to have Sary fall from grace as has already been described.

Sihanouk's association with Chau Seng lasted longer and was of a more chequered character. A member of the generation of Cambodian students who had studied in France in the 1950s and had become communists there, Chau Seng had come to Sihanouk's attention shortly after he returned to Phnom Penh through a report he prepared on the problems of secondary education in Cambodia. He was intelligent and, like Sam Sary, hardworking. But with these qualities went a seemingly inexhaustible capacity to irritate, annoy and offend others. Yet he repeatedly occupied important government positions under Sihanouk, ultimately becoming the head of the prince's own secretariat. Why did Sihanouk tolerate this *enfant terrible* of Cambodian politics, and more than that, allow Chau Seng an extraordinary degree of freedom to publish his views in the press? The answer seems to lie in the almost guilty admiration Sihanouk felt for the robust way in which Chau Seng expressed his anti-imperialist and domestically 'progressive' views. Time and again the prince spoke of how he, too, would have been on the left of politics if he had not been born into the royal family. Moreover, despite the contempt he sometimes expressed for those he termed intellectuals, he was secretly rather envious of those who could claim such an identity, as Chau Seng did.

Yet, again, Sihanouk's judgment was at fault. Although Chau Seng's public posture was that of a leftist, Sihanouk would also have been aware that this critic of capitalism was busily pursuing his own enrichment, through real estate in Phnom Penh and, eventually, a rubber plantation in the provinces. The prince probably found this avaricious side of Chau Seng's character reassuring, for it suggested that his claims to a left-wing identity were ultimately hollow. But finally Sihanouk came to realise that Chau Seng was both commit-ted to radical change and linked to the prince's bitter enemies in the *maquis*. Heeding a public warning from Sihanouk delivered over Radio Phnom Penh, Chau Seng fled Cambodia. This sequence of events, however, was still years away from the early 1960s, when Chau Seng's utility to the prince lay in his ability to write hard-hit-ting anti-American articles.

The fact that only a few Cambodians could do this led to Sihanouk's reliance on French advisers and journalists to fulfil his demands for an admiring press and to interpret legal and technical issues for him. There were perhaps a dozen such Frenchmen working for Sihanouk in the early '60s. Debate continues about the degree of influence they exerted. The most prominent of them, and the tasks they performed, provide valuable insights into Sihanouk's Cambodia in the period when the prince rode high.

The two most important foreigners in Sihanouk's employ were the Frenchmen Charles Meyer and Jean Barré. It was they who oversaw the production of much of the newspaper and magazine material published by the Cambodian government. The weekly semi-official newspaper, *Réalités Cambodgiennes*, was edited by Barré. He and other Frenchmen in Sihanouk's employ produced *Kambuja* and the *Sangkum*, two magazines Sihanouk established during a period of enthusiasm for journalism in the early 1960s. French speechwriters wrote for Sihanouk and, upon instruction, produced summarised and bowdlerised versions of his speeches for the official news bulletin (*AKP*) put out by the Agence Khmère de Presse. Frenchmen provided the published reports of the prince's daily doings. These did not take the form of 'court circulars', with brief accounts of people seen and places visited. Rather, in trembling baroque prose more suited to another age, they invested each of Sihanouk's actions with immense import. By 1960 it was not unusual to find Sihanouk described as 'the man whom heavenly wisdom has provided at the appropriate time so that Cambodia may travel forward in order and peace to the destiny reserved for it'.

By 1960, Charles Meyer was almost certainly the most important foreigner in Sihanouk's employ. A Frenchman with known left-wing views, he was seen by some, particularly Americans, as a singularly malevolent influence on the prince. Despite being so identified, he was a man of some mystery. Born in Alsace, he had begun his association with Indochina in Saigon, where his role in the tangled events that surrounded the end of French rule and the accession to power of Ngo Dinh Diem is tantalisingly obscure. Trained as a geographer, and on all later evidence skilled as a cartographer, he first came to wider notice as an 'adviser' to Bay Vien, the leader of the Saigon-based Binh Xuyen, a quasi-military gangster group which had controlled the lucrative rackets associated with gambling and prostitution in Saigon since the end of the Second World War. As France painfully conceded defeat in 1954, the Binh Xuyen was powerful and ambitious enough to make its own bid for a share of the power in the emerging South Vietnamese state. Just how Meyer reconciled his association with these gangsters is not clear, for it was an odd marriage of convenience given his already known sympathy for left-wing causes. If Bay Vien and his band of scoundrels identified with any political tendency, it was not with the left.

Just how Meyer gained Sihanouk's confidence and came to play such an important part in shaping the prince's public image is also a mystery. Clearly, Sihanouk recognised in Meyer a man of intelligence and energy. Probably, his readiness to employ Meyer also reflected an attitude similar to that which he adopted towards Chau Seng. In Meyer he had as an employee a man who was ready and able to express anti-American views that even Sihanouk was reluctant to put into print. Finally, it would not have escaped the prince's eye that by employing Meyer he gained the services of a man whose considerable talents could be turned to a range of tasks. Once again, however, Sihanouk failed to recognise that the man to whom he entrusted the polishing of his image would finally turn to bite the hand that had paid his wages.

Although Sihanouk and Meyer later became disillusioned with each other, the French adviser clearly revelled in the early years of his association with the prince. His duties were multifarious: writing speeches, editing those the prince had prepared himself, contributing to *Réalités* and giving press conferences on the government's behalf to foreign journalists. Meyer was responsible for some of the most sophisticated promotional material published about the kingdom, material in which his talent for cartography was abundantly evident. He was always ready to act as a guide to those who came to Cambodia with an intention to report favourably on the country. His range of contacts was extensive, and included not just the French community, both official and private, and Cambodians, but also the Chinese embassy (his wife was a Hong Kong-born Chinese), and the Vietnamese communists' representatives in Phnom Penh.

Still, it is difficult to assess his influence over Sihanouk and the policies the prince pursued. I see no reason to change a judgment I made in an earlier attempt to analyse this fascinating man: that Meyer's influence was never as pervasive as some observers thought and probably more fitful than most realised. That noted, there is no doubt that he was an important figure in reinforcing Prince Sihanouk's distrust of the United States, and without question no other foreigner came close to matching the opportunities Meyer had for steering Sihanouk toward a pro-Chinese stance in foreign policy and a continuing readiness to maintain close links with France.

The only other foreigner who came close to equalling Meyer's role as an adviser to the prince was Jean Barré, the editor of *Réalités Cambodgiennes*. While they shared a commitment to left-wing views, the two Frenchmen had little else in common. Meyer, at least in the early 1960s, was reclusive, seldom seen at diplomatic receptions. He projected an almost ascetic air—the British journalist Dennis Bloodworth once suggested that he looked like a younger Molotov, with his round glasses and nondescript hair surmounting a square face. His long years in the tropics had left him looking trimly fit. Jean Barré was very different. By 1960 he was already fat. A dedicated gourmet who once engaged in a spirited published debate with Sihanouk about the merits of particular types of pâté de foie, Barré was a 'regular' on the official cocktail circuit and a habitué of Phnom Penh's better restaurants. On these outings he was usually accompanied by a young Cambodian man; he felt no need, in a city that was extremely tolerant in sexual matters, to hide his homosexuality. A faint air of scandal hung about him for another reason. He was said to have been pro-Vichy in his early life and for this reason reluctant or unable to return to France.

As editor of the country's semi-official newspaper, Barré may have seen Sihanouk as often as Charles Meyer did, but most thoughtful observers in Phnom Penh doubted that he exerted as much influence over the prince as his colleague. He was much more Sihanouk's willing tool, displaying energy belied by his unhealthy physique, but always ready, as was Meyer, to sharpen the anti-American tone of a draft given to him. Sitting close to the prince at news conferences, Barré had an instinctive capacity to know what Sihanouk wanted to say; if the prince hesitated in an answer he would look to Barré to complete the thought.

Meyer and Barré were the most prominent of the men who worked for Sihanouk and kept his propaganda machine functioning. Others who played an important part included Donald Lancaster, Sihanouk's English-language secretary and a former British foreign service officer, and the French journalists Pierre Fuchs and Bernard Hamel.

In combination, Sihanouk's 'courts' played their part in obscuring the reality of Cambodia from most foreign observers, if not from many Cambodians. More importantly for the course of later events, those who were closest to Sihanouk, both in his work and in his frequent search for diversion, tended to disguise if not actually hide from the prince many of the less attractive and more worrying realities of the kingdom. In the company of his cronies, Sihanouk could all too readily turn his back on those aspects of the state that should have been a cause for concern. Those close Cambodian advisers upon whom he relied to carry out his wishes and to administer the state on his behalf seldom felt able to contradict Sihanouk and warn him of difficulties or problems arising from the policies that he laid down. As for the foreign representatives who followed Sihanouk from ceremony to ceremony, their presence catered to his desire to be regarded as important beyond Cambodia's frontiers. When they sought audiences with him, he listened happily to those who praised his policies and reacted negatively to any suggestion that those policies might need adjustment.

All the while his French experts, his scribes, were writing the adulatory copy that his ego demanded and gladly propagating the 'anti-imperialist' views that they shared. Years later, Sihanouk described his failure to recognise the extent to which elite opinion was turning against him as 'unpardonably naive'. In reality, he was more than naive. He was a victim of his own readiness to ignore fact in favour of self-deluding fantasy and to indulge his vanity at the expense of any attempt to view himself and his country in a balanced fashion. So long as domestic and foreign threats to his position were contained, as they were in the early '60s, the indulgence inherent in Sihanouk's behaviour could be ignored. That would not always be the case.

Notes

As with the previous chapter, much of the material in Chapter 11 reflects my personal observation of developments in Cambodia in the period 1959–61 and in subsequent years, and information given to me by private sources in Phnom Penh. Useful insights into the atmosphere described in this chapter may be found in Martin, *Le Mal cambodgien*, and Meyer, *Derrière*. For examples of adulatory writing on Cambodia by foreigners, see Han Suyin's novel *The Four Faces of Shiva*, London, 1963, and Wilfred Burchett's *Mekong Upstream*.

For one of the few published accounts of Sihanouk's inner court in operation, see *Réalités*, 6 February 1970.

Dennis Bloodworth in his *An Eye For The Dragon*, London, 1970, pp. 176–9, discusses Meyer's activities in Saigon. See, also, Edward Lansdale, *In The Midst Of War: An American's Mission to Southeast Asia*, New York, 1972, Chapters 9–11, which discusses the 1954–55 period in Saigon and identifies Barré as a propagandist for General Hinh, one of Ngo Dinh Diem's opponents.

I have written on the personalities of Chau Seng, Charles Meyer and Jean Barré in my *Before Kampuchea: Preludes to Tragedy*, Sydney, 1979.

A striking example of Jean Barré's aiding Sihanouk when in a state of high emotion the prince was lost for words, was at a press conference broadcast on 13 August 1966 which I heard in Phnom Penh.

12

Sihanouk's Cambodia: Foreign friends and enemies

In the early 1960s, not only did Sihanouk appear invulnerably dominant within Cambodia, but he also appeared to have found a formula, or perhaps a series of formulas, for ensuring that his country's international interests were protected. This was no easy task, given the hostility of Thailand and South Vietnam. But the fact that both China and the United States, in their very different ways, lent support to his regime allowed Sihanouk considerable latitude in the conduct of Cambodia's foreign relations. Although he criticised the United States repeatedly for not reining in the governments in Bangkok and Saigon for supporting Cambodian dissidents, particularly Son Ngoc Thanh, he felt he could bank on the US to stop his neighbours from committing outright acts of aggression against his country. At the same time, and as a result of the assurances given to him earlier by Zhou Enlai, he believed China would protect Cambodia from his ultimate nightmare: the kingdom's domination by the Vietnamese communists.

Like the majority of his countrymen, Sihanouk privately feared Vietnamese of all political persuasions as traditional enemies and potential destroyers of the Cambodian state. Over the years, he has been cautious about expressing this view publicly, since he has judged that circumstances, at one time or another, called for appeasement or cooperation with the Vietnamese communists. But no such inhibitions affected his dealings with Ngo Dinh Diem, whom he regarded as an American puppet. Sihanouk's dislike of Diem was deep and visceral. So, too, was his antipathy towards

151

Marshal Sarit, the dictator who was still in control of Thailand at the beginning of the '60s. Since Sihanouk's feelings were reciprocated by both Diem and Sarit, who regarded the prince as a stalking-horse for communism in the region, the record of relations between Cambodia and its neighbours was marked, in the period around 1960, by frequent of border incidents, accusations and recriminations. In all of this, Sihanouk depicted and perceived himself as the embodiment of Cambodia, so that any action by the hostile neighbours was portrayed to the Cambodian public as if it were an attack on him personally.

Amid this equilibrium of despite, Sihanouk worked hard to give greater substance to Cambodia's proclaimed neutrality. In part he pursued this goal through the device of state visits. Over the years Cambodia played host to a steady procession of heads of state and senior figures from countries on both sides of the political spectrum. President Sukarno came to Phnom Penh, and managed to annoy his hosts by the boorish behaviour of his pug-ugly bodyguards and his own too-familiar embrace of Bopha Devi at the end of a performance by the royal ballet. Princess Alexandra of Kent and later Princess Margaret came to Cambodia as representatives of the British royal family. President Liu Shao Chi came from China and Lee Kuan Yew from Singapore. The last, Sihanouk later confided to one of his associates, he found difficult to understand, since he did not behave like any of the Chinese he knew.

Beyond Cambodia, Sihanouk looked to the United Nations as the institution through which his country's point of view could be brought to world attention. He had attended the 1958 General Assembly, but it was at the Fifteenth General Assembly in 1960 that he made the greatest impact. His account of his visit, published after his return from New York, is one of the purest distillations of Sihanouk's views on world leaders and the policies they followed on their countries' behalf. Describing his experiences in New York, the prince was mocking, outraged, malicious and falsely humble. As a bravura example of Sihanouk's reaction to the conduct of international affairs, his account is worth noting at some length.

Reporting to his compatriots on his experiences, Sihanouk left no slight, imagined or otherwise, unmentioned. It was not his personal vanity that was at stake, he insisted, but rather that of the nation, which while it might be small had a longer history than many of those represented at the UN, including the 'young United States of America'. There follows a catalogue of mistakes, slights and inappropriate behaviour, by United Nations officials, the City of New York, the government of the United States, and the representatives of the international community. Nikita Khrushchev had wrongly been given credit for raising representation in the general debate to the level of head of government, but he, Sihanouk, had already led the Cambodian delegation to the General Assembly two years before. This and his status as Cambodia's chief of state seemed forgotten as the 'greats' of the Third World were accorded privileges denied to Sihanouk. Indonesia's Sukarno, Sihanouk noted, was provided with 'detectives, bodyguards and uniformed police escorts', whereas he was assigned a single policeman. Nkrumah occupied a whole floor of the Waldorf Astoria, Sihanouk recorded, with his 'multitude of collaborators and attendants who seldom left the elevators'. Sukarno, 'a veritable Javanese princely friend of the arts . . . insisted on decorating his suite with very beautiful, very conspicuous, very captivating "flowers of the Indonesian islands" '.

Beyond the preoccupation with personal slights, Sihanouk's experience in New York had a very serious aspect. The behaviour of the representatives of the great powers at the General Assembly reinforced prejudices already well established in his mind. The contrast between the favoured treatment accorded the leaders of major states and that which he and his delegation received in New York strengthened Sihanouk's view that the United States simply did not regard Cambodia as important. A further reason for Sihanouk to feel disenchanted with the United States related to his meeting, in New York, with President Eisenhower. Although the meeting appears to have been relatively amicable in tone, Eisenhower failed to give a firm and positive response to Sihanouk's request for additional US funding for the Cambodian armed forces. The prince's feeling that the Western powers did not take him or his country seriously was then further reinforced by a contretemps with the British delegation at the General Assembly. Harold Macmillan, the British prime minister, invited Sihanouk to the United Kingdom, but indicated that for protocol purposes, the visit would not be 'official'. Sihanouk was clearly furious at what he regarded as a gratuitous slight. He was not mollified when, in the face of his displeasure, the British foreign secretary, Lord Home, offered to upgrade the status of the proposed visit. By then Sihanouk was not inclined to go to Britain at all. It was yet another example, he remarked, of the 'bad luck' that always appeared to attend his relations with Britain.

153

The tumultuous events of the General Assembly convinced Sihanouk that his reserved view of the Soviet Union was entirely justified. Not only did he resent the extraordinary attention given by the American press to Khrushchev's every word and action, but he thought the Soviet president's extravagant gesture of beating on his desk with his shoe to show displeasure represented a total lack of decorum. He was equally critical of the way in which various African delegations behaved, indicating their views with shouts as well as applause. For Sihanouk, as for most of his compatriots, black Africans were uncouth figures of fun.

Of all the countries represented at the Fifteenth General Assembly, only two earned Sihanouk's unqualified praise: France and Yugoslavia. All the others failed him in one way or another. The Soviet Union and its allies were displeased by some aspects of his address to the General Assembly and failed to applaud as he would have wished, though they partially redeemed themselves by attending his reception *en bloc*. He felt that the United States and the United Kingdom had patronised him. Curiously, China's role was barely mentioned.

During 1961 and 1962, Sihanouk felt sufficiently confident about his grip on both Cambodia's domestic politics and its international security to seek an active role in solving some of the world's more intractable political problems. Moreover, he had been particularly buoyed by the International Court of Justice's decision in 1962 that Thailand had no right to occupy the Angkor-period temple of Preah Vihear, which it had seized four years before. The decision seemed a further testimony to the correctness of the policies he was following. He promoted the concept of an international conference to bring peace to Laos in 1961, was involved in efforts to find a solution to the Sino-Indian dispute in 1962, and in the same year was a voice in support of most radical causes at the meeting of the Nonaligned Movement in Belgrade. These were not idle diversions, for Sihanouk had a genuine if less than realistic belief in his capacity to solve the problems of others. But such initiatives were soon to be replaced by other concerns as the guerrilla war in next-door Vietnam began to intensify and as Cambodian domestic politics again seemed likely to slip from his absolute control.

As 1962 drew to a close, Sihanouk grew increasingly concerned with developments in South Vietnam. His personal antipathy towards President Ngo Dinh Diem was as sharp as ever, but now he began to worry that the guerrilla war between the Saigon regime and communist insurgents in the countryside could pose a long-term threat to Cambodia. Against this background he began to consider his options, most particularly the desirability of being a recipient of aid from the United States. Might it not be better, he mused, to forgo such dependence both as a true indication of neutrality and as a means of indicating his sympathy for the cause of anti-imperialism?

Notes

Detailed examination of Sihanouk's foreign policy involvement during this period is provided by Roger M. Smith in *Cambodia's Foreign Policy*, and Michael Leifer, in his *Cambodia: The Search for Security*.

The most accessible version of Sihanouk's commentary on his visit to the Fifteenth General Assembly of the United Nations is the translation in John P. Armstrong's *Sihanouk Speaks*, New York, 1964.

13

From hope . . .

One great difficulty in analysing Prince Sihanouk's long career lies in judging the extent to which he considered the consequences of his actions and decisions. All the evidence suggests that Sihanouk seldom looked far into the future, except in the most general terms. He feared for Cambodia's eventual fate at the hands of its hostile neighbours, and he believed that he alone had the capacity to preserve the kingdom's stability. But repeatedly, he made decisions that held within them the seeds of dissent, disunity and disaster. From 1963 onwards, the transitory nature of the calm evident at the beginning of the decade became increasingly apparent. Slowly, but as hindsight now shows surely, Sihanouk's control over the state began to slip away.

Despite the prince's vigorous espousal of anti-imperialist causes in the international arena, his policies towards the domestic left reflected his continuing belief that communism did not offer an answer to Cambodia's problems. He held this view not least because he rightly saw that a communist Cambodia would have no place for him. He had shown his antipathy to local radicals before. Now, having triumphed in the referendum of 1960, he was determined to ensure that the radical left was neutralised as a political force. If those who held leftist views worked within his mass movement, the Sangkum, he was ready to have them voice their anti-imperialist, most particularly anti-American views. What he would not tolerate was a leftist critique of his own policies. Sihanouk's approach posed a dilemma for those of a genuinely radical persuasion, for they faced a stark choice between knuckling under and playing by Sihanouk's rules, or going underground. The starkness of that choice was made increasingly apparent from late 1961 onwards. Representatives of the embattled leftist-front Pracheachon party were harassed by the security forces and publicly humiliated by Sihanouk. In the run-up to the June 1962 elections, a number of Pracheachon figures were arrested. They were subsequently tried and sentenced to death, but their sentences were later commuted to life imprisonment. During the same period, the long-time radical who had become leader of the recently formed Khmer Workers' Party, Tou Samouth, was killed, almost certainly assassinated by Lon Nol and Kou Roun's security forces. In this atmosphere of violent repression, those who continued to espouse leftist views within the open political system, such as Khieu Samphan, Hu Nim, Hou Youn and Chau Seng, recognised that they could do so only under the strictest limitations, while professing loyalty to the prince and to the Sangkum.

This, indeed, was what the young leftists elected to parliament in June 1962 did. Initially given a surprisingly free hand by the prince, they sought to influence the government's economic policies, drawing in part on the arguments Khieu Samphan had advanced in his French doctoral thesis, which criticised the continuing 'colonial' character of Cambodia's economy. But whatever the left's belief in the possibility of bringing real change to Cambodia's politics, its hopes received a body blow in the first half of 1963. In February of that year, while Sihanouk was visiting China, riots broke out in Siemreap which found echoes, on a lesser scale, in other urban areas of the country. The immediate cause of the Siemreap riots was antagonism that had been building for some time between students and the police. During the violence, photographs of Sihanouk were destroyed and anti-Sangkum slogans shouted. These were unexpected and unprecedented developments.

When Sihanouk returned from China, his security forces told him that elements linked to Son Ngoc Thanh were responsible for the riots. His own inclination was to blame men of known anti-monarchical views. Then, responding to information given to him by Lon Nol, Sihanouk in March released a list of 34 'subversives' whom he said were working to bring down the government. Five leftist members of the Sangkum who held seats in parliament, including Khieu Samphan and Chau Seng, were on the list, as were

Saloth Sar and Ieng Sary, the future Pol Pot and his deputy. Surprisingly, the release of their names did not end the participation of the five deputies in open politics. Although Khieu Samphan and Hou Youn left the cabinet of the day, they continued as members of parliament. The event of real historical importance was the decision by Sar and Sary to go underground and into hiding in eastern Cambodia. With their disappearance from Phnom Penh and Sihanouk's green light to the security services to counter nascent radical challenge by any means, the left was counted out of Cambodian politics for a full three years. Largely unrecorded and certainly with Sihanouk's full approval, despite his later protestations to the contrary, Lon Nol and Kou Roun's henchmen pursued their task of harassing the radical left with brutal diligence. In the absence of an opportunity for the left-wing politicians to present a critique of Cambodian society, political debate increasingly centred on the issues of the economy and relations with the United States. To these two intertwined issues must be added a third: Cambodia's increasing involvement in the clandestine supply of the communist forces fighting in the escalating Vietnam War.

The upheavals of the Siemreap riots aside, no-one in Cambodia in 1963 thought Sihanouk faced any serious challenge. Certainly he did not think so himself, and his speeches continued to emphasise the necessity of his own leadership to the country's survival. He remained preoccupied with the issue of who would eventually succeed him and made clear his belief that his overall policies would continue to guide the state when his successor came to power. This thinking lay behind his designation of one of his sons, Prince Norodom Naradipo, to succeed him as head of the Sangkum and eventually as chief of state—Naradipo was Sihanouk's son by Princess Monikessan and at this time was in his seventeenth year. His decision to name a successor and its timing, in November 1963, were both significant. In nominating Naradipo as his political heir, Sihanouk acted much more as a tradition-conscious member of the Cambodian royal family than as a politician aware of the currents of opinion in the state over which he presided. Like his royal ancestors, Sihanouk was seeking to ensure that he would be succeeded by his nominee rather than the choice of any other group, domestic or foreign. And Naradipo, who was a student in Peking, occupied a position remarkably similar to that of earlier Cambodian princes who were educated in the Thai court—the court of

Cambodia's suzerain. But in making his choice and in doing so with every expectation that his policies would guide Cambodia indefinitely, Sihanouk betrayed the degree to which he was beginning to lose the apparently sure touch he had demonstrated between 1955 and 1960.

To a large extent, Sihanouk's firm grip on Cambodian politics began to slip because of his lack of understanding of economic issues. Yet the kingdom's economy was increasingly the focus of political debate and manoeuvring. This was the result of several factors. The conduct of foreign affairs was firmly in Sihanouk's hands and, until the very end of his rule, none dared challenge this fact, particularly as Sihanouk so successfully and consistently portrayed himself as the target of external criticism and threat. And so far as internal policy was concerned, a number of important issues were not susceptible to extended or meaningful discussion because of their sensitive nature. The issue of corruption was a notable case in point.

Throughout Cambodia's independent existence the problem of corruption has been admitted, condemned, and then ignored. Sihanouk's uncle Prince Monireth had sought to confront the problem in the early years of independence, but his efforts came to nothing. According to his cousin Prince Sisowath Entaravong, Sihanouk rebuffed Monireth when he presented the prince with evidence that his own father and mother were benefiting from corruption. The inability of any Cambodian government to reduce corruption to manageable proportions reflected in part the pervading necessity for a system of extra-legal financial gain in a state in which no civil servant received adequate remuneration. This 'functional' corruption, a pattern of rewards given for services rendered, was an accepted way of life under Sihanouk. Because it was so widespread, it was not an easy target, even for those on the left. Nor was it easy to campaign against the corruption that occurred on an even larger scale. Sihanouk acknowledged the existence of such 'grand corruption', whose participants set no limits to their greed and venality. But he confessed he was powerless to deal with it. The pursuit of wealth through rackets and illegalities of the most complex and varied sort was part and parcel of life in Cambodia from the highest circles in the royal family and the government down.

By its very nature, much of the corruption that occurred was beyond legal proof, even if there had been any readiness to bring offenders to account. It was an index of the pervasiveness of this culture of corruption that members of the Phnom Penh elite were so ready to discuss who they thought benefited from which corrupt deal or racket. Sihanouk's mother, Queen Kossamak, was widely believed to take rake-offs from the owners of Phnom Penh's more exclusive brothels. His aunt Princess Rasmey benefited personally, it was said, from her position as president of the Cambodian Red Cross. Part of any donation to that body was supposed to remain sticking to the princess's hand. Whether correctly or not, Sihanouk's courtly economic adviser Son Sann was also spoken of by his critics as being corrupt, his links to the country's principal distillery said to provide a rewarding source of unearned income. Even politicians who were regarded as proponents of radical social and economic policies were not above ensuring their material comforts through dubious means, as the case of Chau Seng, mentioned earlier, showed. Indeed, in the world of open politics in Phnom Penh during the 1960s, what made Khieu Samphan so remarkable to his compatriots was the absolute certainty that he, in contrast to so many others, was incorruptible. As he presided over Cambodia, Sihanouk was not personally corrupt. He had no need to be. His fault was to ignore the danger that failing to confront the problem of grand corruption posed.

With corruption an untouchable issue in the early 1960s, the economy was one policy area that was not off-limits to those left-inclined politicians who had remained within the Sangkum. In practical terms, men such as Khieu Sampan and Hou Youn had little immediate impact on economic developments within the country. They had accepted places in the cabinet appointed after the June 1962 elections, as secretaries of state for planning and commerce respectively, but later had to resign because of conservative opposition. Nevertheless, their arguments, not least concerning the desirability of greater national self-sufficiency, were not entirely ignored by Sihanouk. The prince himself had long argued that Cambodia should seek to rely on its own resources. Although he had earlier rejected the implication of his leftist critics that the acceptance of Western aid compromised Cambodia's neutrality, he had, by 1963, come to believe that the country did, indeed, risk becoming a client of the United States in the same fashion as Laos and South Vietnam, if Cambodia's economic posture was not radically changed. At the same time, the prince concluded that Cambodia's political independence was put at risk by the fact that all major commercial and industrial activity in Cambodia was in the hands of foreign nationals, principally French and Chinese. Accordingly, in November 1963, Sihanouk announced far-reaching economic reforms that involved the nationalisation of the country's export–import trade, the nationalisation of certain other industries and services, including banks and distilleries, and the renunciation of all US aid.

Sihanouk made his decisions against the advice of Son Sann, the most experienced and best-qualified economic adviser in the prince's close circle of senior officials. In the months leading up to the decision Sihanouk's health had been poor and he had alternated between brief periods of manic elation and depression. His English-language secretary, Donald Lancaster, has told of how during this time Sihanouk was given to making speeches cast in apocalyptic terms. Addressing an admiring but bewildered peasant audience, Sihanouk predicted disaster for Cambodia. The hostile neighbours would invade and he would be forced to retreat to the hills. Then, because of his friendship with the Chinese, they would send an army to liberate the country and he would return to rule over a kingdom at peace with itself. Whether he consciously intended it or not, Sihanouk's stark scenario evoked an image deeply held in Cambodian folk memory of the conquering ruler who, having been defeated by his enemies, returns in glory after having gained strength while sheltering in the mountains.

As Sihanouk weighed up possible courses of action, other factors played their part. The appointment of a new American ambassador, in the latter part of 1963, had an unsettling effect on him. After a generally untroubled relationship with Ambassador William Trimble, he found the new US envoy, Philip Sprouse, a much less sympathetic figure. More deeply disturbing for Sihanouk, in his agitated state of mind, was the coup in Saigon at the beginning of November that led to the deaths of Ngo Dinh Diem and his brother Nhu. Three years earlier Sihanouk and his closest associates had been gleeful when it briefly appeared that an earlier attempted coup in Saigon would succeed and that Diem would be overthrown. He saw things differently now, believing that the United States' complicity in the coup and abandonment of the Ngo brothers showed what it might be prepared to do to work its will in neutralist Cambodia. If he was hesitant to take the steps he had been contemplating for some time, Diem's overthrow was a final spur to action. Sihanouk announced the sweeping economic policy changes on 10 November.

The next several weeks were full of fevered activity as Sihanouk justified the changes and railed against the United States for supporting the governments in Bangkok and Saigon that allowed anti-Sihanouk rebels to broadcast from their territory. It was also a period of 'might have beens': President Kennedy briefly showed an interest in trying to prevent further deterioration in relations with Cambodia, only to be assassinated in Dallas almost immediately afterwards.

On 19 November, Sihanouk appeared before a hastily convened national congress of the Sangkum to explain his economic decisions and the rejection of the United States aid. He also used the gathering as an opportunity for savage political theatre, bringing before the assembled crowd two Khmer Serei rebels, representatives of the dissidents linked to his old enemy Son Ngoc Thanh, who were displayed in cages. Asked to admit that Son Ngoc Thanh was supported by the United States, one confessed and was immediately released; the other, who had remained mute as he cowered before the abuse of the crowd, was shortly afterward condemned to death. His execution, in early 1964, was captured on film at Sihanouk's order and shown in cinemas throughout Cambodia. Two years later Cambodians still spoke of the revulsion many had felt at the sight of the rebel's body, riddled with bullets, slumping at the execution stake.

Far away in Washington, a day after the national congress had met, President Kennedy's senior advisers had brought Sihanouk's rejection of American aid to his attention. Previously, Cambodia had occupied little of the American president's time. In contrast to Vietnam most particularly, but also to Laos, Cambodia had seemed a minor concern to the United States, despite what was perceived as Sihanouk's unpredictable behaviour and dubious friendship with China. The rejection of aid had changed this perception, for it might presage a more hostile Cambodian stance that would complicate America's increasing problems in Vietnam. At the core of the problem, Kennedy learnt, was Sihanouk's anger at American links to the Khmer Serei rebels, links, as David Chandler has pointed out, about which Kennedy knew nothing.

Whether the US president would have intervened to distance his country from any association with the rebel radio broadcasts that gave Sihanouk such offence can never be known, for two days later he was killed in Dallas. Lyndon Johnson, his successor, sent assurances to the Cambodian leader that the United States was not lending support to the Khmer Serei, as did Undersecretary of State Averell Harriman. These soothing words were insufficient to lower the political temperature in Phnom Penh, where Sihanouk was now, unsuccessfully, seeking to promote an international conference to guarantee Cambodia's neutrality. When on 8 December 1963 the Thai dictator, Marshal Sarit, died, Sihanouk gave full vent to the anger he felt towards his neighbours and the United States. Speaking on Radio Phnom Penh, the prince welcomed the deaths of Diem, Kennedy and Sarit. Terming the late American president the 'great boss', Sihanouk said the three would 'all meet in hell'. He called on the population to celebrate the deaths of these foreign leaders by wearing red armbands and assembling to listen to music performances near the royal palace. After the Cambodian ambassador to the United States, Nong Kimny, was upbraided by a state department official for the tone of Sihanouk's broadcast, the entire Cambodian mission to Washington was recalled to Phnom Penh. A complete break in diplomatic relations did not seem far off.

Surprisingly, given the intensity of Sihanouk's feeling, that break was still more than a year away despite a series of events that further heightened tension between the two countries. There was a relatively small student demonstration in January that included the United States among its targets. Then, in March, a much larger demonstration occurred, this time with Sihanouk's full approval and with state backing. Directed against both the United States and British embassies, the demonstration included students, soldiers in civilian clothes and peasants trucked into the capital for the day. According to Donald Lancaster, Sihanouk personally gave the order that the embassies should be looted but that no blood should be shed. Remarkably, given the size of the demonstration, this order was honoured. Substantial material damage was done to both diplomatic missions, but no-one was injured.

From this point on, Cambodia's relations with the United States deteriorated steadily. The heart of the problem was Vietnam, and American policy towards that country. By early 1964, those in Washington who advocated increased US involvement in South Vietnam were in the ascendant. For these men and their colleagues, such as Ambassador Henry Cabot Lodge in Saigon and his military advisers, Cambodia was becoming an unacceptable irritant. Although not aware of all the details, they correctly suspected that substantial quantities of supplies were reaching the communist forces in South Vietnam through Cambodia, with some degree of official assent. They also knew for certain that Vietnamese communist forces were using border areas within Cambodia as safe havens. In these circumstances there was little sympathy for Sihanouk's efforts to promote conferences on Cambodian 'neutrality' nor for Cambodian complaints about cross-border incursions by South Vietnamese forces assisted by United States advisers.

As the months passed, dealings between the two countries became a dialogue of the deaf, and as the war in South Vietnam intensified, bringing further border incursions into Cambodian territory, Sihanouk became reinforced in his conviction that the Vietnamese communists would win the conflict. He saw no need to make concessions to the United States by in any way counteracting the use of Cambodian territory by communist forces. On the diplomatic front, he took pleasure in refusing to accept the credentials of the American official sent to replace Ambassador Sprouse, allowing Randolph Kidder to stew in Phnom Penh before sending him back to the United States. A visit to China in September 1964, where he was, as ever, received with the greatest marks of courtesy, buoyed his belief that in distancing himself from the West he was riding the wave of history. Few voices in Phnom Penh were ready to question his foreign policy. When what little concern was expressed came from men such as the French-trained lawyer Douc Rasy, who was clearly identified as a conservative, the prince came to believe that he had chosen the right path. His French idol Charles de Gaulle was already making clear his reservations about American policy in Vietnam, and this did not escape Sihanouk's notice. And in Cambodia itself his retinue of French advisers and assistants praised his courage in standing up to the country which they so disliked. With the cost to lives and property from border incursions stirring genuine popular anger against the South Vietnamese and United States governments it is a fair estimate that, for the moment, Sihanouk's policies had widespread approval.

When the break in relations between Cambodia and the United States finally came, it was triggered by an event that in other circumstances, and in another country, might have been regarded as Gilbertian. In April 1965 Sihanouk departed from his usual policy of refusing entry to journalists working for Western news organisations and allowed a reporter from *Newsweek*, Bernard Krisher, to come to Phnom Penh. Quite why Sihanouk should have relaxed his rule in this way is not certain, though Phnom Penh gossip had an explanation. The reporter, it was alleged, had once procured a woman for Indonesia's President Sukarno, who had now interceded with Sihanouk to allow him to come to Cambodia. This is far from a fully satisfactory explanation, since by this time Sihanouk held a fairly jaundiced view of the Indonesian leader. Whatever the true explanation, and Krisher's own explanation written in 1989 is less than satisfactory, in the course of his visit to Phnom Penh the reporter spoke to Donald Lancaster, Sihanouk's English-language secretary. Usually extremely discreet, Lancaster

Je dédie ce Film aux F.A.R.K.
En témoignage de ma profonde affection
et de ma vive reconnaissance pour les ser-
-vices éminents qu'elles ont rendus à notre
Patrie bien-aimée. *N. Sihanouk*

Sihanouk, cinematographer
Sihanouk is shown directing the filming of his first feature film, 'Apsara'. The handwritten inscription accompanying the photograph dedicates the film to the Cambodian army.

Dramatis personnae in 'Apsara'
General Nhiek Tioulong played the part of an ageing roué, General Rithi, who finally married his mistress, Rattana, played by Royal Air Cambodge flight attendant, Saksi Sbong.

Lon Nol and Sirik Matak
Shown here in official portrait photographs, Lon Nol (*above*) and Sirik Matak (*below*) were the key figures in Sihanouk's deposition in the coup of March 1970.

Mao: — Devine voir le beau cadeau que je t'apporte pour le Nouvel An Khmer.

Sihanouk : — C'est sûrement la "chose", Maître.

Sihanouk: Mao's puppet obsessed with sex
The Lon Nol regime that overthrew Sihanouk constantly stressed the prince's links with China. In this cartoon from the Phnom Penh Army's magazine of April 1971, Mao offers Sihanouk a skull as a New Year's gift, while Sihanouk is shown dreaming of a sexual encounter.

Sihanouk.— Camarade, les gens peuvent crever.
Ce qui compte pour moi, c'est le pouvoir.

Sihanouk in alliance with the Vietnamese
The regime that overthrew the prince in 1970 spared no efforts to denigrate
him and to emphasise his links with the Vietnamese communists. In this
cartoon from the Phnom Penh Army's magazine of August 1971, Sihanouk
is shown telling a Vietnamese soldier amid the chaos of war, 'Comrade, the
people can die. What counts for me is power.'

Sihanouk with his former enemies
When Sihanouk visited Khmer Rouge-controlled territory in Cambodia in 1973, he came face-to-face with men whom he had denounced only a few years before. In this photograph, he is seen with Khieu Samphan (*second from left*) and Hu Nim (*second from right*).

Sihanouk and Monique at Banteai Srei
The highpoint of Sihanouk's visit to Cambodia in 1973 organised by the Khmer Rouge, was the period spent near the Angkor ruins. In this photograph he is shown with Monique at the exquisite 10th century temple of Banteai Srei, a little to the north of the provincial capital of Siemreap.

Starting from 'Year Zero'
While Sihanouk was held a prisoner in the royal palace, Pol Pot and his associates set out to transform Cambodia into a radical new state. This involved the destruction of symbols of the previous regime such as the National Bank (*above*) and private cars (*below*). (*Author's photographs*)

The legacy of the Pol Pot years
Estimates vary of the human cost of the Pol Pot years. Few would argue with
the estimate put forward in this book of between 500 000 and a million
persons dying as the result of the regime's policies, with at least 200 000
having been executed. This assemblage of skulls was taken from a mass
grave close to Phnom Penh exhumed in 1981, and shows that the victims
were executed by blows to the head. (*Author's photograph*)

**A royal imposter, 'Prince
Norodom Soryavong'**
As an index of the continuing
appeal of royalty to the
Cambodian population years
after Sihanouk was deposed,
an imposter 'prince' came
briefly into prominence in the
chaotic period following
Vietnam's toppling of the Pol
Pot regime. Styling himself
Norodom Soryavong and
claiming kinship with
Sihanouk, this otherwise
obscure figure, whose real
name was André Okthall,
preyed on refugees along the
Thai-Cambodian border in
early 1980. (*Author's
photograph*)

Drama in a refugee settlement
After the 1978–79 Vietnamese invasion of Cambodia, several hundred
thousand Cambodian refugees flocked to the Thai–Cambodian border.
Sustaining occasional attacks from the Vietnamese, with results as shown in
this photograph taken at Mak Moon camp in 1980, the refugees became a
major political factor in efforts to find a solution to the Cambodian
problem. (*Author's photograph*)

Vietnamese occupation troops in Cambodia
After toppling the Pol Pot tyrannical regime, Vietnamese forces remained in
Cambodia for over a decade. The troops shown here were southern
conscripts being drilled in the provincial town of Kompong Chhnang in
1981. (*Author's photograph*)

on this occasion let slip the fact that Sihanouk's mother owned the land on which many of Phnom Penh's brothels were sited. Translated into magazine copy as part of a sensationalist article that rehashed details of Sihanouk's amatory life, Queen Kossamak's ownership of the land became ownership of the brothels themselves by a woman who was 'money mad'. The fact that the article did not depart too far from the truth in the latter respect did not matter. Sihanouk raged against this further insult. There were further demonstrations and in May 1965 the prince announced that diplomatic relations with the United States had been severed. As a curious, even extraordinary footnote to this affair, Krisher was ultimately able to rehabilitate himself in Sihanouk's eyes and to collaborate with the prince in the production of a book, *Charisma and Leadership.*

The drama of worsening relations with the US had taken place alongside growing evidence that Sihanouk's new economic policies carried costs he had not anticipated. Although respectable arguments may be advanced for the desirability of some of the measures Sihanouk instituted in 1963, since there certainly was a need to reduce Cambodia's reliance on foreign aid and on a restricted range of exports, the weapons he used were economically crude and through poor administration and continuing corruption failed, even in the short term, to achieve the kind of transformation that Sihanouk had in mind.

The reforms struck a blow at foreign traders operating in Cambodia by nationalising the import–export industry. Long-established foreign firms either closed down or elected to operate at a reduced profit through Cambodian holding companies. European and Chinese importers and exporters became, in theory, dependent upon the transactions of a new commercial organisation, SONEXIM (the National Company for Export and Import). National banks and a national insurance company replaced the existing foreign institutions and the state engaged in the sale of imported goods at both the wholesale and retail level.

At the same time as these sweeping changes were being introduced, Sihanouk's decision to end American aid to his country abolished a substantial proportion of Cambodia's income. In the years 1960–62, the United States had provided aid equal to nearly 14 per cent of Cambodia's annual revenue. Not least, the rejection of American aid meant the end of the main source of foreign assistance to Cambodia's armed forces. The US had provided over 30 per cent of the armed forces budget in 1962, exclusive of the supply of equipment. At a stroke, Sihanouk's decisions ensured both that the nation's economy was put under strain and that an essential element of his support within the country, the armed forces, would be disadvantaged.

Sihanouk's state was ill-equipped to adjust to the changes he had so brusquely decreed. There were, it is true, a number of able young officials who were drafted to take up positions in the new, nationalised banking services and in SONEXIM. Their expertise was no match for an economic problem that was as much a reflection of Cambodia's unsolved social and political dilemmas as of its economic circumstances. Although the new measures, with their emphasis on nationalisation and austerity, initially helped to reduce Cambodia's external trade deficit, the longer-term results were much less encouraging. To understand why, one must take account of features of the Cambodian situation outside the realm of classical economic analysis.

From the start, important sections of the Phnom Penh business community found it was possible to adjust to the new situation. Foreign firms, such as Denis Frères or the Hong Kong and Shanghai Banking Corporation, may have found that Cambodia was no longer a profitable base for operations, but the Chinese and Sino-Cambodian firms operating in Phnom Penh soon discovered that there were ways to evade, or at least to dilute, government control of the import–export trade. Bribery flourished as the result of the state's entry into commerce. Although the state was involved in some wholesale and retail selling, the private sector continued to participate, and by illegal means ensured that, after an initial reduction, imports of luxury goods increased again, to the point where external trade deficits reappeared. If some Cambodian officials sought to prevent such a development, just as many, probably more, were prepared to boost their incomes by providing additional import rights to those rich and discreet enough to pay for the privilege. In the export field, the state's theoretical control over the shipping of rice was systematically circumvented after 1963 as more and more of this most important commodity was sold clandestinely to Vietnamese communist forces, both across the border into Vietnam and in the border regions of Cambodia itself. In this way, customs duties were avoided and revenues lost to the state. Beyond doubt, Sihanouk was aware of the broad outlines of all this, but he cared little for what was happening to the rich, declared himself unable to prevent continuing corruption, and thought that the cost of cultivating the friendship of the Vietnamese communists was worthwhile.

While the very wealthy in Cambodia found it was possible to circumvent the new regulations, the economic reforms had another effect, particularly on the Cambodian population of Phnom Penh. One of the results of the functional corruption so prevalent in Cambodia before 1963 had been the filtering of money from the highest ranks of the administration down to the lower echelons so that rewards were to be had, if in differing degrees, at all levels. Foreign aid and the presence of large numbers of foreign nationals in Phnom Penh had not only brought financial gain to the wealthy and powerful—though certainly they profited the most. Senior officials could afford to invest in real estate which was leased at astronomical rents to Americans working in Phnom Penh. These same men benefited from the bribes that accompanied the conclusion of contracts with foreign firms and the awarding of export and import licences. At the same time, the trickle-down effect of Cambodia's institutionalised corruption meant that people at lower levels of the administration also benefited. Not only did the clerk in the customs service take advantage of his position, in an obvious fashion, but members of all branches of the administration gained from the opportunities for small-scale corruption afforded by foreign aid. Since corruption was pervasive, the elimination of a key financial reservoir from which corrupt benefits could be drawn had pervasive effects.

Even before the full effect of Sihanouk's decisions was felt, many members of Phnom Penh's elite questioned the wisdom of his new economic regime. For some years wealthy Cambodians, including a number of Sihanouk's relatives, had been availing themselves of the services provided by the Bank of Phnom Penh. Managed by a Thai citizen, Songsakd Kitchpanich, who probably had links to the CIA, the bank operated by more flexible standards than such foreign institutions as the Hong Kong and Chartered Banks, providing discretion and a return on investment that appealed to its patrons. Barely a month into Sihanouk's reform program, the nationalisation measures had taken their toll. In December 1963 the bank failed and Songsakd decamped from the capital, taking with him what remained of the funds held on deposit, the substantial sum of $US4 million. The fact that Sihanouk did not hide his amusement at the embarrassment many in the elite suffered as the result of this episode did nothing to endear him to men and women on whose support he had previously been able to rely.

Most important of all, the Cambodian armed forces were hard hit by the prince's 1963 decisions. This cannot be overemphasised. As a largely agricultural country, Cambodia, provided peace reigned, was self-sufficient in many respects. The peasantry in the countryside did not want for subsistence. The fact that many foreign aid projects, such as the factories provided by China, were uneconomic, did not greatly impinge on the bulk of the population. Even the economic discontent of the Phnom Penh elite might have been sustained for a long time. But the effect of Sihanouk's rejecting American aid was critical and, in terms of his own position, ultimately disastrous. Cambodia's armed forces, particularly its army of 30 000 men, had relied heavily upon American assistance at all levels. Not only had the US supplied the funds that paid the salaries of officers and men, and provided equipment and training in Cambodia, but Cambodian officers had been sent to service colleges in the United States. Although the Cambodian officer corps owed much to the French military tradition in which many of its senior officers were trained, until the break in 1963 it was the United States that played the most important role in making the army a functioning body.

So the end of American aid was a savage and unexpected blow to the armed forces. Despite the promised, and the more limited actual aid from the Soviet Union, France and China, the aid cut resulted in a significant depletion of the armed forces' capabilities. The inventory of weapons was steadily reduced through attrition and the lack of spare parts. In addition, the inventory became increasingly inefficient because of the mixture of supplies donated by other countries. Apart from a few prestige units, such as the paratroopers, the army was even short of uniforms. In provincial bases more than half of the military vehicles became unusable through a lack of spare parts. And for those that could be operated, the cost of Sihanouk's economic policies meant that there was frequently no petrol or oil available to fuel and service them.

Some or even all of these problems might have been weathered if the army had been required only to play the civic action role that had been its chief task since 1955. Moreover, the army's involvement in clandestine dealings with the Vietnamese communists enabled many officers to maintain their lifestyles unchanged. But border clashes with Thailand and the growing threat of peripheral involvement in the Vietnam war, together with the incursions and terrorist acts of Son Ngoc Thanh's Khmer Serei forces, forced the army to operate under the most adverse conditions. By 1966 many, including Sihanouk, knew that there was deep dissatisfaction within the army. Yet despite Sihanouk's awareness of the situation, and his later publicly proclaimed judgment that many in the officer corps would look favourably on a rapprochement with the United States, he did little to ameliorate the situation. Not least, he remained convinced that General Lon Nol would never turn against him.

Notes

As with all discussion of the role of the left in Cambodian politics throughout this book, Ben Kiernan's *How Pol Pot* is invaluable for the detail of the left's travails in the early 1960s. Laura Summers, in her introduction to a translation of Khieu Samphan's Paris thesis (Summers ed., *Cambodia's Economy and Political Development*, Ithaca, N.Y., 1979), provides valuable discussion of the policies advocated by the Cambodian left in the early 1960s, along with a detailed account of the 1963 student riots and demonstrations.

Sihanouk's unconvincing implication that he had no knowledge of the campaign unleashed against the left by Lon Nol, or that Lon Nol acted without his knowledge, is contained in *My War With the CIA*, pp. 117–18.

On the designation of Prince Naradipo as Sihanouk's political heir, see *AKP*, 18 November 1963.

Some of Sihanouk's frankest comments on the problem of corruption may be found in *Les Paroles de Samdech Preah Norodom Sihanouk*, April–June 1966, Phnom Penh, n.d., pp. 459–60. Information on Prince Monireth's efforts to take action against corruption was given to me by Prince Entaravong in Phnom Penh in August 1966 (Diary 24 August 1966).

Sihanouk provided his own commentary on his decisions in *Principaux discours, messages, allocutions, déclarations, conferences de presse et interviews de Son Altesse Royale le Prince Norodom Sihanouk, année 1963*, pp. 528–40, which gives the text of a speech delivered at Kep on 6 December 1963.

Donald Lancaster provided me with the account of Sihanouk's doomladen speech in May 1966.

David Chandler's *Tragedy* provides the most detailed published account of Cambodia's break with the United States, pp. 130–39. For discussion of Songsakd's probable links with the CIA, see *Tragedy*, p. 137 and p. 341, n. 37. Further references to information provided by Donald Lancaster in this chapter are drawn from the many conversations I had with him either in Phnom Penh during 1966 or at Cornell University in 1971. Norodum Sihanouk with Bernard Krisher, *Charisma and Leadership*, pp. 173–5 contains Krisher's apologetic account of the 1965 *Newsweek* affair.

On the contribution of United States aid to the Cambodian economy, see R.M. Smith, 'Cambodia', pp. 662 and 668–9.

For discussion of the Cambodian armed forces in this and later chapters, I remain indebted to the late Kim Kosal, a major in 1966, who later rose to general's rank and was killed by the Khmer Rouge shortly after their capture of Phnom Penh in 1975. He was a brave, loyal and incorrupt officer who by 1966 despaired for his country's future.

14

. . . to dangerous stagnation

The economic decline that alienated so many of Sihanouk's important supporters sharpened the divisions in Cambodian political life.
Moreover, the decline took place against a background of intensifying hostilities in Vietnam and the failure of Sihanouk's efforts to
find a way of ensuring international support for Cambodia's neutrality and territorial integrity. This latter aim was, at first glance,
admirable in its conception. Sadly for Sihanouk, his calls for
conferences and declarations were made in circumstances that
offered no real hope of success. In the poisoned atmosphere that
existed between Cambodia and its eastern and western neighbours,
there could be no expectation that South Vietnam and Thailand
would accede to his proposals. And since they would not, their ally
and prime military backer, the United States, was unready to take
a different stand. In any event, there was virtually no sympathy for
Cambodia and its leader in Washington official circles by 1964. To
Sihanouk's chagrin, even Laos displayed an uncooperative attitude,
as Prince Souvanna Phouma showed when he visited Phnom Penh
in March 1964. Despite Sihanouk's entreaties, he made clear that
his country would not give formal recognition to Cambodia's
territorial integrity, a position that reflected the Laotian view that
the Stung Treng region in the extreme northeast of Cambodia
should really be under its sovereignty.

No matter what form Sihanouk's proposals took, he found
himself stymied by one or another country whose recognition of
Cambodian territory or neutrality was fundamental to the success

of his policies. The communist government in Hanoi indicated in March 1964 that it could not unreservedly accept the territorial boundaries that Cambodia claimed, the sticking point in this case being Vietnamese unhappiness with the maritime boundaries in the Gulf of Siam. In 1965 Sihanouk's old friend Zhou Enlai took him aside during the celebrations staged in Indonesia to mark the tenth anniversary of the Bandung Conference and asked him not to proceed with a planned conference intended to achieve international support for Cambodia's neutrality. At a time when China was still wholeheartedly supporting the Vietnamese communists, its leaders feared that a meeting such as Sihanouk was seeking might work to their Vietnamese allies' disadvantage. Faced with this request, Sihanouk, who only the year before had been accorded a place of honour beside Mao Zedong at the celebration of the fifteenth anniversary of the Chinese Revolution in Peking, could only oblige.

The prince did succeed in holding an Indochina People's Conference in March 1965, but since those attending were all communists or supporters of the communist effort in South Vietnam, they had no inclination to back Sihanouk's calls for an end to the fighting in Vietnam. For Sihanouk, this was a period of intense frustration in international affairs. He regarded China as a constant friend, but nonetheless made clear his conviction that it was just as well geographical distance made it possible to sup with Asia's largest power with a long spoon. He saw no signs that the South Vietnamese or Thais would ever be other than irreconcilable antagonists, frequently harking back to his 1963 judgment that the latter acted as they did from their 'simple pleasure of persecuting a nation that the Siamese have habitually humiliated since the fourteenth century'. As for the Hanoi communists, they too were best kept at a distance. Even France did not escape Sihanouk's criticism. Despite a successful state visit to Paris in June 1964, and de Gaulle's support for Sihanouk's proposals for international conferences on the situation in Indochina, by October of the same year the prince was denouncing France as 'the crafty partner of the Anglo-Saxon imperialists' and stating that he had become suspicious of General de Gaulle's calls for Cambodia to show patience in relation to proposals for a conference on Indochina.

Sihanouk's energetic pursuit of some form of international guarantee for Cambodia's continued existence reflected both his long-term gloomy view of the likely course of the war in Vietnam and the immediate fact that the war was spilling over into Cambodia. In mid-1964, while visiting France, he told a *Figaro* reporter that he was now convinced the only way to end the war in Vietnam was for a government to be formed in the south that included representatives of the communist National Liberation Front and the existing Saigon regime. This, he argued, should follow a complete American withdrawal. The new government should then arrange for the reunification of Vietnam to take place over a ten- to fifteen-year period. If this was not done, Sihanouk said, South Vietnam would become communist, and when this happened Cambodia, too, would enter the communist camp.

The prince's long-term fears were joined to more immediate anger at the costs the war was exacting in Cambodian lives. As Cambodian villagers were killed in incidents close to the border Sihanouk was roused to white-hot fury. He launched broadsides of criticism against South Vietnam and the United States and made a series of complaints to the United Nations. His anger was genuine and echoed the feelings of his compatriots. But his deeply felt emotions went hand in hand with the fact that from the beginning of 1964 Sihanouk had secretly approved an arrangement allowing China to ship military aid to the Vietnamese communist forces in South Vietnam through the Cambodian seaport of Sihanoukville. In return, the Cambodian army was rewarded with a 10 per cent 'cut' of material handled in this way. This arrangement and Sihanouk's readiness to tolerate a growing number of Vietnamese communist troops in areas close to Cambodia's eastern boundaries were repeatedly and vigorously denied by the prince and his officials.

In acting as he did, Sihanouk believed he was recognising the inevitability of a communist victory in South Vietnam. He also calculated, correctly, that many in the army's officer corps would profit from his agreement with China and the Vietnamese communists, and that this would temper their concern at the rejection of American aid. What he failed to recognise was that his assistance of the Vietnamese communists would eventually arouse deep concern among conservatives about the extent of the Vietnamese presence. This concern was felt even among officers who had benefited financially from the shipment of arms and the smuggling of rice. This latter clandestine trade by 1966 posed a serious threat to the kingdom's economic stability.

Despite the fact that rice yields in Cambodia were among the lowest in Southeast Asia, rice had always been its major export and its principal earner of foreign currency. In addition the government could count on the revenues produced by a system of internal duties. As the war in Vietnam escalated into a large-scale conflict, the communists' need for rice to feed their troops increased. For rice to reach them from Cambodia all manner of laws had to be breached, but the obstacles were so efficiently overcome that during 1966 between a third and half of the entire Cambodian rice harvest was sold to the communists in South Vietnam. What took place was a massive, even national conspiracy to defeat the regulations laid down by Sihanouk's government. The laws said that farmers should sell their surplus crop to the government, but the government did not pay in cash at the time of the sale and the price it offered was less than that offered by Chinese merchants. Once rice was in the hands of those merchants, they had no compunctions about breaking the laws against illegal exports. In Phnom Penh, Cambodians could quote, each week, the going rate for the bribes that had to be paid to get the trucks carrying the rice through border checkpoints—in May 1966 it was $US1500 a vehicle. Every politically conscious person in Cambodia knew what was going on, as did Sihanouk himself. But he seemed powerless to stop the rot as he continued to fulminate against the divisions between left and right in Cambodian politics.

Little of the atmosphere of tension, disputation and decline that marked political life in Cambodia from 1963 to 1966 was communicated to the outside world. With the exception only of journalists and writers known to be sympathetic to Sihanouk, the world's press was banned from the kingdom. For the most part those on the favoured list were extraordinarily ready to pander to the prince's vanity and to ignore evidence that did not accord with their ideological predilections and his insistence that Cambodia was an 'oasis of peace'. As admirers of the prince, these journalists dismissed allegations of Vietnamese communist troops using Cambodian territory as nothing more than imperialist calumnies.

Yet however ready such complaisant visitors may have been to sing to Sihanouk's tunes, tension was present in Cambodia's domestic politics. It was fuelled by the growing evidence that Sihanouk's sudden economic reforms were not working and by a recognition the prince slowly came to share that he needed to be just as wary of the left as a threat to his vision of Cambodian society as he did of the extreme right. Increasingly, from mid-1964 onwards, his speeches on internal affairs targeted both the left and the right. Armed with information from Lon Nol and Kou Roun, he spoke of his concern that young leftists were preaching subversion in Cambodia's schools and colleges. In his criticism of the left, Sihanouk made clear that he knew Hanoi continued to shelter Cambodian communists. He probably did not know just how many were in Vietnam, and certainly would have been unaware in 1965 that one of them was the future Pol Pot, still at this stage working closely with the Vietnamese.

Yet Sihanouk's denunciations of both left and right did not help to resolve the problems he identified. In the broadest sense, this reflected the malaise that was affecting the country. Sihanouk's international initiatives had failed. His economic decisions had backfired. And those he criticised showed no sign of abandoning their entrenched positions. Nevertheless, as of early 1966, many observers still believed that Sihanouk would be able to regulate and manipulate any domestic challenge that might emerge. By forcing his critics on the left to participate in the process of government in 1962 and 1963 he had done much to prevent them from assuming a significant role in overt politics for the next few years. If they chose to express the most virulent and bellicose criticism of the United States, this did not disturb him, provided they confined themselves to that external target. But if the youthful left was an irritant, in the form of politicians such as Khieu Samphan and Hou Youn, the critical right was also making its voice heard.

Sihanouk in 1966 believed that his long-time close associates such as General Lon Nol, General Nhiek Tioulong, Son Sann, and above all Penn Nouth, would remain loyal to him whatever policies he pursued. That they were conservatives, even extreme conservatives, in matters of domestic policy was well known. Nevertheless, they would follow their prince. Such loyalty, it became more and more obvious, could not be expected from others of a right-wing persuasion. Younger men, such as the French-trained lawyer Douc Rasy, had by the mid-1960s made common cause with older conservative figures such as politician Sim Var and the well-known army officer and journalist Colonel Littaye Soun. Expressed in the newspaper *Phnom Penh Presse*, their criticisms came close to *lèse-majesté*, since it took no special insight to see that virtually any questioning of existing policies was an implicit criticism of Sihanouk.

A further mark of the malaise that affected Cambodia by 1966 was the readiness of a growing number of individuals who were closely identified with Sihanouk's regime to criticise him in private. Such was the case with Charles Meyer, his most important foreign adviser. After years of acting as a spokesman for the prince and his policies, Meyer had become sharply critical of his employer. Not, it is true, to the foreign journalists who were gradually being readmitted to Cambodia in 1966. To men such as Harrison Salisbury of the *New York Times*, I.F. Stone, and Bill Stout of CBS, Meyer still offered a picture of a polymath prince skilfully coping with the complex challenges he faced. He would offer a word of criticism here and there, but the overall impression he gave such foreign visitors was positive. Taking an evening drink with a small group of cronies, Meyer offered a very different picture. Sihanouk, he suggested, was displaying the hereditary mental instability of the Norodom branch of the Cambodian royal family. He was reverting to his earlier tendency to place self-indulgence above the serious interests of the state. This *roitelet*, a sneering French word denoting a 'little king', was no longer 'serious'; he was 'going back to the time when he was the little king with his horses and stage shows'. Only now he spent all his time with his latest passion, film-making, while expecting others, Meyer included, to write the *Réalités* editorials that Sihanouk then signed.

The editor of *Réalités*, Jean Barré, made similar complaints. He bemoaned the fact that he was expected to justify Sihanouk's frequently contradictory pronouncements. How, he asked me at a reception, could he write, as Sihanouk commanded, that Cambodia gave only moral support to the Vietnamese communists when all the world knew that huge quantities of rice were smuggled to them from Cambodia. The Australian left-wing propagandist Wilfred Burchett, who by 1966 was resident in Phnom Penh, expressed similar concerns about the prince's self-indulgence. Meyer, Barré, Burchett, and others who had linked their careers to a particular image of Sihanouk, now had to wonder whether he was going to continue managing the Cambodian state, and whether their own positions in Cambodia were secure. But interesting though these foreign critics were as a reflection of changing times within Cambodia, much more striking was the extent to which Cambodians themselves had become willing to express their concern at the drift now afflicting Cambodian politics.

The range of Cambodians in Phnom Penh who were ready by 1966 to criticise Sihanouk to a foreigner, provided a striking illustration of how far the prince's standing had slipped since his policy shifts of 1963. That Douc Rasy and Littaye Soun were even more critical of Sihanouk's policies in private than they were in the columns of *Phnom Penh Presse* was not surprising. They had deep reservations about Sihanouk's foreign policies, which, as they saw it, were lopsided in their readiness to appease the Vietnamese communists while giving deliberate offence to the United States. They deplored the cult of personality that surrounded Sihanouk and talked darkly of the methods used by Kou Roun's security services. These men were not the only Cambodians who spoke with a mixture of repugnance, fear and gallows humour about the way suspected opponents of Sihanouk's state were treated in the interrogation cells of the grim concrete building not far from the city's central market.

But if criticism was to be expected from such men, given their public, if more muted, critical stance and their known conservative politics, it was much more surprising (despite Sihanouk's continuing anti-US rhetoric) to hear it coming from those who were already identified with leftist positions, or who later proved to have secretly supported the leftist cause. An example from the first category was Poc Deuskoma, a member of one of the old official families of Cambodia. The Pocs had originally been territorial magnates in Battambang and as such had, in the nineteenth century, been ready to work with the Bangkok court when Thailand ruled over that region. Because of this and the later association of a Poc family member with the Khmer Issarak movement, Sihanouk never fully trusted any of family, even though their obvious abilities ensured that they occupied important official positions. Poc Deuskoma's disillusionment with Sihanouk's rule had come when his uncle had been recalled in disgrace from his posting as Cambodian ambassador to Australia—his fault had been failing to respond vigorously enough to a press report critical of Sihanouk. An internal spy in the embassy had reported this 'dereliction' of duty, so bringing about his dismissal. By the mid-1960s, Poc Deuskoma had adopted views that sat uneasily with his privileged background, his Western education and his marriage to a French *bourgeoise.* He approved of Sihanouk's criticism of the United States and its Southeast Asian allies, but he questioned how deeply felt the prince's views were. More important, and despite his own employment in a financial institution, he had become highly critical of the continuing 'capitalist' character of the Cambodian state. The economic changes introduced in 1963, he argued, had done little if anything to alter the basic relationships between rich and poor in Cambodia. Sihanouk knew this and was unprepared to do anything to change the situation. To anyone who heard these frank comments, Poc Deuskoma's subsequent decision to join the communist rebels in the *maquis* in 1968 was far from a surprise.

Defenders of Sihanouk in private conversation were few; critics were numerous. Prince Sisowath Dussady was thought of as a quintessential man-about-town, indeed a playboy. A minor member of the royal family, he had been briefly married to Nhiek Tioulong's daughter before her flagrant infidelities brought the marriage to an end. Renowned as a dancer, he had been recruited by Sihanouk as an extra for the prince's film *Apsara*. By day, he worked in the Magasin d'Etat, the state enterprise responsible for distributing goods to retailers throughout the country. In private, he too had only harsh words for Sihanouk—for his failure to stop the exploitation of his economic reforms by corrupt officials and businessmen, and for his vicious personal attacks on any who displeased him, whether with just cause or not. Dussady joined the Khmer Rouge forces to fight against the Lon Nol regime after Sihanouk was overthrown in 1970.

The list of critics of the regime in Phnom Penh and in the provinces went on and on. And by May 1966 there was a common thread to the views of almost all of them. Now, in addition to concern about the economic slowdown and the direction in which Sihanouk's foreign policy was leading the country, there was apprehension about the prince's increasing preoccupation with film-making. This was an enterprise on which he embarked despite his public admissions that the country's economy was 'blown' and that he was 'beaten' by the problem of corruption.

Sihanouk's passionate interest in the cinema dates back to his early youth. In the years before independence he had produced and acted in two comic films, which had been shown only to a restricted audience within the royal palace. In 1965, he embarked on a much more ambitious project, the production of feature films for public screening both at home and abroad. The genesis of this undertaking seems to have been mixed. Sihanouk apparently received encouragement from the French film-maker Marcel Camus, who had made a film in Cambodia in 1962. But more immediately, he was reacting to the relative commercial success of the film of *Lord Jim*, starring Peter O'Toole, which was made in Cambodia in 1964. Sihanouk was both jealous of the film's success and angered by comments O'Toole had made in a film magazine, depicting Cambodia as a primitive state. Showing his renowned sensitivity, the prince denounced O'Toole's remarks as evidence of the machinations of Western governments to denigrate him and his country. In a long editorial comment on the supposed libel, the prince characterised the remarks as a riposte by the American and British governments to the attacks on their embassies in Phnom Penh in March 1964. By making his own films, Sihanouk planned to give the lie to the image of Cambodia presented by O'Toole.

Sihanouk devoted more and more time to film-making after 1965, to the point where many in Phnom Penh saw his preoccupation as obsessional. By the end of 1965 he was 44 years old. He had been at the head of his nation for nearly a quarter of a century and had been closely and energetically involved in its politics for fifteen years. Because of his style of government, he was at the centre of all that happened, whether for good or bad. Although he took sporadic vacations, he seldom really rested, and since 1963 the demands of government, both domestic and external, had increased. There is every reason to conclude that, by late 1965, Sihanouk was physically and emotionally exhausted. It was in these circumstances that he took up the last of his many fads, which became an escape from the political grind in which he felt himself trapped. Unlike such earlier enthusiasms as horse-riding, *le sport*, and magazine publishing, his film-making was to have very real political consequences.

Sihanouk's first feature length film, *Apsara*, set the tone for those that followed. Written, directed and produced by Sihanouk, it was the first of nine films that he made between 1966 and 1969. The cast of *Apsara* was drawn from the ranks of Sihanouk's relatives and close associates, a few professional actors and comedians, and well-known figures in Phnom Penh 'high society'. In later films both he and Monique played roles. In this first venture, General Nhiek Tioulong, who had been many times minister for Foreign Affairs and for Planning, was one of the male leads, while General Ngo Hou, the head of Cambodia's air force, had a walk-on part. Sihanouk does not seem to have considered whether their energies would have been better applied to their normal official duties any more than he hesitated to mobilise what there was of Cambodia's air force, and a large part of the Cambodian army's fleet of helicopters, for use in the film. His demand for the army's helicopters caused real resentment. No-one dared tell him that there were wounded Cambodian troops waiting to be medevacked from the northern Dangrek mountains after a border clash with Thai troops. The wounded men had to wait an additional day to be moved. For Sihanouk—and this raises serious questions about his judgment—his films were not just a diversion. They were an integral part of Cambodia's national business. As such, they had precedence over other demands on the resources of his state.

As for *Apsara* itself, it was, like all his subsequent films, amateurish in the extreme. Sihanouk has reacted with some hauteur to Charles Meyer's dismissal of his films as the artistic equivalent of an amateur painter's 'daubs'. Perhaps this is true, he has said, but for a chief of state it is 'distracting' and 'restful' to produce 'daubs'. Meyer was right and Sihanouk wrong, and the prince did not indulge his passion simply as a distraction. Indeed, his conduct years after his 1970 overthrow has demonstrated that he still regards his films as a genuine artistic achievement. When *Apsara* was first shown publicly in Phnom Penh in May 1966, the audience was told that the chief of state had produced this film to show a 'fairyland' (*féerie*) in the service of national solidarity.

> A fairyland yes, yet more, for you have these scenes before your eyes every day. But to place them in relief it is necessary, quite deliberately, to eliminate precisely that everyday quality and to choose scenes with the eye of the poet and the sensitivity of the artist.
> Why has this full-length film been made?
> A saying has it that Frenchmen 'know nothing of geography', but for a long time we have observed that this lack of knowledge is not simply the preserve of the French. Let us deal solely with the world of the cinema. For a film producer (even one of real talent) what is Cambodia? The ruins of Angkor . . . and that is all. So, a run-of-the-mill script is hurriedly written, one or two flashy stars are hired, one adds a mixture of eroticism and violence, advance promotion dwells on the same old hackneyed themes (stew made from snake's meat . . . scorpions lurking in boots . . . the poverty of the people . . . a meagre existence that must be defended against tigers, etc. . . . . etc.) and the whole lot is put in motion. That is the image of Cambodia current in the four corners of the globe.
> Is it any longer possible to ignore such ineptitudes, such errors, whether voluntary or otherwise? Certainly not, and the Chief of State, more than any other, has felt this deeply. And so, once again, faithful to his reputation as the 'Pioneer Prince', he has taken up the challenge. So much the better, for who is more qualified than he to provide such a real picture of present-day Cambodia?

These were the words with which the master of ceremonies, a French 'expert', introduced the prince's film to the audience in the Ciné Lux. After an hour-long Chinese documentary on Sihanouk's visit to Peking in 1965, the unedited version of *Apsara* was shown. Sihanouk explained afterwards that there were to be a number of versions of the film. One, destined for the screens of the socialist world, would include a long speech by General Tioulong, playing the part of General Rithi, denouncing the 'imperialists'. The version for the non-socialist world would have this speech excised. What was being shown was the basic story, which lasted two and half hours. That length, Sihanouk assured readers of his own commentary on the film, was not a problem, since no-one worried about how long a good film lasted.

In Sihanouk's script, General Rithi, a rich bachelor, has decided to give up his long-term relationship with the voluptuous widow Rattana (played by the amply endowed Royal Air Cambodge flight attendant Saksi Sbong) in order to seek the hand of the beautiful Kantha Devi (played by the truly beautiful Bopha Devi, Sihanouk's daughter and star of the royal ballet). But the ballet dancer's heart had already gone to another, a young pilot in Cambodia's air force (played by one Prince Sisowath Chivanmonriak). The marriage between Rithi and Kantha Devi takes place but is never consummated. The pilot is wounded while gallantly defending his country against an attack by the Saigon regime and its American allies. General Rithi realises that he must not stand in the way of true love. The pilot and Kantha Devi are united. Rithi promises to marry his mistress. And the pilot's adolescent brother (played by Sihanouk's son, Norodom Narindrapong) provides the closing action of the film. Seeking to learn about life and love, he throws himself into the arms of a nurse in the hospital where his older brother was treated. In another of the many ironies associated with Sihanouk's Cambodia, Narindrapong was later to become a passionate supporter of the Pol Pot regime.

Despite the claims of Sihanouk and his spokesman, *Apsara* had nothing to do with the reality of Cambodia in 1966. In a country where the sun shone constantly, 'high personalities' drove here and there in one luxurious vehicle after another. The instructions from the script offer these details: Scene 1 (filmed at Chamcar Mon, Sihanouk's personal palace), 'A Facel Vega driven by a pretty woman.' Scene 6 (again at Chamcar Mon), 'General Rithi and Rattana get out of his Jaguar.' Scene 10 (On the Kirirom Plateau), 'Along a fine forest road drives a black Cadillac convertible.' Scene 15, 'An overview: arrival of the guests in glistening cars.' Scene 22, 'The [Mercedes] 230 SL stops at the foot of the monumental staircase leading towards the Mohanikay pagoda.'

From start to finish, *Apsara* was indeed a 'fairyland', depicting Sihanouk's fantastical vision of a country Cambodia never had been nor ever could be. Dirt, poverty and disease were absent. The streets of the capital were free of the ubiquitous pedicabs that were so much part of its normal life. 'Life' as portrayed in Sihanouk's film revolved around receptions, parades, languorous moments in palaces and villas decorated in the worst of taste, and knockabout humour provided by Cambodia's best-known music hall comic, who had the distinctly un-Cambodian stage name of Mandoline. Only once, briefly, did the film capture anything that seemed in the least authentic—unless it was the sight of some of the kingdom's less admirable royal and wealthy citizens at play. This was when the royal ballet, with Bopha Devi as its star, danced to the music of the traditional Cambodian orchestra. Yet even here Sihanouk chose to present the famous dancing troupe on the stage of the recently constructed modern conference hall on the banks of the Tonle Sap River rather than in the traditional dance pavilion within the royal palace. Predictably, *Apsara* received the highest praise from the local press. Writing in the official news bulletin *AKP*, one of Sihanouk's French *plumatifs*, Pierre Fuchs, claimed that the sequences in the film that showed the Cambodian army recalled the unforgettable bas-reliefs on the Bayon temple at Angkor.

The screening of the 'rough' version of *Apsara* in May had been for a charity gala, and final points of continuity had not been settled. A print of the film was sent to Paris for reprocessing to improve colour quality. Then, after final editing by Sihanouk, it was announced that the 'World Premiere' of the film would take place on 20 August. This was just ten days before the planned arrival of President de Gaulle, an event already being hailed as of historic importance. But before then, Phnom Penh society and invited foreign guests were to be able to see not only the completed version of *Apsara* but also rushes from *The Enchanted Forest*. The invited foreign guests failed to materialise, but the Chinese government did send its regrets, saying that no delegation would be forthcoming 'because of the Cultural Revolution'.

There was a bizarre element to the whole affair of the world premiere. Throughout the preceding three weeks Sihanouk had displayed almost continuous rage following attacks on a village near the Cambodian–South Vietnamese border in which several people had been killed. A projected visit by Averell Harriman, intended to explore the possibility of improving relations between Cambodia and the United States, had been thrown into doubt by these events. And at the same time as negotiations were going on between Cambodia and representatives of both the communist government in Hanoi and the South Vietnamese National Liberation Front were trying to negotiate a border agreement, Sihanouk was showing public concern about the appeal of left-wing ideas to his country's students. All of these issues, and the continuing decline of the economy, provided a curious background for the prince's devotion to his 'art'. On the basis of the May screening, the Phnom Penh elite were already discussing *Apsara* in terms of the ridicule it would bring on the country. Among the students whose flirtations with left-wing views worried Sihanouk, some brave voices asked out loud questions that others were raising in private: How, in the light of Cambodia's many serious problems, could the chief of state expend so much of his energies making films? As for others engaged in the enterprise, people asked, was General Tioulong edging towards senility when he agreed to play the ageing lover and utter lines of such profound banality? It was a legitimate question in view of the script, which interspersed the Khmer dialogue with passages in French for the benefit of foreign viewers. General Rithi and Rattana made their film exit with the following lines:

> *Rithi:*. . . It is only in misfortune that one knows one's true friends. In you I have a true friend.
> *Rattana:*(ironically) Friend?
> *Rithi:* No! You will be my wife.
> *Rattana:* (overcome with joy) Oh my love. (Rithi takes her firmly in his arms. They fall on the bed.)
> *Rithi:*(gives her a passionate kiss while whispering) My dear one.

Dwelling on Sihanouk's films would not be justified if *Apsara* had only been a passing phase, merely the diversion he later claimed all his films to have been. But it was not. Certainly, Sihanouk continued to involve himself in a myriad issues of state. But such issues necessarily received less of his attention when the making of films absorbed so much of his time. Even with his phenomenal energy, Sihanouk could not make nine films in three years without curtailing the time he devoted to Cambodia's affairs. His approach to the conduct of public business had always been haphazard, but after 1966 it was even more so, as he wrote, directed and produced films, and in a number of cases starred in them. As Charles Meyer has suggested, it may be psychologically significant that Sihanouk chose successively to play the following roles in his films: a spirit of the forest, a victorious general, an intelligence agent, a wounded soldier and a Japanese colonel. At the very least, a picture emerges of a man for whom fantasy was increasingly more attractive than the real world.

Sihanouk was aided in living his fantasies by the sycophantic praise that many, both Cambodians and foreigners, were ready to heap upon him. His courtiers, who surely were aware of the dismay many of their compatriots felt at the amount of time Sihanouk was giving over to film-making, continued to offer extravagant praise. But so did foreigners such as the retired British diplomat and proconsul Malcolm MacDonald. After a private screening of Sihanouk's film *Joie de Vivre*, he likened it to the Sistine Chapel.

The pretence that Sihanouk was a world-class film-maker became institutionalised in the Phnom Penh International Film Festival. It was held only twice, in 1968 and 1969. Cast as a competition, it was in fact a charade: Sihanouk on both occasions won the grand prize, a solid gold statue of an *apsara*, a female heavenly being. Other exhibitors were rewarded with smaller statues finished in gold plate. At the 1969 festival, whose audience had nothing but uncritical praise for the prince, Sihanouk's entry—in a special class with himself as the only competitor—was *Crépuscule* (Twilight), an ironically symbolic title in view of the short time he had left to rule. And he was presented with his prize by that staunch supporter of leftist causes Han Suyin. Evidently her acerbic judgment, forcefully expressed on so many political and aesthetic issues, did not extend to the cinematographic offerings of the hospitable prince.

Equally ironic but more politically significant was the fact that Sihanouk's films did not worry only the elite residents of Phnom Penh. In the countryside, where the prince had commanded that the films be screened for the benefit of his 'children', peasant farmers and their families watched with amazement the scenes of high living depicted in them. For those who were succeeding in convincing the peasantry of the evils of the regime and its leaders, Sihanouk's films became a potent propaganda weapon.

Notes

Much of the material in this chapter reflects personal observation of events in Cambodia between April and September 1966, during which time I kept a detailed journal. That journal later formed the basis for my book *Before Kampuchea*, and was important, also, to my *Politics and Power in Cambodia*. Some of the issues discussed here received more extended treatment in these earlier works.

The flavour of Sihanouk's endeavours to arrange guarantees of Cambodia's neutrality and territorial integrity is best gained from the editorials and records of press conferences to be found in *Réalités* and the official news bulletin *AKP* during 1964 and 1965. Sihanouk's comment about Thailand's long historical antagonism towards Cambodia comes from *Cambodia News* (Washington), VI, 2, 1963. His denunciation of the French is recorded in *The New York Times*, 31 October 1964, reporting Sihanouk's interview with *Le Figaro*. Michael Leifer's *Cambodia: The Search for Security*, is the best accessible survey of Sihanouk's foreign policy manoeuvring during this period.

On Sihanouk's secret agreement for the shipment of Chinese matériel to the Vietnamese communists, see Chandler, *Tragedy*, p. 140. See also my discussion of this question in *Politics and Power in Cambodia*, Chapter 7. The same chapter discusses the clandestine rice trade, as does Chapter 12 in *Before Kampuchea*. Sihanouk's frank admission that he permitted Vietnamese troops to use Cambodian territory may be found in *L'Indochine vue de Pékin*, pp. 94–5.

Sihanouk's criticism of both left and right in Cambodian politics was a growing tendency from 1964 onwards and is abundantly reflected in the published versions of his speeches in *Réalités, AKP*, and the Cambodian Ministry of Information collection of his speeches.

Discussion of the views expressed by Charles Meyer, Jean Barré and Wilfred Burchett is drawn from my 1966 journal. Meyer's remarks are quoted in the entry for 23 May 1966. The references to Poc Deuskoma's and Prince Dussady's views also come from journal entries. On Poc, see also Chapter 8 of *Before Kampuchea* and on Dussady, pp. 123–4 of the same book. Both Poc and Dussady were last reported alive in the period 1975–76. See Vickery, *Cambodia: 1975–1982*, pp. 145–6 and 165.

Sihanouk's admission that the economy was 'blown' comes from a speech published in *AKP*, 3 May 1966. The reference to being 'beaten' by corruption is from a speech published in *AKP* on 30 May 1966.

The introduction to *Apsara* is translated from the text delivered at the showing of the film on 14 May. The dialogue is drawn from a brochure containing the script distributed at the same showing. Also on *Apsara* and later films, see Chapter 5 of *Before Kampuchea*.

The account of Malcolm MacDonald's comment was given to me by a private source in Phnom Penh (Diary 11 February 1970). Malcolm MacDonald had some years earlier published a book unrestrained in its praise of Sihanouk. See his *Angkor and the Khmers*, London, 1957.

For a general comment by Sihanouk on his films, see *Souvenirs*, Chapter XXXIX, pp. 335–43.

15

Farce turns to tragedy

From the second half of 1966, the all-too-often farcical aspects of Sihanouk's Cambodia began steadily to give way to a history marked by tragedy. In the classic fashion of tragedy, what occurred was a result both of the prince's own actions and miscalculations and of events over which he had no control. Arguments as to whether, by the end of 1966, it was possible to foresee the disastrous course Cambodian history was to follow, are ultimately unproductive. Some, including myself, expressed their belief that Sihanouk would not survive the decade as Cambodia's leader in private journals and conversations. Few, if any, did so publicly. None foresaw that Sihanouk's departure from power would plunge Cambodia into a terrible war and end in the terror and brutality of Pol Pot's tyranny.

Sihanouk has never revealed whether he realised how reserved was the reception his compatriots gave to the world premiere of *Apsara*. There had been applause, but only sufficient to satisfy the minimum demands of politeness, certainly not any demonstration of enthusiasm. This was an early sign that Sihanouk risked losing the vital support of the Phnom Penh elite. It may have escaped him, for throughout his passionate involvement in film-making he gave himself over to the fantasy that he was, indeed, a director and producer of world standing. He did, it is true, have a pang of guilt about the amount of time his film-making was absorbing, and wondered if the death by drowning of a young relative might have reflected supernatural displeasure with his activities. But this concern soon passed. Moreover, in late August 1966 he was looking forward to the visit of the President of France. This visit by Charles de Gaulle, the prince's idol for more than twenty years, had become invested with almost mystical qualities. De Gaulle, Sihanouk had come to assume, would provide answers for the problems afflicting Cambodia. He would, Sihanouk fervently hoped, be able both to give the assurance of international support that a vulnerable Cambodia needed and play a role in bringing the war in Vietnam to a halt. Whereas Sihanouk had previously seen China as Cambodia's bulwark against its enemies, the disruption of the Cultural Revolution had cast into doubt the extent to which he could now rely on Peking. The prince also thought that de Gaulle might offer Cambodia increased economic aid to take up the now abundantly apparent slack following the break with the United States. With all these hopes in mind, he set about preparing a spectacular welcome for the French president.

For weeks before de Gaulle's visit, virtually all government business was subordinated to this task. Phnom Penh was scoured clean. Along the routes the president would travel, the trunks of the trees were whitewashed and private houses were ordered repainted. Secondary schooling ground to a halt as students were rehearsed for a giant ceremonial welcome in the capital's 'Olympic' stadium. In a striking illustration of the lack of confidence that still pervaded Sihanouk's relationship with Cambodia's former colonial ruler, the ode to be declaimed at this mass welcome was composed by a French schoolteacher who worked in Phnom Penh, not by any of the perfectly competent Cambodians who could have handled the job.

Briefly, Phnom Penh took on the raffishly vivacious face so characteristic of the years around 1960. There was an influx of foreign journalists, most of them French and all with money to spend in the bars and restaurants that had fallen on hard times in the previous three years. The bar girls, whose standard of living had plummeted after 1964, suddenly appeared in their bikinis with their foreign catches beside the swimming pool at the Hôtel le Royal. In an atmosphere of widespread euphoria, de Gaulle was welcomed as the 'great son of France' of his countryman's ode and cheered as he rode along the boulevards in an open limousine with the prince and as he made the obligatory visit to the ruins of Angkor. Sadly for Sihanouk, his idol delivered very little. The conversations that the French foreign minister accompanying de Gaulle, Couve de Muirville, had with a representative of the North Vietnamese government achieved nothing so far as the Vietnam

War was concerned. And what de Gaulle was ready to offer Sihanouk by way of aid was much more meagre than the prince would have wished. Beyond the rolling cadences of de Gaulle's speeches, critical of the United States but full of praise for Sihanouk, was the offer of a phosphate factory, finance for a second *lycée*, and new uniforms for the Cambodian army. While the last was undoubtedly welcome to forces which, by this stage, were desperately short of equipment of all kinds, the truth of the matter was that de Gaulle's visit did little more than raise Sihanouk's spirits for a brief period, after which temporary euphoria was rapidly replaced by deepening despondency.

From the middle of the year, Sihanouk's security services had been telling him about the growing number of pamphlets circulating in the kingdom which denounced his regime and called for the overthrow of the 'capitalist' Cambodian state. These reports enraged Sihanouk, just as the critical pamphlets found during Operation Sammaki had done thirteen years before. As his resentment of the left mounted, he made a decision of considerable moment. In August, with elections for the National Assembly due the following month, he announced that in a break with past practice he would not nominate the Sangkum candidates. As Cambodia's shrewdest politician, particularly in relation to short-term tactics, Sihanouk would have been fully aware of the implications of his decision. By opting out of the selection process, he was aiding the most conservative elements in Cambodian politics. If there was more than one candidate for the Sangkum mantle in each constituency, it was fairly certain that the man able to disburse the greatest rewards during the campaign and with the most money to spend on political propaganda would win. And this, for the most part, was what happened.

In the September 1966 election, money was the key consideration. Votes were bought and sold. Some of those ambitious to be deputies in the assembly even paid rival candidates to withdraw from the contest. There were exceptions to the general pattern, both on the right and the still-legal left of the Sangkum. Douc Rasy, the right-wing lawyer, gained his seat despite the fact that one of his competitors was given tape recordings in which Sihanouk bitterly denounced Rasy. Since the tapes came from the Ministry of Information, it was widely assumed that Sihanouk had authorised their broadcast throughout the electorate in an effort to discredit Rasy. At the other end of the political spectrum, Khieu Samphan won his seat, as did his fellow leftists Hou Youn and Hu Nim. Samphan was elected despite harassment by Kou Roun's security

services which included the jailing of some of his campaign workers. But his victory, and those of a limited number of his leftist
colleagues, were essentially exceptions to the broad triumph of the
right. The National Assembly elected in September 1966 was more
conservative in outlook than any that had preceded it and most of
its members did not owe political debts to Sihanouk. If the right
was not yet clearly in the saddle, it stood firmly on the mounting
block.

After the elections, Sihanouk briefly withdrew from politics for
medical treatment and rest in hospital. By the second half of
October he was ready to take stock of what he later called the 'most
reactionary and corrupt assembly' he had ever faced. This was a
retrospective judgment, made after he was deposed in 1970. Yet
the assembly's highly conservative cast was a direct result of
Sihanouk's decision to stand aloof from the selection of Sangkum
candidates. Moreover, once the election was over, it was with
Sihanouk's approval that Lon Nol stood for and was elected to the
prime ministership. Once he had gained that post, Lon Nol
recruited to his cabinet some of the best-known older conservatives,
such as Kou Roun, and younger men of a right-wing persuasion,
such as Douc Rasy.

Only after Lon Nol became prime minister did Sihanouk realise
that the balance of Cambodian parliamentary politics had changed
in such a way that his capacity to influence future events could
come under threat. His solution, conceived as ever in immediate
tactical terms, was to introduce an institutionalised counterweight
in the form of a 'counter government'. The purpose of this new
body, whose members were selected by the prince, was to give those
with left-wing views the opportunity, through a regular news bulletin, to put forward alternative policies to those of the government
in power. No matter how Sihanouk chose to justify this innovation,
its effect in the world of Cambodia's factious politics can only be
described as bizarre. Having supported Lon Nol's bid for the prime
ministership, he was deliberately providing a platform for those
who sought to undermine the recently installed government. The
result was a resurgence of the factional politics which had caused
him so much despair before.

In October and through November he gave full vent to his
unhappiness with the course of Cambodian politics. In speech after
speech he told his compatriots of his anguish over the persistent

divisions within the kingdom. Claiming, probably inaccurately, to have instituted the counter government at the behest of others, he seemed more capable of describing the sterile arguments and counter-arguments of the rival political camps than of finding a formula for ending them. He reacted sharply to foreign press suggestions that Cambodia was close to a political crisis, insisting that what was taking place should properly be seen as the natural ebb and flow of political life. But his own repeated expressions of concern belied such an interpretation, and he found himself under sustained pressure of a kind he had not experienced for many years.

In the face of left-wing criticism, Lon Nol offered his resignation at the end of October. Sihanouk refused to accept it. Politicians on the left pressed Sihanouk to form a new ministry, believing that if he did so they would have more chance of advancing their views. This, too, the prince refused, just as he refused to accept right-wing calls for the suppression of the young leftists. In yet another of his marathon speeches at the beginning of November, Sihanouk declared that not even forecasts of a right-wing coup backed by the army disturbed him. Amid all the public rehearsal of his concerns, one point stands out. As he discussed the prevalence of disunity and the sterility of the clash between right and left, Sihanouk never once entertained the idea that he might not remain the indispensable centrepiece of Cambodian politics. In this confident frame of mind, he left Phnom Penh for France in early January 1967. His mood was reminiscent of late 1953. Then, he had retreated to Siemreap so the politicians in Phnom Penh could come to their senses. Now, in 1967, he believed his departure for France would have a salutary effect on both political camps. Within a month of Sihanouk's departure, agrarian unrest broke out in scattered parts of the country and shattered any remaining illusions about Cambodia's internal unity. Right and left were now engaged in limited but serious armed conflict that went far beyond political skirmishing in its threat of future disaster.

Contrary to Sihanouk's expectations, Cambodian politicians did not abandon their increasingly entrenched positions in the wake of his departure. This is the more readily understandable now that hindsight has revealed just how deep was the malaise affecting all sections of Cambodian society. By the beginning of 1967, a probable majority of the elite was ready at least to question the assumption that there could be no alternative to Sihanouk and his policies. The still-small clandestine left could see no place for Sihanouk in the future they planned, while those leftists, such as Khieu Samphan, who continued to operate in the world of legal politics, feared for their lives and had already begun to contemplate going into the *maquis*. Research since Sihanouk's overthrow has also made clear the extent to which the educated youth in Phnom Penh had become politicised by 1967. For some this transformation involved approval of the increasingly trenchant voices being raised on the right of politics. For others, disillusionment with the failures of Sihanouk's policies, not least his inability to offer employment to many high school and university graduates, led them to adopt left-wing views and join the slowly growing ranks of dissidents in the countryside.

While Sihanouk was still in France, Lon Nol and his colleagues served notice that they were prepared to govern independently of the prince. In an effort to overcome the loss to government revenues caused by the contraband sale of rice to the Vietnamese communists, Lon Nol's government despatched officials into the countryside to urge peasants to sell their rice only to authorised agents. To back up the officials, the prime minister and his colleagues took two steps. First, they deployed the army to enforce compliance with their request. Second, Lon Nol and his fellow cabinet members embarked on a fact-finding tour of the countryside, assessing the peasants' discontent and exhorting them to follow the government's directives on rice sales.

Lingering in France, Sihanouk began to receive disturbing reports from the kingdom. Lon Nol's progress through the countryside had drawn large crowds, a privilege the prince believed was his alone. But there was worse to come after Sihanouk returned to Cambodia on 9 March. Responding to heavy-handed actions by the military to enforce the collection of rice in the northwestern province of Battambang, angry peasants attacked the soldiers on 2 April 1967, killing two of them. The insurrection that has come to be known as the Samlaut Rebellion had begun, and with it Cambodia's descent into full-scale civil war.

The reasons why unrest flared into open conflict in the Samlaut region are complex. The rebellion was not simply a result of plotting by the radical left, though small pro-communist groups had been established in this part of Battambang province for many years. Certainly, communist agitators played a part in fanning peasant discontent, but they were aided by widespread resentment at falling crop prices, indebtedness and the high-handed behaviour of the military. A decade later the Cambodian Communist Party was to praise the revolutionary aspirations of those who fought against Lon Nol's soldiers at Samlaut, but the revolt itself was more an outbreak of largely spontaneous resistance to government actions than the first orchestrated challenge from the radicals.

On his return to Phnom Penh, the prince faced a political scene that was evolving outside his control. General Lon Nol had recently been injured in an accident, and he was still convalescing when a noisy demonstration led by high school and university students called for the prime minister's removal and for the army's withdrawal from Battambang. Sihanouk now had to contend with a dilemma that arose in large part from his own imperfect understanding of events in Cambodia and from his instinctive inclination in a crisis to side with those who refrained from criticising him personally. While the right of Cambodian politics was now calling for policies that explicitly rejected those the prince had previously advocated, they continued to profess loyalty to his person. Those leftists who remained active in legal politics found it increasingly difficult to make this distinction. The extra-legal left in the countryside no longer tried. Faced with spreading peasant unrest, Sihanouk was ready to sanction its brutal repression. He also increased his verbal attacks on the prominent left-wing deputies Khieu Samphan and Hou Youn, and began to suggest that the Cambodian army should perhaps play a similar role to that of the Indonesian armed forces, which were engaged in a brutal purge of leftists in the wake of the September 1965 Gestapu affair. By the end of April 1967 Samphan and Youn, fearing with good reason for their lives, had slipped away into the *maquis*.

The outbreak and suppression of rural unrest in the Samlaut region of Battambang province signalled a new development in modern Cambodian politics. For the first time rural insurgency on a substantial scale had taken place against an independent Cambodian government rather than a colonial regime. Moreover, the measures taken to suppress the insurgency reflected the state's readiness to to achieve its goals through violence on a scale unprecedented in independent Cambodia. Lon Nol and Kou Roun had mounted witchhunts before, but their targets had been individuals or small groups. Now, repression was being directed against whole communities. The brutality inflicted on the peasants linked to the Samlaut Rebellion was an ominous foretaste of the ferocity that was to be such a feature of the later full-scale civil war.

In the wake of the first outbreak of anti-government violence in Samlaut, first Lon Nol and then Sihanouk urged the army to exact retribution. For Lon Nol, the peasants' actions were an intolerable challenge to the state's authority. For Sihanouk, they were a personal outrage. He vowed that his forces would be merciless, and they were. Bounties were paid for the severed heads of villagers accused of participating in the insurrection and trucks brought these grisly trophies to Phnom Penh as evidence of the army's success. Villages were put to the torch. By the end of May the Samlaut affair was said to be at an end. How many lives were lost in crushing it is not known for certain. Sihanouk himself has offered wildly differing estimates of the number of peasants killed, suggesting 10 000 when he spoke to Jean Lacouture in 1972 but amending this to fewer than 100 in later memoirs. With no reliable records kept of the army's killings, and with enthusiastic civilian volunteers assisting them in the violence, a realistic estimate of the death toll would have to put the cost in lives in the hundreds, at a minimum.

The Samlaut Rebellion and the rising tide of armed resistance to Phnom Penh's authority through 1967 received very little attention outside Cambodia. To the extent that international interest was focused on events in Asia, two much bigger stories dominated the media: Vietnam and the Great Proletarian Cultural Revolution in China. Yet while events in Cambodia received little mention, Sihanouk was striving to resolve dilemmas that were vitally linked to what was taking place in Vietnam and China. For Sihanouk the events in Samlaut underlined the extent to which the foundations of both his domestic and foreign policy assumptions had come under threat. Always fearful of a future communist-controlled Vietnam, the prince had hoped that his policy of clandestine appeasement, which allowed materiel to be transported through Cambodia to the Vietnamese communist forces, would ensure that his regime survived whatever happened across his eastern boundary. At the same time, he believed his cooperation with the Vietnamese communists would inhibit their assisting the small domestic communist movement within Cambodia. As vital reinsurance Sihanouk looked to China, and to his friend Zhou Enlai, for further protection, assuming that, should the worst come to pass and a communist

Vietnam became a threat, Peking would be able to restrain his eastern neighbour.

The events in the Samlaut region and the growth of resistance elsewhere threw these assumptions into doubt. In speech after anguished speech, Sihanouk declared that what had happened in Samlaut was the work of local 'reds' acting under the orders of a 'great chief' who could be Cambodian or a foreigner. In hinting at foreign direction of the Samlaut Rebellion—a charge that he later firmly attached to China—Sihanouk was repeating a view he had long held. He accepted that there were home-grown leftists in Cambodia, but he remained convinced that they were directed from outside the country. Previously he had believed that Vietnam posed the greatest threat; now China's role was an increasing worry as young ethnic Chinese and Sino-Khmers in Cambodia combined vocal support of the Cultural Revolution with criticism of the Lon Nol government. Nevertheless, whatever the degree of foreign involvement, Sihanouk blamed prominent Cambodian leftists for a large part of the unrest in Battambang province. Singling out Khieu Samphan, Hou Youn and Hu Nim as his targets, he threatened that Red Khmers would be treated in the same way as right-wing Khmer Serei rebels. Emphasising this point, he had three of the latter executed and once again had their executions filmed for public showing.

In speeches throughout April Sihanouk rehearsed old themes in the light of new circumstances. He deplored the disputes between conservative 'blues' and leftist 'reds' and between prominent political personalities such as Sim Var and Chau Seng. He pointed to the conflicts in Vietnam and Laos as examples of what happened when political disputes could not be settled peacefully. Confident in his own mind that it would never come to pass, he said that he would accept a communist regime in Cambodia if this was what the people voted for. And he once more threatened to play his now rather tattered trump card. If the squabbling politicians could not come to their senses, he would resign from public life.

Finally, at the end of April 1967, Sihanouk decided to accept Lon Nol's resignation as prime minister and to replace his ministry with a new 'government of national union', led by Son Sann. Although Sihanouk claimed that the new government incorporated men with a range of political outlooks, its character was essentially conservative. As a principal policy plank, the prince declared, the new government would seek reconciliation with the rebellious peasants in Battambang; he offered an amnesty to all who would lay down their arms. In June, in an act that was as much a reflection of hope as an accurate assessment of the true situation, Sihanouk declared that the Samlaut Rebellion was at an end.

Scattered rural violence continued on a sporadic basis, however, with the army taking harsh repressive measures whenever the opportunity arose. Much of this was obscured, for Cambodian and foreigner alike, by the political drama occurring in Phnom Penh, where two intertwined themes came to dominate political discussion. The first was the widespread speculation over the fate of the two prominent leftist deputies Khieu Samphan and Hou Youn, who had disappeared at the end of April. The second was the reverberations of the Chinese Cultural Revolution on Cambodia's domestic and external politics.

When Khieu Samphan and Hou Youn fled into the countryside at the end of April, they did so in genuine fear for their lives. Sihanouk's threats against them had become increasingly frequent and menacing. Their clandestine departure presented Sihanouk with a curious problem. His information was that the two men were still alive. Despite his threats he had not ordered their deaths, and Lon Nol assured him that in this case the army had not killed the two deputies. But the prince could not prove a negative. The conviction rapidly developed among the politically conscious in Phnom Penh and the provinces that the two leftists were indeed dead, brutally executed by the prince's security forces, with his blessing. The ever-active rumour mill in Phnom Penh seemed to be consistent on the details of their deaths. The two men had been tortured, then crushed to death beneath the tracks of a bulldozer. Three years later, after Sihanouk had been deposed, this theory seemed to receive circumstantial verification when the then Cambodian delegate to the United Nations, the veteran conservative Kim Tith, claimed to have seen a police report that stated Khieu Samphan had been burnt to death with acid, while Hou Youn and Hu Nim, who had gone into the *maquis* later in 1967, had been crushed beneath bulldozer tracks. At the time, the disappearance of the first two deputies was a signal for demonstrative acts of mourning by left-inclined students, many of them Sino-Khmers.

As 1967 progressed, support for the goals of the Cultural Revolution became increasingly vocal among ethnic Chinese and Sino-Khmers in Cambodia. What remained of the legal left elected to show its sympathy for the Khmer–Chinese Friendship Association, which had become the chief local supporter of the upheavals taking place in China. Hu Nim, in a series of acts of courage, if not madness, continued to defy the prince until Sihanouk threatened him with a military trial and accused him of treason. Finally recognising that he could no longer survive in open politics, he too joined the slowly growing band of urban revolutionaries who had gone into hiding in the countryside.

As relations with China continued to deteriorate, almost ending in a complete break by the end of 1967, Sihanouk began to reassess his foreign policy options. Earlier in the year both the Vietnamese communists and China had given pledges of their respect for Cambodia's territorial integrity and its existing boundaries. If this had happened four years earlier, Sihanouk might not have felt any need to alter his foreign policy course. In the latter half of 1967 matters looked different. Whatever claims he made for external consumption, Sihanouk knew that his country was no longer 'an oasis of peace'. He had become suspicious of China's role in fomenting left-wing unrest, particularly among the youth of the capital, and he had begun to wonder whether a communist victory in Vietnam was likely in the near future. Just as he had long sought to dominate domestic politics by playing off one side against the other, he began to listen to arguments that Cambodia's best interests would be served by a rapprochement with the United States, which would help to counterbalance a policy that had become too heavily weighted towards anti-Western states.

The slow process of restoring links with America began with a visit to Cambodia by Jacqueline Kennedy, the widow of the former president, in October 1967. Here was an event rich with irony and containing a hefty measure of political hypocrisy on both the Cambodian and American sides. Sihanouk, who had exulted in the death of Jacqueline Kennedy's husband, now received her with both honour and courtesy. The American government, for its part, was ready to put Sihanouk's 1963 outburst behind it in terms of its broader strategic interests. Although largely symbolic, the visit's success provided the basis for a more substantive visit by the American ambassador to India, Chester Bowles, two months later in January 1968. During this visit Sihanouk's prime minister, Son Sann, made clear Cambodia's desire to resume relations with the United States, a resumption that finally occurred before the end of the same year. But more fundamentally important was the fact that during the Bowles visit, Sihanouk signalled a shift in position that had vital immediate and longer-term consequences. Tacitly acknowledging that Vietnamese communist forces did, indeed, make use of Cambodian territory—a fact strenuously denied officially—Sihanouk told Bowles that he would not object to US forces crossing into Cambodian territory if they were in hot pursuit of their enemy. This concession was a basis for the later restoration of relations between the two countries. In terms of the ground war raging in Vietnam, the US forces were now able to exert greater pressure on their enemy and so drive the communist troops deeper into their Cambodian sanctuaries. Most fatefully of all the consequences, and notwithstanding the denials of Henry Kissinger, Washington twisted Sihanouk's readiness to accept the principle of hot pursuit to justify the intensive bombing of Cambodia between 1969 and 1973, which resulted in massive destruction and loss of life. For the moment, Sihanouk was increasingly preoccupied with other concerns. As 1968 began, there was growing evidence that despite the army's repression resistance to Phnom Penh's authority was growing throughout the country.

A remarkable feature of commentary on Sihanouk's life has been the extent to which the darker side of his nature has been hidden or obscured from public view. There are several reasons for this. Probably most importantly, the horrendous record of the Pol Pot years of tyranny and death has pushed the excesses of Sihanouk's final years in power into the historical background. Added to the horror of the Pol Pot period is the fact that the Lon Nol regime which emerged after Sihanouk's overthrow was characterised by gross incompetence and brutality. This has predisposed many to treat Sihanouk's rule with less rigour than it deserves. Finally, but far from exhaustively, those who have paid due attention to the 'warts' on his image have mostly been academic writers read by an academic audience. Accounts of Sihanouk aimed at a more popular audience have often been uncritically sympathetic, whether for personal or ideological reasons.

Yet the record of Sihanouk's use of the harshest measures against his enemies is clear, and documented in part in his own words. During 1968 and 1969, as the dissident challenge to the government in Phnom Penh grew in intensity, the government, with Sihanouk's direct encouragement and explicit orders, waged a campaign of brutal repression. The picture that emerges from the last two years before Sihanouk's downfall is of the prince swinging between an ever-intensifying search for diversion, particularly through his passion for film-making, and a determination to wreak dreadful punishment on the rebels whom he saw, as ever in highly personal terms, as offending against his right to rule.

We shall probably never know the full extent of the resistance mounted against Phnom Penh during 1968 and 1969 nor how much of what was happening was apparent to the prince. The records of his speeches over these years show him alternating between repeated enumerations of the *réalisations* of the Sangkum—so many schools built, so many clinics opened—and a blunt readiness to state his satisfaction with the number of insurgents killed in fighting with the army or subsequently executed. He was particularly incensed by reports of resistance among the hill peoples of the northeast. After an outbreak of anti-government activity among the Brao people, the army went into action, killing indiscriminately. In May 1968, Sihanouk allowed the official *AKP* news bulletin to record his triumphant claim that he had ordered 200 rebels summarily executed in the northeast. This was not the only public boast Sihanouk made, nor his only direct intervention to order executions. According to sources used by Ben Kiernan, it was on Sihanouk's own orders that 40 schoolteachers suspected of treason were thrown to their deaths from the mountainous heights of Bokor above the provincial capital of Kampot. While the left was Sihanouk's principal target, he was still ready, on occasion, to threaten the right of Cambodian politics with his vengeance. Speaking in Takeo in June 1968, he threatened to send Sim Var and Douc Rasy 'to another world without asking for the lifting of their parliamentary immunity'. But this was an exception to the general rule in which the left was Sihanouk's main concern.

As the security situation deteriorated, conservatives increasingly dominated the government in Phnom Penh. With the army operating virtually untrammelled in the countryside, the press was placed under stricter control. By the end of 1967 the remaining avowed leftists within the Sangkum found that their position was perilous. The most prominent remaining spokesman for left-wing views, Chau Seng, was placed under house arrest before he fled to France. Other men whose left-wing sympathies were well known disappeared into the *maquis* in late 1967 or early 1968. The evolution of politics clearly favoured the right, a fact made clear when, in April 1968, Lon Nol returned to the cabinet as minister of defence.

Yet as the security situation became an ever-greater cause for concern, Sihanouk showed an even more intense interest in film-making. In November 1968, not content with acting in, writing and directing his own films, he instituted the Phnom Penh international film festival. Quite apart from the resentment this event caused among the Phnom Penh elite for its lack of relevance to Cambodia's many problems, the festival's cost prompted bitter comment at a time when rumours of the corrupt activities of Sihanouk's consort, Monique, were arousing growing indignation. Few knew the full nature and extent of the dealings of Monique and her circle, of which her half-brother Oum Mannorine was the most prominent member, but ugly stories flourished that she had set her sights on aggrandisement at all costs and by any means. Even if exaggerated, the rumours had a destructive political effect, just as had been the case with the rumours associated with Ngo Dinh Nhu and his wife in Saigon five years earlier.

The widespread belief among many members of the Phnom Penh elite that Monique was pursuing wealth through a program of corruption was only one of a range of developments that pointed to the decline of Prince Sihanouk's regime. While right-wing politicians and military leaders were still unready to seize power, the social and political climate was poisoned by the unfettered pursuit of wealth in a situation of increasing uncertainty over both external and internal developments. For senior Cambodian army officers in the late 1960s there was no insuperable contradiction between thinking of a future in which close relations with the United States might be resumed and engaging in large-scale contraband with the Vietnamese communists. But the issue had become more complicated. First, when Sihanouk did rouse himself to discuss the problems of the state, he increasingly portrayed internal resistance as a product of external, largely Vietnamese, direction. Second, the Vietnamese communists who had proved such a useful source of additional illegal income for the army were no longer confined to a limited number of border regions. It was gradually becoming clear to the military that in addition to the domestic resistance they were asked to suppress they now faced a growing and uncontrolled Vietnamese presence within Cambodia.

Hindsight has made clear how far the governance of Cambodia had passed from Sihanouk's control by the end of 1968. He still felt able to affirm, yet again, that Cambodia was an 'oasis of peace', as he did in a speech on 10 October, but this description no longer coincided with the everyday experience or knowledge of many of his compatriots. His country's relations with the Vietnamese communists had reached a critical point, and were to approach flashpoint the following year as growing numbers of Vietnamese troops made use of Cambodian territory. The situation called into question Sihanouk's claim that he was unchallenged, and unchallengeable, in his capacity to direct the Cambodian state and its foreign affairs. At the same time the economy continued to stagnate and the nation's finances to decline, twin problems that encouraged conservative politicians to risk pressing ever harder for a reversal of the policies followed since 1963.

As 1968 drew to a close, evidence began to grow that political groupings were working to consolidate their positions for the uncertain future. The name most frequently mentioned in this context was Prince Sirik Matak. A cousin of Sihanouk's and once a firm supporter, Sirik Matak had come to hold critical views of the prince which led to his occupying positions of relative unimportance over the years. As an ambassador abroad, even in such an important post as Peking, Sirik Matak had been removed from the cut and thrust of domestic politics for most of the 1960s. Yet even in 'exile' he loomed as a figure of potential importance for two key reasons. Monique was indebted to him, for she had spent much of her childhood in his household, and he was one of Lon Nol's patrons. By late 1968 it was apparent that he had by no means abandoned his ambition to play a major role in Cambodia's domestic politics. As the politically conscious in the capital took account of this, regional unrest continued to grow and the state of administration outside Phnom Penh varied between areas in which provincial governors were unready to act on their own responsibility, and those in which the senior officials acted as if they were unrestrained by any direction from the centre.

Although conservatives spoke of their grievances in private, they still hesitated to challenge the prince in public. The result was a situation in which reality had little to do with the picture of progress presented by Sihanouk; yet nothing was done to correct the results of error and neglect. Sihanouk still spoke of the Cambodian monarchy, symbolised in his mother, Queen Kossamak, as a vital factor in preserving the unity of the state. And he continued to refer to the ultimate succession of his son, Norodom Naradipo, to the leadership of the country. The most important critics on the left had long since abandoned trying to work through the system Sihanouk defended and had gone into clandestine dissidence. The critics on the right were still unready to mount their challenge, but they were no longer convinced that Sihanouk's leadership was indispensable. If most still shrank from the thought of removing him from power, they were certainly beginning to believe that his single-handed determination of Cambodia's major policies, whether external or internal, must be curbed.

Notes

For some discussion of the atmosphere in Phnom Penh at the time of General de Gaulle's visit, see my *Before Kampuchea*, pp. 157–61.

Discussion of Sihanouk's decision to abstain from selecting Sangkum candidates for the 1966 elections may be found in Chandler, *Tragedy*, pp. 153–6, Osborne, *Politics and Power*, p. 93, and *Before Kampuchea*, Chapter 17.

Sihanouk's comment on the nature of the National Assembly elected in September 1966 is in *L'Indochine vue de Pékin*, p. 82. Also useful for this period is the discussion in Elizabeth Becker, *When the War Was Over: The Voices of Cambodia's Revolution and its People*, New York, 1986, pp. 116–17. On the counter-government, Chandler, *Tragedy*, Meyer, *Derrière*, and Osborne, *Politics and Power* all provide commentary.

The most accessible and detailed discussion of the Samlaut Rebellion may be found in Kiernan, *How Pol Pot*, Chapter 7. Discussion in Chandler, *Tragedy*, pp. 163–7, is particularly valuable. In his *Souvenirs*, pp. 325–6, Sihanouk denies that what took place at Samlaut was a 'popular revolt'.

On bounties for severed heads see Donald Lancaster, 'The Decline of Prince Sihanouk's Regime', in J.J. Zasloff and A.E. Goodman, eds, *Conflict in Indochina*, Lexington, Mass., 1972, pp. 47–56. On repression generally, see Meyer, *Derrière*, pp. 193–4. Sihanouk's reference to the deaths of 10 000 people is in *L'Indochine vue de Pékin*, p. 90. His revised and much lower estimate is in *Souvenirs*.

For Sihanouk's earliest extended commentary on the outbreak of insurgency in Samlaut, and his recognition that it reflected, in part, an attack on the Lon Nol government, see FBIS reporting Radio Phnom Penh on 3 April 1967. A later, extended commentary by Sihanouk is his address of 30 April, also reported by FBIS.

A valuable discussion of the growing problem of anti-government activity in 1967 and 1968 is Michael Leifer, 'Rebellion or subversion in Cambodia', *Current History* February 1969, pp. 89–93. As always, the review of this period by David Chandler in his *Tragedy* is a valuable summation of the available evidence. Although Sihanouk was ready, on occasion, to give a frank account of the level of resistance to the Phnom Penh government, treatment of developments in the semi-official *Réalités* often sought to minimise the extent of unrest. Moreover, foreign commentary was given short shrift. A notable instance was Sihanouk's riposte to the article by Jacques Decornoy in *Le Monde* in early 1968—Decornoy's article was published in the 2 February 1968 issue of the newspaper and drew a sharp response from Sihanouk, published on 7 March.

My discussion on the speculation surrounding the disappearance of the leftist deputies reflects conversations held in Phnom Penh in December 1967. As late as August 1970, and despite their having been named as members of Sihanouk's government-in-exile following his deposition, there was doubt about the three men still being alive. Kim Thith's account was reported in the *New York Times*, 22 August 1970; the report quoted Sihanouk's long-time associate Charles Meyer as saying he believed Khieu Samphan and Hou Youn were dead, but was uncertain about the fate of Hu Nim.

For some discussion of the period of difficult relations between Sihanouk and China, see R.M. Smith, 'Cambodia: Between Scylla and Charybdis', *Asian Survey*, VII, 1, January 1968, pp. 72–9. Contemporary Cambodian comment may be found in *Réalités*, 8 and 15 September and 11 November 1967. See also *New York Times*, 15 and 19 September 1967.

William Shawcross's *Sideshow: Nixon, Kissinger, and the Destruction of Cambodia*, New York, 1979, and subsequent expanded edition, 1981, provide an essential and invaluable discussion of how America came to bomb Cambodia.

On Sihanouk's boast of having ordered the execution of two hundred people, see *AKP*, 25 May 1968. The ferocity of Sihanouk's views and orders is best learned from transcripts of his speeches to be found in FBIS and BBC Shortwave Monitoring reports. On the execution of the teachers, see Kiernan, *How Pol Pot*, p. 276. Douc Rasy recalled the threat made against him and Sim Var in a letter he sent to *Le Figaro*, reproduced in *Réalités*, 11 September 1970, quoting Sihanouk on 19 June 1968.

The October 1968 reference to an 'oasis of peace' was recorded in *Les Paroles de Samdech Preah Norodom Sihanouk*, October–December 1968, Phnom Penh, n.d., p. 583.

On the nature of the Cambodian economy and its decline during the 1960s, see R. Prud'homme, *L'Economie du Cambodge*, Paris, 1969.

16

Exit a prince

In his many reviews of his fall from power at the beginning of 1970, Sihanouk has repeatedly charged that the coup which toppled him was engineered by his old adversary, the CIA. As this chapter will show, his perhaps understandable knee-jerk reaction was wrong, though the involvement of some American intelligence services is now beyond dispute. More importantly, Sihanouk's emphasis on the foreign element associated with his overthrow diverts attention from the vital indigenous feature of Cambodian politics during 1969: the fact that during this year Sihanouk's hold on power steadily slipped away. When he left Phnom Penh for rest and medical treatment in France, in early January 1970, he was little more than a political figurehead. But it was by no means impossible that he could have continued as an honoured if largely powerless chief of state. What occurred in March 1970 was, in the end, the result of miscalculations, by both Sihanouk and others, a sequence of unpredictable developments, and the culmination of accelerating political, economic and military decline within Cambodia.

Politics in Cambodia in 1969 took place amid a steadily deteriorating security situation. A visitor could easily fail to recognise this. Phnom Penh was calm, as were the major provincial capitals. Travel by day on the country's excellent trunk road network was unimpeded, as was rail travel. But this impression of calm was misleading. Away from the provincial centres and main roads the leftist-led insurgency continued. Both sides—the army and the 5000 or so insurgents—were locked in an increasingly brutal conflict in which neither side hesitated to kill cruelly and indiscriminately. Bizarre stories reached the capital of rebel captives having their heads sawn off while still alive and of severed heads being exposed in market-places as a warning to others. For their part, the rebels matched the army's savagery with attacks on civilian targets, with innocent bus passengers massacred to reinforce warnings against cooperat-ing with government troops. Particularly bloody exchanges took place in the mountainous regions of the northeast, where the resistance of the hill people—wise in the ways of the forest and readily able to ambush their opponents—brought savage retribu-tion from the army.

Although indigenous Cambodian communists played a vital part in inciting resistance in widely scattered areas of the kingdom, it remains unclear whether the central committee of the Commu-nist Party of Kampuchea, secretly based among the hill people of the northeast, was the controlling force in the insurgency or whether local leaders determined the extent to which resistance waxed or waned in particular regions. Indeed, if the challenge to the government in Phnom Penh had come solely from indigenous Cambodian leftist forces, the best retrospective judgment would have to be that there was, in 1969, no threat that could not be contained for at least the medium term. But there was another threat, even though it was, at this stage, still potential. By 1969 there were tens of thousands of Vietnamese communist troops sheltering inside Cambodia. This fact began to concentrate the minds of politicians in Phnom Penh and to call into question the fundamentals of Sihanouk's foreign policy.

Stated baldly, Sihanouk believed he could appease the Vietnam-ese communists while gaining a measure of reinsurance by renewing relations with the United States. In principle, this was a policy of essential good sense for a small, weak country located next door to a war between much larger powers. Justifying himself, the prince frequently quoted a proverb common to many Asian societies: 'When elephants fight, ants should stand aside'. He was powerless to prevent the Vietnamese from crossing into Cambodia and using its territory, so acquiescence seemed the better choice. To have resisted would have risked conflict. Moreover, Sihanouk knew that the presence of Vietnamese troops inside Cambodia had contributed money to line the pockets of the army's officer corps as the result of contraband rice sales. The only other alternative was inconceivable. To have cooperated with the Saigon regime would have dragged Cambodia into the Vietnam War and so have destroyed Sihanouk's most enduring achievement: preserving his country from the hostilities throughout the 1960s. Why did others not judge matters in the same wasy as the prince? The fact that the Vietnamese troop presence was now so large certainly played its part in shaping contrary opinion. But more was involved as the economic and social consequences of Sihanouk's rule alienated the elite and the middle class whose support was vital for his survival.

By 1969 the Cambodian economy was plagued by stagnation and corruption. Rising rural indebtedness was leading to the movement into the cities, and particularly Phnom Penh, of landless peasants who added to the already large number of urban unemployed. Declining rice yields testified to a rural malaise that central authority was unable to address. Cambodia's main export crop apart from rice, rubber, contributed less to government revenues as world prices fell and production, in the most easterly regions of the kingdom, was affected by chemical defoliants that drifted across the border from South Vietnam. The industrialisation program that had been such a source of pride to Sihanouk was financially wasteful and, in terms of the products produced, inefficient. The plywood from a Chinese-donated factory cost more than competing products available on the world market. The same was true of the Russian aid gift, the cement factory near Kampot, and the tractors assembled in a Czech-donated factory were unsuited to agricultural conditions in Cambodia.

Nothing suggests that Sihanouk even tried to understand the costs of these industries. What was important for him was that Cambodia should show the world it was more than a former colonial backwater dependent on agriculture for its economic survival. The concept of cost-benefit analysis was utterly alien to his way of thinking. Similarly, he saw the state as a source of endless funds for the construction of buildings and facilities which, by their existence, would contribute to Cambodia's prestige. This was the basis for the construction of state residences in Phnom Penh and in the provinces, of a state dance hall, a state golf course and a state cinema. Cost was his last concern and he angrily dismissed from his presence those few advisers who were brave enough to tell him the country was in economic trouble. Son Sann, one of his closest advisers since before independence, tried to bring the seriousness of the situation to Sihanouk's attention only to be shown the door, so bringing to an end the two men's long association.

In the face of Cambodia's accumulating difficulties Sihanouk increasingly distanced himself from day-to-day politics. Rather than contemplate the hard choices that were needed to turn the economy around, he instead sanctioned the opening of casinos in Phnom Penh and Sihanoukville (Kompong Som). In terms of raising revenue for the state, the casinos were an instant success. But their social cost was high, as Cambodians from the richest to the poorest surged through the casinos' doors intent on beating the odds. These were no elegant gambling clubs modelled on establishments in Monte Carlo or Mayfair. In an atmosphere thick with the smell of stale sweat and cigarette smoke, men and women struggled toward the crowded tables amid a permanent din as croupiers shouted and the patrons proclaimed their success or failure at the top of their voices. The only dress code enforced in the casinos was the requirement that all patrons should wear shoes, which many of the poorer gamblers did not possess. The problem was overcome by an enterprising Chinese businessman, who set up a shoe hire service for the pedicab riders and urban labourers who, along with their more affluent compatriots, flocked into the gambling halls. Within weeks of the casinos' establishment in early 1969 there were rumours of suicides by people who had lost their life savings. Whether true or not, the stories were believed and more thoughtful Cambodians came to wonder at the wisdom of Sihanouk's decision to raise money in this way.

For much of 1969 Sihanouk was absorbed in the production of his last two films, *Crépuscule* and *Joie de Vivre*. These were no better than his previous cinematic ventures. Impervious to the irony of his action, Sihanouk allowed *Crépuscule* to be placed in a special category in which he was the only competitor so that he could collect the premier award at the second, and last, international film festival held in Phnom Penh in November 1969. *Joie de Vivre* was in many ways a rerun of the prince's first film, *Apsara*. Once again General Nhiek Tioulong played an ageing roué, and once again the female lead was the full-bosomed former airline hostess Saksi Sbong. The storyline revolves around Saksi's unfaithfulness as she bed-hops from minor prince to minor prince. But, as in *Apsara*, she finds true love in the end, this time with Tioulong, with whom she is shown embracing on a beach in a direct copy of the beach scene between Burt Lancaster and Deborah Kerr in *From Here to Eternity*. As I noted in my journal after attending (with a handful of others) a screening at Phnom Penh's state cinema in January 1970: 'It was dreadful. The technical standard was just as bad as *Apsara* . . . The royal family is depicted as constantly absorbed with lust and gambling—perhaps this is not so far wrong—and shows them living in villas furnished at great expense and in the worst tastes, driving everywhere in Cadillacs. After two hours I could bear no more and left.'

The prince's preoccupation with films and what many saw as their dubious subject matter threw into even sharper relief his country's problems, which now had become a matter for public discussion. In the past, Sihanouk's handling of foreign affairs had generated almost continuous praise in the press, and even those who criticised his domestic policies in private conceded his idiosyncratic skill in keeping Cambodia out of the Vietnam war. But as awareness spread of the presence of Vietnamese communist troops on Cambodian soil, so did doubts deepen about the wisdom of Sihanouk's past policies. Although refraining from direct criticism of the prince, the Phnom Penh press by early 1969 was expressing the concern of many that large areas of eastern Cambodia had passed out of the government's control. Reiterated assertions of friendship for the government in Hanoi and its southern allies now appeared side by side with worried reflections on what was happening and what it meant for Cambodia's national sovereignty. For Sihanouk's opponents, the time to change policies had come.

Well before he was deposed in March 1970, Sihanouk's domestic opponents showed that they were strong enough to counter his long-established policies. In response to intensifying criticism over the country's economic problems Sihanouk agreed, in August 1969, to accept the resignation of the government that had held office since January 1968. The new ministry, designated the 'government of salvation' and inaugurated after much manoeuvring, was led by General Lon Nol, who had as his deputy Prince Sirik Matak. It was the latter who soon demonstrated that Sihanouk's control of the state had greatly diminished, after Lon Nol was injured when a jeep driven recklessly by Sihanouk overturned. When Lon Nol departed for medical treatment in France in October 1969, Sirik Matak assumed direction of the government and showed his determination to disregard the wishes of the chief of state. In a series of confrontations on both domestic and external issues, he refused to change his policies despite Sihanouk's displeasure. Backed by the parliament, he worked to dismantle the economic structures established by Sihanouk in 1963 and 1964. He sought to reactivate a civil service that had stagnated for years because of the unreadiness of successive ministries to act counter to Sihanouk's wishes. With Sihanouk's grudging approval, Sirik Matak also encouraged the Cambodian army to reestablish a presence in the northeastern provinces, where there was the greatest concentration of Vietnamese communist troops.

Sirik Matak's policies were a direct challenge to Sihanouk. When, after calling a national congress at the end of 1969, Sihanouk found that Matak's ministry intended to persist with policies that ran counter to his own wishes, the chief of state left for France to undergo a much delayed health cure. Sihanouk's own commentary on this period is ambiguous. Discussing the events that led up to his overthrow, he has argued that he knew power had passed from his hands and that a major new effort was needed to rejuvenate the Cambodian state. He had recognised, he has insisted, that from July 1969 onwards real power was in Lon Nol's and Sirik Matak's hands. At the same time he has admitted that his great error was to trust Lon Nol and to believe that he would never betray him. In these circumstances, and feeling the need to reflect on the future, he departed for France on 6 January 1970.

The public record does not support much of Sihanouk's account. That the prince recognised the extent of the challenge to his policies and his control of the state is beyond dispute, but his actions once the 'government of salvation' had been inaugurated in August 1969 indicate no passive acquiescence in the drift of power from his hands. Discussing events during the last few months of 1969, Prince Sisowath Entaravong told me, in February 1970, that in the face of the opposition he was encountering, Sihanouk was contemplating remounting the throne. He had discussed this possibility with his mother, Queen Kossamak, who had firmly rejected the idea, arguing that the prince would make a fool of himself were he to do so after his repeated vows that he would never again become king. Charles Meyer later recorded a similar report, adding that the prince had considered holding spectacular ceremonies to mark the occasion. Although it is true that Sihanouk made fewer speeches and public appearances, absorbed as he still was with his films, when he did speak he tried repeatedly to demonstrate that in issues of major policy his was the determining decision. When Sirik Matak and his supporters, backed by a National Assembly that did not disguise its wish to see Sihanouk's policies reversed, would not be swayed from their chosen path, Sihanouk made his decision to go abroad. Repeating the tactic he had used so many times before, he removed himself from the political scene in Phnom Penh in the belief that his absence would bring his opponents to their senses and rally his flagging supporters to his side. He still believed he was indispensable. Surely those who had dared to oppose him would come to recognise this too.

The flaw in Sihanouk's assessment lay in his belief that among the Phnom Penh politicians whose hands rested on the levers of power he still had some unwavering supporters. For years he had spoken of dissatisfaction in the army; but he believed this dissatisfaction would never be directed against him because of Lon Nol's personal loyalty to his leader. Even among the factious politicians, Sihanouk probably believed his status was sufficient to inhibit any decisive action against him, whatever criticism these men might voice against his policies. Probably, too, Sihanouk left for France at the beginning of 1970 with a continuing conviction in the importance of peasant support for his leadership. Throughout his rule Sihanouk had evoked demonstrative affection from the peasantry, and though he regarded them as 'children' with no views of their own, he also thought of them as a permanent support base. In these several judgments Sihanouk was wrong. Under duress, Lon Nol proved ready to lead the army into the anti-Sihanouk camp. Politicians, following Sirik Matak's example, finally proved ready to depose Sihanouk despite his regal aura and the long years during which he had directed Cambodia's affairs. And the peasantry, however much some of them may have regretted Sihanouk's deposition, were ill-placed to translate their feelings into action.

Yet if Sihanouk left for France burdened by these incorrect judgments, his opponents in Phnom Penh were making assumptions that were even more grossly incorrect. As David Chandler has succinctly summarised them, these were four in number. First was the assumption that Sihanouk would be prepared to accept a figurehead role; this was perhaps the most understandable, since he had not been prepared to challenge Lon Nol and Sirik Matak head-on. Next was the assumption that the Vietnamese communist forces would meekly leave their privileged sanctuaries in Cambodia to return to battle in South Vietnam. The third unwarranted assumption made by Sirik Matak and his allies was that Cambodia could be isolated from the war going on in Vietnam. And, finally, Sihanouk's opponents appear to have concluded that the domestic Cambodian communists would abandon their goal of gaining power.

Hindsight shows how wrong these assumptions were, but for Lon Nol and Sirik Matak in January and February 1970 the future seemed open and positive. They may not have decided finally to overthrow the prince, but they took satisfaction in having humbled him. Buoyed by the support of an urban elite disenchanted with Sihanouk, they genuinely, if misguidedly, believed they could confront the Vietnamese communists. They most certainly did not realise that they were poised before an abyss of terrifying and tragic proportions.

Controversy still surrounds the *coup d'état* that toppled Sihanouk in March 1970. Much evidence has emerged that there was an extraordinarily tangled web of conspiracy, but many of the alleged details of the plotting lack corroboration. Moreover, Sihanouk's own lengthy commentaries on the affair are less than fully frank and distorted by his determination to sheet home responsibility to the CIA. What follows is an attempt to tease out a sequence of events on which there is general, if not universal, agreement.

Central to understanding what happened in March 1970 is a recognition of the changed political mood in Phnom Penh following Sihanouk's departure for France. The spell of Sihanouk's invincibility had been broken as the urban elite and the bourgeoisie counted the cost of his economic policies and gossiped nervously about the implications of a foreign policy that had led to more than 40 000 Vietnamese communist troops camping on Cambodian soil. Instead of the leader whose boundless energies had dominated political life ten years earlier, they now saw a man whose chief concern seemed to be the production of embarrassingly amateurish films. While the standard of living of many urban Cambodians had declined since 1964, they were convinced that Sihanouk's consort, Monique, and members of her clique, particularly Oum Mannorine, were growing ever richer through corruption on a grand scale. With Sihanouk out of the country and with a political leader in Sirik Matak who was ready to make his own decisions, there was hope abroad of a new beginning. Some even doubted Sihanouk would come back to Phnom Penh. As one extremely knowledgeable foreign observer put it to me when I visited Cambodia in February 1970, Sihanouk might not be given a visa to return.

Apart from the conspirators themselves, no-one at the time knew the extent to which Sihanouk's removal from power was already being plotted. By late 1968 or early 1969, both Lon Nol and Sirik Matak were considering a coup, and Lon Nol appears to have established clandestine contacts with elements of the American military in South Vietnam. Lon Nol was looking for an assurance that he could expect American support if Sihanouk were overthrown. From his viewpoint, this was a prudent precaution, since he clearly thought in terms that linked Sihanouk's deposition with efforts to end the Vietnamese communists' use of Cambodian territory. Lon Nol's contacts seemed to provide such an assurance, though the level at which this was approved is a matter of dispute. The contacts went further, suggesting that ethnic Cambodian mercenaries could be used to assassinate Sihanouk, a proposal that Lon Nol rejected out of hand. Sirik Matak, according to one account was, in contrast, quite ready to contemplate such a step.

The picture that emerges is of Lon Nol keeping his options open and of Sirik Matak favouring a coup but being unable to act without the certainty of support from Lon Nol's military. In September 1969 Lon Nol secretly made contact with Sihanouk's old enemy, Son Ngoc Thanh, who was now living in South Vietnam. According to Thanh's brother Son Thai Nguyen, whom I interviewed in Saigon in January 1971, Lon Nol began tentative discussions about overthrowing Sihanouk at this time. While there seems no doubt that Lon Nol was in touch with Son Ngoc Thanh, the purpose of his approach may not have been unqualifiedly malevolent, despite Son Thai Nguyen's testimony. Rather, as David Chandler has suggested, Lon Nol may well have had Sihanouk's approval for an approach to Thanh that aimed to recruit ethnic Cambodians from South Vietnam to fight against the Vietnamese communist forces in Cambodia. Several hundred pro-Thanh rebels had rallied to the Phnom Penh government earlier in the year. While many now doubt that their actions were genuine—judging that they were part of the developing plan for a coup—Sihanouk himself greeted the ralliers with joy. In the event, Lon Nol's contacts with Thanh were broken off when the general was injured in his jeep accident and went to Paris for medical care.

Lon Nol was still in Europe when Sihanouk left Cambodia at the beginning of January 1970. Sihanouk maintains that American agents were in touch with Lon Nol while he was in hospital in Paris. This is possible, but not certain. What is clear is that when the prince reached Rome, en route to his holiday home in the south of France, Lon Nol travelled to see him and urged Sihanouk not to stay away from Cambodia for too long. This final meeting between Sihanouk and Lon Nol suggests that the latter had still not decided to act against the prince. This havering and uncertainty fits well with what is known of Lon Nol's personality. Although he was probably confident that he could rely on some form of American assistance following a coup against Sihanouk, the decision to act against the man he had served for so long was an awesome step which he still hesitated to take.

Back in Cambodia, however, Lon Nol showed that he was ready

to react with uncharacteristic vigour to the continuing presence of Vietnamese communist troops on Cambodian soil. Probably with Sihanouk's approval, Lon Nol demonetised all 500-riel banknotes then in circulation. This was a shrewd move to deprive the Vietnamese of the funds they had accumulated in large-denomination notes to pay for rice and other contraband goods. More overtly hostile and serious was the government's decision in February to start shelling areas occupied by the Vietnamese forces. Whether reluctantly or not, Sihanouk seems to have accepted this shift in policy. But it must all have seemed very far away from Dr Pathé's clinic in Grasse, which he had entered to lose weight. Just before he started his cure, the readers of *Réalités Cambodgiennes* were told on 6 February, in a report that summed up the sense of unreality now surrounding Sihanouk, that the prince had eaten 'his last good meal' of trout with almonds and chicken cooked with Provençal herbs at the 'modest but charming inn, Chez Dany'.

In Phnom Penh matters started coming to a head when government-organised demonstrations were held in front of the North Vietnamese and National Liberation Front's diplomatic missions on 11 March. Sihanouk approved these demonstrations, but he had not expected that the police would lose control as they did, or that the two buildings would be sacked and set on fire. Speaking on French television the next day, the prince lashed out at the demonstrators, rightists and Vietnamese communists. It was an echo of the old Sihanouk. He would, he said, return to Phnom Penh to reestablish Cambodia's policy of neutrality and non-alignment. While he blamed rightists for the sacking of the diplomatic missions, commenting a shade naively that there were rightists 'even in the government', he even-handedly attacked the Vietnamese communists for failing to respect Cambodia's neutrality and for interfering in Cambodia's internal affairs. Looking to the immediate future, he posed a key question when he observed that everything would now depend on the attitude of the army. 'It is very royalist. Will it agree to remain poor? In fact, we are only aided by France. Peking and Moscow do not help us in an effective fashion.' The question Sihanouk asked was the right one, but his comments on China and the Soviet Union seemed curiously misjudged in light of his hopes that these two countries would press the Vietnamese communists to scale down their presence in Cambodia.

After the sacking of the Vietnamese communists' missions in Phnom Penh, Sihanouk and Lon Nol each made a fateful decision. Lon Nol, with what degree of thought and consultation is unclear, issued an ultimatum to the Vietnamese troops in Cambodia. They were to leave Cambodia in three days' time, on 15 March. Perhaps only the exultant mood that now gripped so many in the Cambodian capital can explain such a wildly unrealistic demand, which ultimately pitched the weak and poorly trained Cambodian army against battle-hardened Vietnamese. But if Lon Nol was showing signs of disregarding reality, so too was Sihanouk, who elected not to return quickly to Phnom Penh to try and reassert his control but rather to travel back via Moscow and Peking. Evidently he saw those capitals as the best potential sources of pressure on North Vietnam and its southern supporters.

In his own account of the hectic final days before he was deposed, Sihanouk states that he still did not believe Lon Nol would betray him, and this is probably true. Indeed, Lon Nol hesitated to act until the last moment and did so only then under duress. But there was more to Sihanouk's calculations, and even twenty years after the event it is impossible to reconcile all the evidence into a coherent whole. This may well be because Sihanouk himself swung between doubt and conviction about which course to follow. On the one hand and while still in Paris, he spoke of having the members of the 'government of salvation' killed once he returned to Phnom Penh, a threat that unknown to him was secretly tape-recorded. On the other hand, it could be argued that he did not expect to receive any worthwhile assistance from either Moscow or Peking, and that consequently he looked towards forging an alliance with Lon Nol against both the extreme right and extreme left while continuing to improve relations with the United States. Overall, it is not surprising that Sihanouk showed signs of irresolution as matters evolved in Cambodia almost totally beyond his control. Up to the moment before he left Paris on 13 March, and for the first three days of his visit to Moscow, Sihanouk continued to exchange messages with his mother, Queen Kossamak, and to receive daily reports from Lon Nol. Clearly aware that the situation had become very serious, the prince may simply have reverted to the tactic he had so often relied on in the past: if he stayed away long enough, the politicians would come to their senses.

He did not know that his talk of killing the members of the government on his return had reached Phnom Penh and Sirik Matak's ears. Whether or not Sihanouk had meant what he had said, his record of sanctioning violent action against his enemies was not something that Matak felt he could ignore. While Lon Nol still proclaimed his loyalty to the prince, Matak embarked on the final steps towards a coup. After discussions with Sim Var and Douc

Rasy, two of the most committed conservatives, he decided to begin with an oblique attack on Sihanouk by targeting Monique's half-brother, Colonel Oum Mannorine. In a shrewdly calculated move, Matak had Mannorine called before the National Assembly on 16 March to answer charges of having smuggled large quantities of cloth from Hong Kong into Cambodia. But once Mannorine was at the Assembly, where students had been brought to mount an anti-Vietnamese demonstration, Matak's supporters transformed the session into a debate which approved the earlier demonstrations that had destroyed the Vietnamese missions and condemned unnamed senior Cambodian figures who had cooperated in supplying the Vietnamese communists.

The very fact of haling Sihanouk's brother-in-law before the National Assembly had made clear that Sirik Matak was not going to back away from confronting the prince. By stage-managing a debate that offered the opportunity for men such as Douc Rasy to call for war against the Vietnamese and to denounce Sihanouk's long-standing policy of appeasing the Vietnamese forces on Cambodian territory, Matak had brought the kingdom to within a step of overthrowing its chief of state.

Yet according to those who were in Phnom Penh at the time, it was still uncertain that Matak and his allies would take that final step. Preparations had continued for Sihanouk's expected return and at the end of the 16 March session of the National Assembly the deputies voted to send two of their number to Moscow to report on events in Cambodia and ask the prince to return immediately. In a tense telephone conversation with Matak, Sihanouk refused to receive the proposed envoys and indicated that he was still not ready go back.

Events continued to move rapidly in Phnom Penh. Oum Mannorine was arrested and Sirik Matak took over control of the police from Sihanouk's brother-in-law. It was now 17 March and Phnom Penh seemed unnaturally calm after the excitement of the previous few days. The final step that ensured Sihanouk would fall took place in the early hours of the following day. Accompanied by trusted associates, including Major Po Chhon who was subsequently interviewed by David Chandler, Sirik Matak confronted Lon Nol with a demand that he join in a plan to depose Sihanouk. If he failed to sign a document put before him, Matak threatened, he would be shot. In tears, Lon Nol did so. Matak now had the essential military backing he wanted and Lon Nol's long period of prevarication was over. With the army on side, Matak was confident the Assembly would lend him the support necessary to give legislative weight to the coup he had so long contemplated. His calculation proved correct. The knowledge that Lon Nol had finally and publicly changed sides galvanised the members of the Assembly and speaker after speaker now gave vent to the resentment of Sihanouk, his family and his policies that they had been storing up for years. Early in the afternoon of 18 March the members of the National Assembly voted to remove Sihanouk from office as chief of state and, in accordance with the constitutional arrangements hastily put together in 1960, to replace him with the president of the assembly, Cheng Heng. Sihanouk's Cambodia had come to an end.

News of his dismissal reached Sihanouk as he was about to leave Moscow. His visit had not been a success. Premier Kosygin had urged him to return promptly to Phnom Penh to confront the challenge from the right, but this Sihanouk was not prepared to do. His reluctance almost certainly reflected his contemplating seeking permanent asylum away from Cambodia, though this possibility does not receive attention in Sihanouk's own accounts of the period. He had found the final months of 1969 humiliating as Sirik Matak and his ministry consistently ignored his wishes. Exile abroad may have seemed preferable to being little more than a figurehead if he returned home. As for his hopes that the Soviet Union would be prepared to put pressure on the Vietnamese communists, Sihanouk found it was not, thus confirming his long-standing critical view of the Russians.

Things were very different in Peking. Premier Zhou Enlai greeted him warmly at the airport, but for the moment Sihanouk was uncertain about his next move and the possibility of exile in France was still in his mind. In his 1971 account of his arrival in Peking, the prince glosses over the fact that he himself asked the French ambassador whether asylum in France was an option, implying that the ambassador made the offer unprompted and that he, though exhausted, had never contemplated going into exile. Instead, he has recounted, he spent 24 hours mulling over the offer Zhou made to him on his arrival. If Sihanouk was ready to fight, Zhou said, the Chinese were ready to support him. Buoyed by the prospect of China's support and outraged both by the fact of his deposition and by the crude personal attacks that were now being made on him and Monique in Phnom Penh, Sihanouk made his decision. He declared himself ready to fight, little knowing that in doing so he was fated to be first a pawn and then a prisoner.

In the past, far too much ink has been expended debating the extent of American involvement in the March 1970 coup. It is unlikely that Sihanouk himself will ever accept that the CIA was not involved. And he could, with justification, point to the incontrovertible evidence that other American agencies knew of the plotters' plans. The terrible war that subsequently engulfed Cambodia and the later Pol Pot tyranny have also tended to colour views of Sihanouk's Cambodia with a favourable hue, so that his deposition has been seen by many as an act of hideous folly.

Yet however dreadful the consequences of Sihanouk's removal, the fact remains that Sirik Matak and Lon Nol acted in response to growing dissatisfaction in the army officer corps and among the urban elite in Phnom Penh who had come to see Sihanouk's policies as politically and economically ruinous. To dwell on the issue of external involvement in the coup or to deplore the war that raged between 1970 and 1975 does not alter this fact. Beneath the claims of Sihanouk's Ministry of Information lay a reality that accorded ill with official insistence on unruffled calm. Discontent accelerated in 1969, but the factors that produced it were not new. Resentment with the economic situation, felt so acutely in 1969, had long been present among the Phnom Penh elite. In the closing months of 1969 there was certainly an increase in antipathy towards Sihanouk's consort, Monique, and those, including her half-brother, Oum Mannorine, whose interests she promoted. This antipathy, too, had existed for some years. Equally, concern over Sihanouk's preoccupation with film-making was only the latest instance of feeling among his associates and advisers that princely diversions were being placed above the demands of state business.

What was novel in late 1969 was that the urban elite were no longer prepared to accept the status quo. The decline in the economy had finally reached a point where palliatives could no longer stand in the place of root-and-branch cures. Resentment of Monique, and of Sihanouk's indifference to her corrupt activities, was heightened by the belief that her concerns were spreading beyond financial gain into politics. Sihanouk's devotion to the cinema might have been forgiven or ignored in other days, but the problems of the state had never seemed so threatening as in late 1969. Not least, the urban elite and many in the army's officer corps feared the consequences of the permanent presence of tens of thousands of Vietnamese communist troops on Cambodian territory. However misguided the later battles waged against these troops may have been, there is a solid case that it was concern at the Vietnamese presence that finally led to the 18 March coup. Whether the events which began with the demonstrations denouncing the Vietnamese presence were planned, even in Sirik Matak's mind, with the firm intention of deposing Sihanouk is still not clear. But at the end of a tumultuous week of hesitation and manoeuvring Sihanouk's right-wing opponents put their doubts behind them and removed the prince from office. It is often forgotten that Sihanouk's overthrow was greeted with joyful enthusiasm by many in Phnom Penh.

Notes

In addition to impressions and information gained during visits to Cambodia and Vietnam in 1970 and 1971, this chapter benefits from detailed accounts of the coup that deposed Sihanouk in Chandler's *Tragedy* and Kiernan's *How Pol Pot*. Chandler, in particular, has through interviews gone as far as any writer is likely to do in setting out the sequence of the various plots. I am indebted to his book, p. 198, for the account of Sirik Matak's confrontation with Lon Nol on 18 March.

Other useful sources for the period include Maslyn Williams, *The Land in Between*, New York, 1970, and Meyer, *Derrière*, both of which are valuable for providing a sense of the atmosphere in Phnom Penh during the period. See also Thion and Pomonti, *Des Courtisans;* Shawcross, *Sideshow;* and Kirk, *Wider War.*

Sihanouk's own, and not always reliable, accounts of this period are best studied in *L'Indochine vue de Pékin*, *My War With the CIA*, and *Souvenirs*.

Prince Entaravong spoke of Sihanouk's having considered remounting the throne in the course of discussion on 12 February (Diary 12 February 1970). Meyer's reference to this issue is in *Derrière*, pp. 302–03.

17

From pawn . . .

The decade that followed Sihanouk's fall from power was arguably the most tragic in Cambodia's long history. What had been bloody but episodic encounters between the army and leftist-led rebels were now transformed into full-scale war as Lon Nol's forces battled both indigenous Cambodian communists and their Vietnamese allies. When, by the end of 1972, the Vietnamese troops were withdrawn from Cambodia, the conflict became a civil war that was fought with unremitting savagery by both sides. Adding to the loss of life and destruction wreaked by the war was the devastating campaign of strategic bombing carried out by American B52s until it was halted by Congress in August 1973. When the Cambodian communists, the Khmer Rouge, finally gained their victory in April 1975, the agony of war was followed by the terror of a peace that in less than four years saw the death of hundreds of thousands of people through executions, disease and forced labour. In all of this, Sihanouk's role was limited. Until the Khmer Rouge's victory he was useful as a symbol. Afterwards, he was not even needed in that role, and from late 1975 until the Pol Pot regime was overthrown at the beginning of 1979 he was, as he has termed himself, a 'prisoner of the Khmer Rouge'.

Sifting through the accounts Sihanouk has given of his first few days in Peking after the news of his deposition, one gains a picture of initial confusion, depression and bewilderment followed by fierce anger and a determination to bring down those who had overthrown him, at all costs. While he has chosen to gloss over his hesitations and thoughts of long-term exile, his state of mind is revealed in his admission that when he saw the Vietnamese prime minister, Pham Van Dong, on 22 March he had not slept since receiving news of his overthrow in Moscow four days before.

In accepting Zhou Enlai's proposal to fight on with Chinese support—the prince was later to say that the offer of help came from Mao himself—Sihanouk recognised that he was making a fateful choice. Previously he had seen China as a bulwark against potential Vietnamese domination. Now, he was committing himself to join an alliance that would bring together not just the Chinese but the Cambodian communists, whom his forces had pursued throughout the 1960s, and the Vietnamese communists, whom he had previously condemned for assisting his domestic enemies. Several factors were at play in his mind. Above all was his deep sense of resentment and betrayal, particularly in relation to Lon Nol, but more generally at the Cambodian elite and urban bourgeoisie for turning against him. At the same time, for a while at least, he was ready to concede that he might have been wrong to distrust and persecute those on the left of Cambodian politics. He had once said publicly that he would have been a leftist himself if he had not been born a prince. Now, stripped of power, he found something to admire in those of his fellow countrymen who were ready to fight the new Phnom Penh regime.

Sihanouk was flattered at the attention the Chinese paid him and impressed that they could arrange for Pham Van Dong to fly from Hanoi to Peking within hours of his deciding that he would, indeed, fight to oust Lon Nol and Sirik Matak. Sihanouk's breakfast meeting with Dong could not have seemed other than odd to both men. They had last met some five months before at Ho Chi Minh's funeral in Hanoi. At that time, and despite the occasion and Sihanouk's effusive public demonstration of grief, Pham Van Dong had bluntly complained to Sihanouk about Lon Nol's failure to deliver rice to Vietnamese communist forces for which the general had already been paid. In the dramatically changed circumstances in which Sihanouk now found himself, it was the Vietnamese premier who was ready to be a supplier—of a very different commodity, instructors to train the Cambodian forces that would be used to fight Lon Nol.

There could scarcely be a more striking illustration of politics making strange bedfellows. China and Vietnam, two countries with a long record of distrust for each other, were combining to support a Cambodian communist movement that now took as its nominal head the man whose government had persecuted them throughout the previous decade. Sihanouk gives little indication of having reflected on the irony of the situation. Revenge was his guiding preoccupation. Moreover, at this stage his own understanding of the Cambodian communist movement was both flawed and incomplete. He was unaware that an indigenous movement existed which, while still benefiting from association with the Vietnamese, was determined to become master of Cambodia in its own right and which viewed the necessity of accepting Vietnamese assistance with distaste. Certainly, Sihanouk did not know that at this time of high drama the future Pol Pot, Saloth Sar, was in Peking, though probably not playing any principal role in the feverish manoeuvring that immediately followed Sihanouk's arrival.

On 23 March, the day after his meeting with Pham Van Dong, Sihanouk announced his intention to establish a National United Front of Kampuchea. Speaking over the radio from Peking, he denounced those who had driven him from office and called on the Cambodian population to join in a guerrilla war against the new regime in Phnom Penh.

Sihanouk's call to arms had mixed results. Recorded on cassettes and played in the countryside by Cambodian communists, it undoubtedly was instrumental in recruiting additional fighters to the leftist cause. But it did not result in a sudden groundswell of mass rural protest against the new government in Phnom Penh. Local leftists led violent demonstrations against Sihanouk's deposition in Kompong Cham, Kampot and Takeo. Once they had been forcefully suppressed there were no further rural protests against Lon Nol and Sirik Matak's seizure of power. Many peasants were undoubtedly disturbed and unhappy at what had happened, but the essentially passive nature of the peasantry's support for Sihanouk was now made clear.

Meanwhile, in the first weeks after Sihanouk was toppled, there was abundant evidence that his departure was welcomed by a large proportion of the capital's youth. They flocked to the colours—many to their death. With Sihanouk now heading a front against the Phnom Penh regime, there was no longer any reason for the Vietnamese communist troops within Cambodia to show restraint. As poorly led and ill-equipped young Cambodian soldiers went into battle, the hardened Vietnamese veterans slaughtered them. Slaughter of a different kind took place in Phnom Penh, where Lon Nol allowed his troops to carry out a savage pogrom against the city's Vietnamese population, several thousand of whom were killed in late April and early May. It was rapidly becoming clear that the war taking place in Cambodia would be deeply stained by ethnic antipathies, as Lon Nol and his associates portrayed themselves as fighting for the survival of the Khmer race.

During the early months of his long exile in Peking Sihanouk regained the energy and the sense of purpose that had been so lacking during his last year in Phnom Penh. His deeply wounded *amour-propre* was salved by the flattery and attention showered upon him by Pham Van Dong and by the Chinese government. His new Cambodian communist comrades in arms made the shrewd choice of sending Thiounn Mumm, Cambodia's only *polytechnicien*, from Paris to serve as their principal contact with the prince. Scornful though he often was of intellectuals, Sihanouk secretly admired those who had excelled academically in France. And Mumm, though long a dedicated communist, was well versed in the decorum Sihanouk expected from his compatriots. The son and grandson of powerful court officials, he readily fitted in to Sihanouk's diminished royal household, though Sihanouk later criticised him for showing insufficient respect and for trying to turn others against him. Mumm's replacement, the following year, was the very different, abrasive hard-liner, Ieng Sary.

Accommodated by his Chinese hosts in the considerable comfort of the former French embassy in Peking, Sihanouk set about translating his wish to see the downfall of the new regime in Phnom Penh into practical terms. At the end of April 1970 he presided over a Summit Conference of the Indochinese Peoples, which was attended by Vietnamese, Laotian and Cambodian communist representatives. Then he lent his name to a political program, drafted by Thiounn Mumm, for the front of which he was the titular leader when the program was released in Peking on 3 May. Revealingly, it made no mention of any future role for Sihanouk in Cambodia once the Lon Nol regime was overthrown. Indeed, in the thirteen pages of text of the French version published in Paris, Sihanouk is mentioned by name only once, and in terms of position twice, in references to his broadcast of 23 March. The program was anti-imperialist in tone and aimed at securing the broadest possible support without giving more than the barest hints of the aims of the Cambodian communists.

Despite Sihanouk's voluminous commentaries on these early

months in Peking it is difficult to tell to what extent he recognised that he was being used and slowly but steadily turned into a political pawn. He made much of being head both of a royal government in exile and of the united front of which he was president. In letters, cables and interviews, the prince insisted on his continuing popularity within Cambodia, his centrality to the country's affairs, and his lack of responsibility for the ruthless suppression of the Samlaut Rebellion in Battambang province in 1967. As was the case before his overthrow, no criticism was too distant or obscure not to warrant a reply. Thus, the leader of the New Zealand parliamentary opposition, Norman Kirk, found himself under attack for remarks about Sihanouk reported in the *New Zealand Monthly Review*. These, Sihanouk stated, were 'violent, injurious and unjust', and came from a man who lent support to his 'fascist friend Lon Nol'.

His treatment by the Chinese would certainly have inclined him to believe he still had a major role to play. He was particularly delighted by the attention he received from Mao Zedong, who accorded him a long audience on 1 May 1970. Still mentally alert, Mao played on Sihanouk's almost limitless appetite for praise. Well briefed by his aides, he spoke approvingly of Sihanouk's earlier decision to open a casino in Phnom Penh, clearly aware that its closure while the prince was still in France had been offensive to him. Like his premier, Zhou Enlai, Mao assured the prince that China did not seek a communist Cambodia, simply one that was neutral in international affairs.

Yet it is inconceivable that Sihanouk did not have doubts about the future course of an alliance with men whom he knew were dedicated communists. Thiounn Mumm could present the reasonable face of Marxism to Sihanouk, but how could he believe that Khieu Samphan, Hou Youn and Hu Nim would put aside their past differences with him? These were men he had threatened with trial and death. He knew they were communists and, his brave words to journalists such as Jean Lacouture notwithstanding, it defies belief that he truly expected—even in 1971—they 'would respect the Buddhist beliefs of our fellow citizens'.

The presence of doubt in Sihanouk's mind would go some way towards explaining his repeated insistence in 1970 and 1971 that he did not wish to return to Cambodia to assume any position of power. He spoke of how he had become a 'new' Sihanouk, a person who was conscious of his past errors, of the need to control his 'explosive personality'. Perhaps he would allow his compatriots to name him as chief of state, he suggested, but even if they did he would not seek to exercise power. And while he would be happy to represent Cambodia at international gatherings, he would want to live away from the capital. Phnom Penh held too many memories for him, he maintained, both of his efforts to embellish it and of the humiliation he had suffered at the hands of his former associates in that city. The image of Sihanouk contemplating a voluntary relinquishment of the opportunity to exercise power is unconvincing, but he may well have begun to understand how little time his communist allies had for his services.

Whatever illusions he may have held about the true nature of his communist allies, these were severely undermined with the arrival in Peking of Ieng Sary in 1971. A committed communist since his time in Paris in the 1950s, he had gone into the *maquis* in 1963. Sent to the Chinese capital by the Communist Party of Kampuchea, Ieng Sary's task was to ensure that Sihanouk did not in any way undermine the image of a united front fighting against the Lon Nol regime. Almost immediately Sihanouk reacted hostilely to Sary, whom he found rigid, dogmatic and personally offensive. For the moment, however, he did not voice these feelings publicly. He was still charged with the energy generated by his resentment of his overthrow and outraged by shifts in American policy towards Cambodia, in particular the military incursion into the country ordered by President Nixon in May 1970.

He was even further angered by his condemnation to death at his trial *in absentia* in July 1970 (Monique was sentenced to life imprisonment) and by the treatment his mother, Queen Kossamak, and various of his children and relatives had received from the new regime, which had declared Cambodia a republic in October 1970. His outrage at his mother's fate was deeply felt. He found it intolerable that she should be a virtual prisoner in Phnom Penh, deprived of most of her privileges and denied the opportunity to go into exile. Yet even as he expressed his anger over this situation, Sihanouk could not hide his long-standing ambivalence towards his mother. As well as condemning her treatment, when he spoke to Wilfred Burchett in 1971, the prince thought it necessary to detail how his mother had mistakenly trusted men such as Sim Var and In Tam who now supported the Lon Nol government in Phnom Penh.

By early 1973 the tide of battle had swung decisively in favour of the communist-led forces in Cambodia and the Cambodian com-

munist party was firmly embarked on eliminating Vietnamese influence from within its ranks. The military incompetence of Lon Nol's
forces had been brutally exposed and the indiscriminate nature of
their attacks, combined with resentment of the continued American bombing, had driven increasing numbers of peasants into the
Khmer Rouge ranks. By this time, too, the corrupt character of the
Phnom Penh regime was abundantly apparent, leading many in the
capital to reassess their earlier enthusiasm for the new leadership
and some to join the insurgents, whom they mistakenly believed
were actually led by Sihanouk. The time was ripe for a *coup de
théâtre* in the form of a visit by Sihanouk to Cambodia's liberated
zones.

Although the Cambodian communists had been deliberately
minimising the importance of the prince within the areas they
controlled, their leaders recognised his continuing value in terms
of influencing international opinion. To be able to show him
visiting Cambodia and being greeted by those who were said to be
fighting in his name would be a major public relations success,
particularly at a time when international abhorrence at the hostilities throughout Indochina was gathering momentum. Chinese and
Vietnamese cooperation was required for this exercise, and the
leaders in both Peking and Hanoi may have seen the proposed
journey and their support for Sihanouk as a way of protecting their
influence in Cambodia, for it was increasingly apparent that the
Cambodian communists were inclined towards a chauvinistic independence that paid scant attention to the interests of their allies.

Beginning in late February 1973, Sihanouk, Monique, the
ever-present Ieng Sary as 'minder', and more than a hundred
Vietnamese to assist and supervise travel down the Ho Chi Minh
trail, left southern China headed for Cambodia. Travelling in
Soviet-made jeeps, they reached Cambodian territory after eight
days on the road and were met by Hu Nim, whom Sihanouk had
regarded as a bitter enemy only five years before, and Son Sen, a
leading military figure in the Khmer Rouge. Travelling on, they
were joined by Khieu Samphan and Saloth Sar, the future Pol Pot,
and later again by Hou Youn and Sar's wife, Khieu Ponnary.
Sihanouk now had about him the three men whom many had
assumed he had condemned to death; men whom he had repeatedly castigated as traitors and enemies while he was still in power.

The prince's party ended its journey at Phnom Kulen, just to
the north of the Angkor ruins. From this base, over several days
in mid-February Sihanouk and Monique took part in a series of
ceremonies recorded on movie film and in still photographs and

designed to show that Sihanouk was, indeed, the leader of the forces fighting against Lon Nol and Sirik Matak's regime. The pictures have a surreal quality, showing as they do the prince and Monique dressed in the black peasant costume that was the Khmer Rouge 'uniform'. In photograph after photograph, Sihanouk is seen smiling, surrounded by the communist leaders, in front of Angkorian period ruins, and before massed ranks of stern-faced Khmer Rouge men and women soldiers. Monique's diary, written in the course of their travels, reveals a naive pleasure in the attention and consideration she and Sihanouk received. The prince himself has written little about his feelings during this journey of more than a month. He has described being under bombardment from American aircraft and of being shocked by the evidence he saw of the devastation caused by US bombing. He has written, too, of his surprise that relations between the Vietnamese communists and their Cambodian allies were tense, so much so that he was asked by a senior Vietnamese official not to speak favourably of the assistance given to the Khmer Rouge by the Hanoi government, 'because our Cambodian comrades are so touchy on the subject'. But he has not mentioned what it was like to be so obviously used by the Cambodian communists. And by now, his relations with Ieng Sary and even the less abrasive Thiounn Mumm had reached a point where his resentment at the diminished role he was allowed to play conflicted with his passionate determination to bring down the Phnom Penh regime.

This conflict of emotions burst into the open shortly after his visit to Cambodia. During a round of visits to countries that supported the Cambodian front, Sihanouk allowed his feelings to boil over. In a widely quoted interview with the Italian journalist Oriana Fallaci that was published in *The New York Times Magazine*, Sihanouk insisted that he fully supported the Khmer Rouge, then launched a direct personal attack on Ieng Sary and admitted that he knew that when he was no longer of use to them the Cambodian communists would 'spit him out'.

But despite the poor treatment he received from his communist compatriots, despite their criticism of his still lavish dining habits, which included importing *foie gras* from France at Chinese expense, Sihanouk genuinely believed that it was his patriotic duty to stay linked to men who he knew despised him. Whatever else, the Cambodian communists were showing that they had the capacity to defeat the Lon Nol regime.

The story of why the republican regime that replaced Sihanouk did not fall earlier to the Khmer Rouge–led forces has been told many times elsewhere. To Lon Nol's military incompetence was linked his physical frailty—he had a stroke in 1971—and a devotion to mystics, astrologers and geomancers that placed a belief in the supernatural above the harsh practicalities of politics and war. But he was not without political ambition, and he saw his deputy, Prince Sirik Matak, as too obviously a potential challenger. Under pressure from demonstrations orchestrated by Lon Nol's brother, Lon Non, in early 1972, Matak declared he had opted out of politics. Later the same year, Son Ngoc Thanh, Sihanouk's old enemy, who had come to the capital soon after the 1970 coup to claim a long-desired position at the heart of Phnom Penh politics, accepted that there was no place for him in the Lon Nol regime and returned to South Vietnam. A weak and frightened man was now in charge of the Cambodian government, propped up by United States aid and surrounded by self-serving advisers.

Even in the face of imminent defeat, or in some cases perhaps because of it, many of those linked to the Phnom Penh government were ready to accept a decline in even the most rudimentary standards of public administration. For many of the elite Phnom Penh became a sink of corruption. Military officers profited by drawing the pay of soldiers who were no longer members of the units they commanded, and in some cases sold weapons directly to their enemy. Conditions within Cambodia deteriorated atrociously as peasants driven out of the countryside by the fighting and the American bombing flocked into Phnom Penh and provincial capitals. By early 1974, Phnom Penh was swollen with hundreds of thousands of refugees and under irregular but frequently fatal bombardment by rockets and artillery, which the insurgents fired into the capital with no regard for the civilian casualties they caused.

Yet victory still eluded the Cambodian communist insurgents. Despite the corruption and weakness that characterised the leadership in Phnom Penh, there were still government troops who were ready to fight under the most extreme conditions—including, as the renowned Australian news cameraman Neil Davis reported, resorting to cannibalism to feed themselves during a prolonged siege. But in the end the raw courage that many government units displayed could not prevent what had become an inevitable progression towards a Khmer Rouge triumph. Efforts to establish a dialogue with Sihanouk's united front failed. As early as August 1973, Sirik Matak had sent an open letter to his cousin that combined criticism of the prince's past policies with an emotional appeal for him to bring the war to an end. Sihanouk rejected all advances, including those that came belatedly from the United States. However strained his relations with his communist allies, the prince was now determined to see the total humiliation of Lon Nol and his supporters. More to the point, he was no longer in a position to determine the united front's policy even if he wanted to. There were some limited possibilities for him to act on his own initiative, but these were in matters far removed from the great issues of war and peace. So, in early 1975, as the insurgents' forces drew ever nearer to capturing Phnom Penh, he wrote to the American president, Gerald Ford, asking for the United States embassy in Phnom Penh to find and send him any copies of his films that remained in the capital. President Ford, who had previously earned Sihanouk's gratitude by arranging for Queen Kossamak to leave Cambodia in 1973, acceded to this request and some of the prince's films were preserved for posterity.

The end of the Cambodian Republic came on 17 April 1975. By that date Lon Nol and his family had fled the country, as had many other wealthy and well-placed members of the government and armed forces. Those leaders who remained behind had few illusions about their fate. Long Boret, republican Cambodia's last prime minister, was executed shortly after the Khmer Rouge entered Phnom Penh. So, too, was Prince Sisowath Sirik Matak, who had written a bitter letter to the American president shortly before Phnom Penh fell, denouncing the United States for abandoning Cambodia in its most desperate hour of need. If these executions might have been expected at the end of a bloody civil war, nothing prepared Cambodia's non-combatant population for the events that followed immediately upon the communist victory. Within days, hundreds of those linked with the defeated regime were executed and the bulk of Phnom Penh's population was forcibly driven out of the city. 'Year Zero' had begun and with it the horrors of the Pol Pot regime. In Peking, Sihanouk issued a statement lauding the insurgents' victory and glorying in the defeat of American imperialism.

Notes

This chapter draws on Sihanouk's own writings, notably *L'Indochine vue de Pékin*, *Souvenirs*, *War and Hope: The Case for Cambodia*, London, 1980, and, above all *Prisonnier des Khmers Rouges*, Paris, 1986. As with previous periods, David Chandler's *Tragedy* provides an essential overview of the events described. Other useful insights for the period up to the Khmer Rouge victory in 1975 can be gained from Kirk, *Wider War*; Becker, *When the War Was Over*, Shawcross, *Sideshow*, and Craig Etcheson, *The Rise and Demise of Democratic Kampuchea*, Boulder, Colorado, 1985.

For detail on developments within Khmer Rouge ranks during this period, Kiernan, *How Pol Pot*, is once again the key text, with Chandler's more recent *Brother Number One* providing valuable additional material as the result of further research.

The quotation from Sihanouk's letter concerning Norman Kirk is contained in an undated pamphlet published in Paris under the title *Prince Norodom Sihanouk replies to Mr Norman Kirk, M.P., Leader of the Opposition (New Zealand)*, and the quotation concerning Buddhist beliefs is from *L'Indochine vue de Pékin*, p. 157. The prince provides his account of the 'new Sihanouk' on p. 117 of the same book.

For Sihanouk's comments on his mother's having mistakenly trusted Lon Nol and Sim Var, see *My War With the CIA*, pp. 217–18.

Sihanouk provides a brief account of the 1973 visit to Cambodia in *War and Hope*, p. 16 and following. Chandler, in *Tragedy*, p. 227 and following, quotes from Monique's journal kept during this visit. In a personal communication, David Chandler has told me that Sihanouk may deal with this period in more detail in as yet unpublished further memoirs.

The interview with Oriana Fallaci was published on 12 August 1973. Other interviews echoing that which he had with Fallaci may be found in *Le Monde*, 27 October 1973 and *The Guardian*, 18 September 1973.

Neil Davis's account of cannibalism is in Tim Bowden, *One Crowded Hour*, Sydney, 1987, pp. 297–8. Davis gave me a detailed account of this development in a series of conversations in Bangkok and provincial Thailand in late 1979.

For Sirik Matak's letter to Sihanouk in August 1973, see FBIS 27 August 1973.

18

... to prisoner

Despite the robust tone of his victory message, Sihanouk remained in Peking. Three months earlier, while participating in New Year celebrations in Hanoi, he had spoken of his plans for the future to Ieng Sary, in the presence of the Vietnamese leadership. With victory achieved, Sihanouk told Sary, he would resign his public office and return to live in Cambodia as a simple citizen. Now that victory had been achieved, he was uncertain what he should do and made no move to carry out his foreshadowed retirement. For their part, the Khmer Rouge leaders showed no inclination to hasten the prince's return to Phnom Penh. Although Sihanouk did not fully realise what was happening at the time, he had now become an embarrassment to the Khmer Rouge and a cause for difficulty between them and the Chinese government, which had been such an important supporter of their cause while the war was still being fought. For a time, his sense of unease was subordinated to concern for his mortally ill mother, who finally died on 27 April, but by the middle of the year he was prey to conflicting emotions. On the one hand, he had been absorbing the worrying accounts that were emerging of the radical measures being enacted by the Khmer Rouge victors in Cambodia. Incomplete and limited in detail though these were, the picture they presented was unrelievedly grim. On the other hand, he remained attached to Cambodia and felt humiliated that he, as president of the united front that had won victory, was not able to return to the country where that victory had been achieved.

In his desire to return to Cambodia, Sihanouk had two trumps to play. He had the support of China and North Korea, and of those two countries' leaders. With Mao, Sihanouk believed he enjoyed something approaching a father–son relationship. With Kim Il-Sung, for reasons that have never been very clear, Sihanouk found comfort in an extraordinary exchange of mutual admiration. To this foreign support was added the fact that he still held some value to the Khmer Rouge leadership as the acceptable face of the front that defeated Lon Nol, provided they were able to control his activities. So, in September 1975, more than four months after the Khmer Rouge capture of Phnom Penh, Sihanouk was permitted return to his country.

The prince has written of his return to Phnom Penh and of his later enforced sojourn in Cambodia from January 1976 until January 1979 in his lengthy memoir *Prisonnier de Khmers Rouges*, which he compiled with the assistance of a French sympathiser, the writer Simonne Lacouture. Composed in a rambling, stream-of-consciousness style, the book is both self-indulgent and revealing, as Sihanouk cannot pass up the opportunity to refer self-pityingly to the 'splendour' of his past while recording with pain the humiliations he endured as a political prisoner. The record of what he saw and suffered is interspersed with idiosyncratic references to the gauche dining habits of the Khmer Rouge leadership and the pleasure he took in the behaviour of a family of mice that lived in his quarters. Although he expresses pain over the fate of his compatriots and grieves for the loss of his children and close relatives at the hands of the Khmer Rouge, the book is imbued with his intense preoccupation with self. What is more, although at times he was plagued by illness and plunged into despair—even times when he genuinely wondered if his own life was at risk—the memoir reveals that, physically, the prince's house arrest was far from arduous. He and Monique were accommodated in the royal palace and even enjoyed air conditioning, a blessing for the prince since he 'does not like the heat'.

But his trials and tribulations were still to come when he left Peking for Phnom Penh in September 1975, carrying in his mind the admonition given him by Chairman Mao shortly before his departure. He should remember, said Mao, that the reasons for accord between him and the Cambodian communists outweighed the reasons for discord. For nineteen days Sihanouk, nominally chief of state of Cambodia, remained in Phnom Penh, only once leaving the palace compound for a river trip. His account of this period makes contradictory reading. While still in Peking he had received many reports of the forced evacuation of Cambodia's cities and of the systematic killing of senior officials in the Lon Nol regime. Sihanouk says he was 'bowled over' by the sight of Phnom Penh as a dead city. But he professes to have believed Khieu Samphan and other Khmer Rouge leaders when they claimed that the city's population was now working in the countryside—working hard, it was true, but doing so of their own free will.

Possibly, Sihanouk simply did not know what to believe. Certainly, he was eager to accept the assurances of those relatives and former associates who had linked their fortunes to the Khmer Rouge before the fall of Phnom Penh when they extolled the spartan virtues of the new regime. In some measure, Sihanouk's claim that he found his first, brief stay in Phnom Penh 'relatively agreeable' can be read as a justification for the visits he now made on the new government's behalf to the United Nations and to an assortment of countries, including China, North Korea, Syria, Roumania, Tanzania and Yugoslavia, that recognised the new regime and showed some sympathy towards it. But his ambivalence about his new circumstances was apparent in the offer he made to his personal staff while visiting Peking in October. He would, he declared, return to Cambodia at some future date, but he was not going to insist that they accompany him. Most chose not to do so.

By December 1975, Sihanouk was in Pyongyang enjoying the attentive hospitality of Kim Il-Sung. It was here, in the North Korean capital, that he received a letter from Khieu Samphan which provided the clearest indication of the position Sihanouk might expect to occupy when he returned to Phnom Penh. Nouth Chhoeurm, a former spokesman for the prince, had told representatives of the Western press what he had heard of conditions in Phnom Penh from members of Sihanouk's party who had accompanied the prince to Cambodia in September. The sombre picture he painted was seized on by newspapers in France and Hong Kong and eventually came to the notice of the Khmer Rouge leadership in Phnom Penh. Writing to the prince on behalf of his colleagues, Khieu Samphan upbraided Sihanouk for the calumnies put abroad by his former employee, making clear that the prince was being held responsible for the information Nouth Chhoeurm had given the press. Samphan concluded his letter with an unveiled warning that Sihanouk found deeply insulting. In acting as he had, the prince was told, 'you have nothing to gain and everything to lose'.

Sihanouk briefly considered resigning his position as chief of state and going into exile in France. Once again he endured sleepless nights, but in the end he decided to return. He had to do so, he has written, because of his love for his people and his need to share their fate. This is believable, as is his description of that love as being so intense that it was 'carnal' in character. Notwithstanding his later assertions, he can have had few illusions about what was happening in his homeland, so his decision to return was indeed brave. To some extent it was also forced upon him. Mao's injunction still applied: the Chinese expected him to return and Sihanouk could not easily disregard their wishes. Finally, though he does not list it among the motives that were involved in his decision, it is probable that the prince, forced to choose between returning to Phnom Penh and going into exile, reflected on how history would judge him if he chose the latter course. It had not been his choice to spend the years between 1970 and 1975 in Peking. Now the choice *was* his, and he had often expressed his near contempt for the kind of life lived by another former Indochinese monarch, the exiled Vietnamese emperor Bao Dai. At times, when he had been in France, Sihanouk had even been mistaken for Bao Dai. To be a permanent exile was singularly unattractive prospect. Reluctantly, on 31 December 1975, Sihanouk went home. Three years were to pass before he next crossed his country's borders.

Sihanouk's doubts about what lay ahead were reinforced as soon as he stepped from the aircraft at Phnom Penh's Pochentong airport. There was an honour guard, but more striking to Sihanouk was the assembled crowd of workers, dressed in black peasant clothing, who greeted his arrival with shouted slogans extolling the peerless virtues of *angkar*, the shadowy 'organisation' in whose name the Khmer Rouge forces had fought and which now, more than the formal government of the state, controlled Cambodia. As Sihanouk, Monique, Monique's mother and a few close members of his household took in the scene, Sihanouk records that his 'fixed smile was itself ridiculous'.

So began Sihanouk's life in what he himself terms his 'gilded prison'. To the Khmer Rouge leadership, he was already only marginally important. They saw some value in having him preside over a meeting that endorsed a new constitution for Democratic Kampuchea on 5 January 1976, but beyond this they had no intention of giving the prince any substantive role to play. He, Monique and his tiny 'royal' household were lodged, comfortably enough, in the royal palace. Despite the destruction the new masters of Phnom Penh had wreaked elsewhere, the living quarters of the palace were largely untouched and Sihanouk had access to a library, received newspapers from abroad and was able to listen to the radio. In the early weeks of his confinement, he was even able to entertain the ambassadors of those few countries that had sent diplomats to Phnom Penh after April 1975 at dinners, which were also attended by senior Khmer Rouge figures. But reality was soon to trouble this 'unreal world'. In February 1976, Sihanouk accompanied Khieu Samphan on a provincial tour which, for the first time, allowed Sihanouk to see what life under the new government was really like.

He was shocked, he recalls in his memoir, though it is not always apparent what shocked him more—the fate of the masses he saw labouring in the fields or the damage done to the buildings in which he had once received famous foreign visitors. His concern for the anonymous black-clad workers hunched over their tools seems to have been equalled by his sadness at the destruction of a provincial villa in which he had entertained such visitors as 'Prince Raimondo Orsini of Italy, the famous German actor Kurt Jurgens and Tunku Abdul Rahman, the prime minister of Malaysia'. Photos of his progress through the northern provinces of Cambodia show him smiling his familiar public smile. It was a smile that he wore clearly believing he had no other choice if he was to remain alive. He still had no firm understanding of the extent of the new regime's capacity for evil, but he had seen enough to decide that he could no longer lend his name to Democratic Kampuchea. Back in Phnom Penh he decided in March to resign his position as chief of state and to seek the government's permission to travel to Peking for medical treatment.

Sihanouk's hope that he could extricate himself and his entourage from Cambodia was in vain. As David Chandler has shown, drawing on records of the Communist Party of Kampuchea's standing committee, Sihanouk's letter of resignation evoked a sharp response from Pol Pot. The Khmer Rouge leader dismissed the suggestion that the prince could resign, observing that he had already done so in 1971—a reference to the year when Ieng Sary had gone to Peking to be Sihanouk's 'minder'. In Pol Pot's eyes, the prince was indeed an embarrassment, but he could still be of some use to the communists if he remained in Cambodia. On the one hand, his continuing presence was a counter to Vietnamese criticism of the Phnom Penh regime's radical character. On the other, to allow him to leave might cause problems with the Khmer Rouge's major patron, the Chinese government. Sihanouk's valued supporter, Zhou Enlai, had died in January, but the Khmer Rouge could not assume that others in the Chinese leadership would not be concerned about his fate. In the light of these considerations, Khieu Samphan was sent to tell Sihanouk that he should withdraw his resignation and remain in Phnom Penh.

There is some doubt about what happened next. The records that Chandler has consulted indicate that a now terrified Sihanouk begged Samphan to be allowed to resign and that only after a further meeting of the Khmer Rouge leadership was it decided to accept his resignation and to spare his life. His resignation, dated 2 April 1976, was then accepted.

The account provided by the communist records has the ring of truth. Sihanouk's version of this fateful period is less detailed. He writes in his memoir of the efforts made by senior Khmer Rouge leaders to dissuade him from resigning, but links their final decision to act against him to his suggestion that if he were allowed to attend a Nonaligned Movement's meeting in Colombo he might use the occasion to seek his liberty. After he had spoken in this bold fashion, Sihanouk has written, Khieu Samphan told him that his wish to resign would be examined in the light of what the prince had said.

The two accounts are not necessarily contradictory. Whatever the details of events in late March and early April 1976, the final outcome was absolutely clear. On 16 April, a day short of a year since the Khmer Rouge forces had entered Phnom Penh, and without further consulting Sihanouk, Samphan announced the chief of state's resignation. The prince, he said, was a 'great patriot'. In recognition of this, he was to be honoured by a statue and would receive an annual pension from the state of $US8000. For all practical purposes, Sihanouk was now removed from Cambodian political life. While they honoured neither of their undertakings—no statue was erected and no pension was paid—the Khmer Rouge chose not to kill Sihanouk. Why they did not do so will never be entirely certain, for they had no hesitation in eliminating many of his children, grandchildren and other close relatives. Concern for foreign, particularly Chinese reaction is probably the principal explanation, coupled with the notion that at some future date the prince's international prestige might just be of use to the regime. With these and perhaps other calculations in mind, they were prepared to allow Sihanouk a relatively comfortable confinement, sheltered from the barbarities that were now the normal, awful fate of so many of his compatriots.

While Sihanouk uses the word 'unreal' to describe existence during his confinement in Phnom Penh, his deeply personal and detailed memoir of this period often suggests that 'surreal' might be a better description. Sihanouk had effectively become a 'non-person' to the Khmer Rouge, yet in his limited dealings with its leaders he chose to address them formally, and they to show him, in the words they used at least, the respect due to a former king. But while Sihanouk could bring himself to congratulate Khieu Samphan on his 'gripping success' at the meeting of the Nonaligned Movement held in Colombo in August 1976, the new regime did not reciprocate by showing any readiness to grant the prince's requests to be allowed to travel to Peking, first for medical treatment and then, in September 1976, to attend Mao Zedong's funeral. As Sihanouk wrestled mentally with the ambiguities of his position, he watched with dismay as the grounds of the royal palace slowly deteriorated and the buildings scattered through the palace compound became more and more dilapidated. Uncertainty was his greatest enemy and in November 1976 he could contain himself no longer. To Monique's deep distress, he vented his feelings to Khieu Samphan, demanding to know if he was to be kept a prisoner for life, prevented from travelling even in his own country. If this was the case, Sihanouk dramatically concluded, 'let *angkar* shoot me'.

Four months elapsed before the Khmer Rouge leadership reacted to Sihanouk's anger and frustration. He was unimportant in their greater scheme of things. The disastrous reorganisation of Cambodian society was continuing, with vast rural and hydraulic works being undertaken through the use of forced labour. Perhaps even more important to the communist leadership were the signs of dissent and disagreement that had emerged within their own ranks and which led, by the second half of 1976, to increasingly savage purges by Pol Pot and his closest associates. A still mysterious aspect of this period was the publicly announced resignation of Pol Pot as prime minister in September. Whatever the reason for this brief retirement, for he took up his office again the following month, it can, at the very least, be regarded as an index of instability and disarray in the top ranks of the Khmer Rouge. By comparison, Sihanouk's position barely rated consideration. But eventually, there came a response to the prince's remarks. On 30 March 1977, a Khmer Rouge functionary brusquely told the prince that domestic servants would no longer service his household. What Sihanouk has described as 'the punishment of *angkar*' had begun.

After all the uncertainties of the previous months, Sihanouk,

Monique and his small entourage feared that the withdrawal of their domestic staff was at last the sign of their impending death. Their fear was heightened by the fact that they received no supplies of food for three days. But, after sleepless nights as they waited to be taken away, food was once again brought in. Monique now shared the task of cooking with her female relatives, and life within their quarters again settled into an approximation of normality.

Normality was increasingly a relative concept and the strain that this period imposed on Sihanouk is abundantly apparent in his memoir. A little more than two weeks after this new level of 'punishment' had begun, his faithful *aide de camp*, Ong Meang, disappeared. One of his regular chores was to take the household garbage away from their living quarters in a wheelbarrow and throw it into the Tonle Sap River in front of the palace. On 18 April he never returned from this task. Sihanouk was certain that he had been seized and murdered by the Khmer Rouge. Mourning this loss, the prince was further depressed by the continuing degradation of the royal palace buildings and grounds. Buffalos, sheep and goats were driven into the royal compound to feed in the gardens and the Khmer Rouge soldiers who lived and slept in the palace buildings showed no concern for their upkeep.

With deepening despondency, Sihanouk listened to international shortwave radio broadcasts, which provided an increasingly sombre picture of developments within Cambodia. He has recorded the dreams he had during this period, believing them to be predictive in character—a psychologist would see in them at the least a reflection of a deeply worried individual. By now Sihanouk was pondering the extent of his own responsibility for the fate of his relatives, as he tried unsuccessfully to learn what had happened to those of his children and grandchildren who were held outside the palace grounds. Adding to his distress was the presence, living with him, of his son Narindrapong, who had become a vehement partisan of the Khmer Rouge and an unrestrained critic of his father. In sum, the middle months of 1977 were the time when Sihanouk's spirits were at their lowest ebb.

Outside the palace in which the prince was confined, momentous developments were taking place. Of the greatest importance for the future course of Sihanouk's life was the rapid deterioration in relations between the government in Phnom Penh and the Vietnamese government in Hanoi. More immediately impinging upon him was the revelation, in September 1977, of the existence of the Communist Party of Kampuchea. For Sihanouk, as for the rest of the world, the true character of *angkar* was now, at least in part, revealed. Throughout its existence the Cambodian communist movement had been intensely secretive. Before 1975 its leaders had seen this as necessary for the party's survival. Once in power, Pol Pot and his close associates relied on secrecy to consolidate their position against those they judged internal enemies. The revelation of the party's existence in 1977 reflected, in part at least, pressure from China on its clients to acknowledge their true political identity at a time when they depended on Peking for assistance against Vietnam. The pretence that Democratic Kampuchea was a state like others, and that the parliamentary deputies had a role to play following the elections that had been held in March 1976, was no longer to be sustained. In a five-hour-long speech shortly before he went to Peking to join in China's national day celebrations, Pol Pot told of the CPK's foundation in 1960, thus emphasising its separateness from Vietnamese communism, and revealed that the party was the supreme authority in Cambodia.

After the revelation of the CPK's existence, Sihanouk was asked to write the party a letter of congratulation to mark the occasion. He hesitated, then complied, believing that if he failed to do so his children and other relatives might pay with their lives. He later learned that this gesture had had no effect and that most of his relatives who were still in Cambodia had been killed during 1976 and 1977. Those killed included Naradipo, whom Sihanouk had named as his successor years before. In one of his frankest admissions of remorse, he has commented that, 'When I knew the truth, I said to myself that my refusal to serve Pol Pot's Kampuchea from April 1976 carried with it, perhaps, some responsibility for the elimination of my relatives. But in working with the Khmer Rouge I would have betrayed the confidence of the millions of my compatriots who were the victims of worse horrors. I torture myself [thinking about this].' Whether this passage should also be read as Sihanouk's acceptance of guilt for the period—1970 to 1976—when he *did* work with the Khmer Rouge is not clear.

From this time on, and to his surprise, the conditions under which Sihanouk was detained began to improve slowly. He writes of being anguished by the readiness of the Chinese government to receive and lend public support to Pol Pot and, in January 1978, he was distressed that he was not permitted to meet Zhou Enlai's widow when she visited Phnom Penh. But his treatment within the palace was better and he had opportunities, once again, to make short trips into the provinces. The reason for this improved state of affairs was not hard for Sihanouk to discern. The rapidly deteriorating relations between Cambodia and Vietnam, which had involved increasingly vicious cross-border raids by both sides, flared into open warfare at the end of December 1977. Intending to give a severe warning to the Phnom Penh government, Vietnamese armed forces advanced rapidly into Cambodia along a broad front.

With their immensely superior armour and artillery, some of the Vietnamese troops reached within 50 kilometres of the Cambodian capital before withdrawing, having inflicted heavy casualties. Just why the Khmer Rouge leadership failed to recognise this limited Vietnamese invasion for what it was—a threat to overthrow them if they did not mend their ways—will remain a matter for debate. Relying on support from China, but more importantly possessed of an almost millennial belief in their own invulnerability, Pol Pot and his closest associates publicly claimed victory and continued to pursue policies that confronted and provoked the Vietnamese. At the same time they set in train a massive purge in eastern Cambodia. Yet, however irrational they were in acting as if they had achieved a victory, they saw some value in a marginal rehabilitation of Sihanouk. To treat him better, Pol Pot appears to have concluded, might be a further factor in ensuring Chinese support.

The fact that he was being partially rehabilitated became clearer to the prince in the second half of 1978, as relations between Cambodia and Vietnam became even more tense. In August 1978, Sihanouk was taken by Khieu Samphan to see the regime's 'achievements' in the countryside close to Phnom Penh. He was again shocked by what he saw, but followed his practice of speaking nothing but praise for the policies of the regime, still fearing that to do otherwise would be to risk death. Early the next month, he travelled with an unnamed senior Khmer Rouge army officer to Kompong Som, the port on the Gulf of Siam previously known as Sihanoukville. As in his description of his travels in February 1976, the prince's account of this excursion blends references to his despair at seeing his compatriots engaged in forced labour with equally profound shock at the way in which the Khmer Rouge had treated his villas in Kompong Som. Taken to meet the Chinese workers who were manning the port's facilities, Sihanouk was convinced that he had been brought to Kompong Som with the express intention of reassuring the Peking government that he was still alive and well.

The need for the Khmer Rouge leadership to provide this

reassurance was daily growing more important as hostilities along the Vietnamese–Cambodian border grew in intensity. China was now the only foreign friend on whom the Phnom Penh government could rely and, as rationality began to triumph over the policies of the Gang of Four, there was growing concern in Peking about the behaviour of its southern client and the treatment of Sihanouk.

In the same month as his visit to Kompong Som, the Phnom Penh authorities told Sihanouk that he and his household were to be moved to a new location, distant from the palace. He was surprised but acquiescent and then pleased, for the new quarters were more agreeable than the by now run-down rooms they had occupied since the beginning of 1976. When he asked Khieu Samphan for his household goods to be moved to his new residence, his request was readily complied with. And to Sihanouk's further surprise he now received another testament to his apparent change of status in the form of delicacies brought back to Phnom Penh by Ieng Sary from a visit to the United Nations in New York. Sihanouk writes with almost audible delight of his pleasure in this sudden unexpected gift of French *pâté de foie*, Swiss cheeses, and sausages from Italy and Germany.

He did not know it, but the reasons for his change of residence went beyond a Khmer Rouge readiness to treat him better as relations with Vietnam soured further. By September 1978 the leadership in Phnom Penh was undoubtedly aware of Vietnamese plans to back a new, protégé front that could eventually be installed in its place. If Sihanouk could be snatched from Khmer Rouge control, he would be a rich prize and might be persuaded to head the new, anti–Khmer Rouge front. Unlike many of their other views, this concern of Pol Pot and his associates was not woven from fantasy, for towards the end of December 1978 just such an attempt was made by a Vietnamese commando unit. The commandos were intercepted by Cambodian soldiers and killed.

However unreal or surreal Sihanouk's experiences since his return to Cambodia at the end of 1975, they scarcely prepared him for the bizarre proceedings that marked his final period of captivity. Hard on the heels of Ieng Sary's gift of delicacies, the prince received a visit from Khieu Samphan, who came to his residence to invite him to dinner. On 28 September, Sihanouk and Monique dined at the former residence of the French high commissioner in Cambodia, a building that had been used during his time in power as a setting for state occasions. Greeted on their arrival by Khieu Samphan and Ieng Sary, Sihanouk and Monique were told that the dinner was being held to honour them. The truth was different. Having endured a long monologue from Ieng Sary on the theme of the invincibility of Democratic Kampuchea, Sihanouk learned that the event had been staged so photographs taken of him and Monique could be used by the Chinese government to suggest that the prince still played a central role in his country.

All the while, a full-scale Vietnamese invasion grew more likely. The Vietnamese government, with which Phnom Penh had severed diplomatic relations at the beginning of 1978, urged the Khmer Rouge regime to reconsider its policies and to negotiate for a peaceful solution. Concurrently, Vietnamese radio trumpeted the success of the National Front for the Salvation of Kampuchea, an organisation led by two defectors from the Khmer Rouge administration, Heng Samrin and Pen Sovan, in battles with Phnom Penh's forces.

As Sihanouk noted the continuing improvement in his living conditions, marked by better and more generous supplies of provisions, the sound of artillery could now clearly be heard in Phnom Penh as barrages and counter-barrages were exchanged to the east of the city. The final weeks of Sihanouk's stay in Cambodia were part of an extraordinary jumble of events. The Khmer Rouge were now under increasing pressure from China to try and improve their tarnished international image. In March 1978 they had permitted a Yugoslav film crew to travel to specially selected sites within Cambodia to present the 'triumphs' of the regime to the outside world. Now arrangements were made for a party of tourists to visit the Angkor ruins, flying in from Bangkok and out again on the same day. And in an unprecedented gesture, two American journalists and a British academic were given the opportunity to travel through the country in December and to interview Pol Pot. This initiative ended with the killing of the academic, Malcolm Caldwell, in circumstances that have still not been fully explained.

Much of what was taking place was unknown to Sihanouk. He continued to follow developments as best he could through short-wave broadcasts, so that he was well and truly aware of the Vietnamese invasion when it finally began during the night of 24–25 December. Without placing the account in a precise time frame, Sihanouk says that right up till his final departure from Phnom Penh on 6 January 1979 he hoped to be allowed to go into the *maquis* with Khieu Samphan and that with this in mind, he and Monique had prepared their black pyjamas and rubber sandals for the flight that now seemed only days away. Given all that he had gone through and all that he now knew about those who had confined him in Phnom Penh, this seems a bizarre assertion that can only be explained in terms of a wish on Sihanouk's part to show, retrospectively, that when it came to resisting Vietnamese aggression he was at least as committed as the Khmer Rouge.

Whatever the prince's true hopes, the Khmer Rouge leadership had other plans for him. On 1 January the nameless official who had accompanied Sihanouk to Kompong Som suddenly appeared to tell him and Monique that they were to leave Phnom Penh with him. The prince feared that this was the end, that execution awaited him somewhere in the countryside. But in a commentary that mixes the banal with the trivial, he describes how he and Monique, accompanied by the members of their household, set off in a convoy of three cars. During his confinement, Sihanouk had become sensitive to the type and size of vehicle his captors provided for any travel away from the capital, seeing these as a measure of his standing—a Ford station wagon had been the low point of his experience. Now, a 'fine black Mercedes' carried the prince at the head of the small motorcade. He and Monique, dressed in black peasant clothing and rubber sandals, brought their Maltese terrier, Miko, with them. With no apparent sense of the ridiculous, Sihanouk comments that 'This kind of clothing is very practical, even for an aristocrat like me'.

As they drove westwards towards the Thai border, the Vietnamese blitzkrieg continued. By the time Sihanouk's party reached Sisophon, only a short drive from the border town of Poipet, on the morning of 2 January, the invading forces were moving steadily towards their initial goal of controlling all of Cambodia to the east of the Mekong. As they waited in Sisophon, Sihanouk was convinced that his party would soon be driven into Thailand and then flown to Peking from Bangkok. So he was greatly surprised when, on 4 January, Khieu Samphan appeared in Sisophon to tell him he was to return to Phnom Penh. The rulers of Democratic Kampuchea had a role for him, and for his old and trusted associate, Penn Nouth, who was travelling with him. They were to return to the capital, which Samphan assured the prince was entirely safe, where they would receive a briefing that would enable them to present Cambodia's case to the world. Sihanouk was to denounce the Vietnamese invaders at the United Nations, while Penn Nouth was to make the same case to those countries friendly to Democratic Kampuchea.

By late afternoon on 5 January, Sihanouk's party was back in

Phnom Penh. The prince noted that all seemed calm in the capital, and that labourers were even continuing to engage in roadwork. By this stage he had had little opportunity to listen to shortwave broadcasts, so he did not know that the previous day, 4 January, the invading forces had gained control of Cambodia east of the Mekong. The calm that Sihanouk observed was, indeed, that preceding the storm as the Vietnamese high command assessed their next moves. Contrary to their initial plans, they now decided to carry the invasion to Phnom Penh and beyond. In the brief calm that lasted while the Vietnamese reached their decision and prepared to push forward, Sihanouk was invited to meet Pol Pot, whom he had last seen during his visit to Cambodia in 1973.

The prince's account of his meeting with Pol Pot leaves no doubt that this was the last, and most surreal, of the many extraordinary episodes that took place in the first few days of January. Quite apart from the desperate military situation confronting the Khmer Rouge's armed forces, this was a meeting between Sihanouk and the man who had sought to destroy all the prince stood for. Yet both men strove to conduct their conversation with perfect courtesy—Pol Pot greeting Sihanouk in traditional fashion and addressing him by his royal title; the prince speaking nothing but praise for the valiant efforts of the Cambodian soldiers and expressing his gratitude for Pol Pot's 'kindness'.

The meeting lasted four hours. Sihanouk was served tea and cakes and drank endless glasses of orange juice while he listened in unaccustomed silence. Pol Pot talked on and on, briefing the prince on the military situation, insisting that his forces had already won striking victories and that more were to come. Within a matter of months the Vietnamese would be driven from Cambodia and their forces destroyed forever. Since this was a certainty, Pol Pot looked forward to once again receiving Sihanouk in Phnom Penh, in three months 'at the latest'.

Echoing almost all who have actually met Pol Pot, Sihanouk records the man's remarkably charismatic presence. His charisma was not manifested in violent or dramatic fashion, but rather through a soft and gentle style of talking that carried a seductive intensity. Sihanouk writes of how Pol Pot put him in mind of 'Bluebeard', who seduced his victims with his manners and soft voice. At last, when Pol Pot finally brought his monologue to a close, the two men parted, each speaking of meeting again 'soon'.

Sihanouk, Monique and their small household flew out of Phnom Penh in the afternoon of 6 January, one day before the invading Vietnamese army reached the Cambodian capital. They left behind most of the personal possessions they had managed to retain throughout their long months of confinement: clothes, records, the porcelain dinner service bearing the royal coat of arms. (Plates from this service—which was from Limoges, not Sèvres as Sihanouk claims—could be bought for a few dollars by visitors to Phnom Penh during the 1980s.)

As their aircraft flew towards Peking, Sihanouk writes of how he was assailed by contradictory feelings of relief at having finally escaped from confinement in Phnom Penh and the ever-present fear of execution, and sorrow at once again going into exile from his beloved country. When they landed at Peking, the newly dominant figure in Chinese politics, Deng Xiaoping, was there to greet him. Deng's presence was an assurance of Chinese esteem and a gesture to soften past blows, for it had often seemed to the prince that the Chinese government placed concern for the Khmer Rouge regime above consideration for him and his interests. Arriving at the temporary quarters his Chinese hosts had prepared for him, Sihanouk was almost overcome with fatigue and emotion. He took a sleeping tablet and lapsed into 'merciful sleep'.

The next evening, news of the fall of Phnom Penh reached the Chinese capital as Sihanouk addressed the crowd attending a banquet of welcome. He called on the assembled guests to drain their glasses in a toast to the future victory of Democratic Kampuchea and referred, incongruously he admits, to the famous words of his hero Charles de Gaulle in 1940, that 'France has lost a battle, she has not lost the war'. He was, he reflected, in an impossible position. His 'people were liberated from Pol Pot's grip', but those same people now had to be liberated from the grip of the Vietnamese. When he returned to his quarters, he took another sleeping pill.

Notes

For the account of Sihanouk's confinement in Phnom Penh, and for all of his words quoted in this chapter, I rely on his *Prisonnier des Khmers Rouges*.

For broader background dealing with the period while Sihanouk was held in Phnom Penh, see Chandler, *Tragedy* and *Brother Number One*; David P. Chandler and Ben Kiernan, eds., *Revolution and Its Aftermath in Kampuchea*, New Haven, Conn., 1983; Michael Vickery, *Cambodia, 1975–1982*, Boston, 1983, and Sydney, 1984; Karl D. Jackson, ed., *Cambodia 1975–1978: Rendezvous with Death*, Princeton, N.J., 1989; and Becker, *When The War Was Over*. This is a far from exhaustive selection from the now extensive literature dealing with the Pol Pot years.

David Chandler deals with Sihanouk's resignation in *Brother Number One*, pp. 14–15.

For a detailed account of Malcolm Caldwell's assassination, see Becker, *When the War Was Over*, pp. 432–3, and Chandler, *Brother Number One*, pp. 161–2, 163.

On the particular issue of forced labour, death and executions during the Pol Pot years, which does not receive detailed treatment in this chapter, François Ponchaud, *Cambodia Year Zero*, New York, 1978, remains of fundamental importance. A dissenting view from the widely accepted picture of what occurred under Pol Pot's rule may be found in the book by Michael Vickery cited above. My own judgments on the Pol Pot years were shaped, in part, by the two periods I spent, in 1980 and 1981, consulting for the United Nations High Commission for Refugees in relation to the Cambodian refugee problem, working along the Thai–Cambodian border. For some account of my findings during this period see C.A. Price, ed., *Refugees: The Challenge of the Future*, Academy of the Social Sciences of Australia, Fourth Academy Symposium, 1980, which contains my essay, 'The Indo-Chinese refugee situation: A Kampuchean case study', pp. 31–68.

Two most helpful analyses of the conflict between Vietnam and Democratic Kampuchea are Nayan Chanda, *Brother Enemy*, New York, 1986, and Grant Evans and Kelvin Rowley, *Red Brotherhood at War*, London, 1985, revised edn., 1990.

19

Escape to exile

On 8 January, the day after invading Vietnamese forces captured Phnom Penh, Sihanouk held a news conference in Peking. In the course of some six hours of questions and often seemingly endless answers, Sihanouk showed that his three years of confinement away from the public eye had done little to alter his personality and his capacity to pour forth words at will. But despite his tendency to retrospective self-justification, his first encounter with the international press for over three years found him facing a dilemma that he could not easily resolve. On the one hand, both in his own visceral feelings and with an eye towards pleasing his Chinese hosts, he bitterly condemned the Vietnamese invasion of his country. But on the other hand, and egged on by the journalists who questioned him, he could not pass up this opportunity to denounce Pol Pot and his regime.

This was a dilemma that he carried with him when, the following day, he set off for New York to speak for Democratic Kampuchea at the United Nations. He was still watched over by Khmer Rouge functionaries. Sihanouk argues that his critics should recognise that he was defending the interests of his country and not those of the Khmer Rouge regime the Vietnamese had overthrown. But his justification of his visit to the UN is less than fully convincing since, as has so often been the case throughout his life, it is less than fully frank. Still, it is easy to feel sympathy for the prince at this emotionally charged period of his life. He had just emerged from prolonged confinement and he was deeply grateful to the Chinese government for the role it had played in preserving his life, as he believed it to have done, and in bringing him back to Peking. He was still uncertain about the fate of many of his close relatives and did not want to jeopardise the safety of any who remained alive under the Khmer Rouge rump that still held sway over parts of western Cambodia. Yet when all these considerations are taken into account, the fact remains that Sihanouk was ready to travel to the UN to speak on behalf of an abhorrent regime, and his culpability in doing so is only blurred by his citation of the nations, most of them Western, which condemned the Vietnamese invasion in UN debates.

Indeed, Sihanouk weakens his own case that he acted according to the principle of 'my country right or wrong' when he writes of the insulting behaviour of Thiounn Prasith, the senior Khmer Rouge figure who had accompanied him to New York, and the effect this had on his plans for the future. Speaking to Sihanouk in the Waldorf Astoria, where the Cambodian party was lodged, Prasith suggested that the prince's address to the United Nations would benefit greatly from the reservoir of goodwill that Ieng Sary had built up at previous UN meetings. For Sihanouk, who had detested Ieng Sary since they first met in 1971, such an observation was, at best, gratuitous. But it was followed by news that, for him, was much worse. Prasith told the prince that when Ieng Sary, in his capacity as foreign minister of Democratic Kampuchea, reached New York for the 34th session of the General Assembly, he would lead the Cambodian delegation. Sihanouk would be his deputy. The prince was outraged. This final insult made up his mind. He decided that after the meeting of the Security Council on 13 January, he would sever his links with the Khmer Rouge regime.

With his mind made up, Sihanouk devised a plan for escaping from Khmer Rouge surveillance. His account loses nothing in the telling. Early in his stay in New York, a police officer assigned to provide security had shown himself sympathetic to the prince. Now that he was determined to slip the Khmer Rouge leash, Sihanouk contrived to pass this man a brief note alerting him to his intention to steal away at 2 a.m. the next morning and asking that he should be taken to the offices of the United States delegation to the United Nations.

Sihanouk had based his plan on the routine of the Khmer Rouge functionaries who watched over him and Monique, and who were staying in the same suite at their hotel. He had noted that his watchers kept to a rigid timetable in which they typed reports until retiring for the night at midnight sharp. So it was with growing dismay that on the night of his intended escape he and Monique listened as the typing continued until 12.30 a.m. But at last the noise of the typewriters stopped and their watchers retired. At 2 a.m. Sihanouk, who had determined that Monique should remain behind while he arranged their future, crept to the door of their suite and into the hall to find four American officials waiting for him. Within minutes, the small party was on its way to the US delegation's offices near the UN building, where Sihanouk was received by the then permanent American representative, Andrew Young. Within hours, the US government had indicated its willingness to let Sihanouk remain in America and to meet his and Monique's costs. It was, Sihanouk writes, a moment 'that did not lack spice'. Here he was, a 'notorious anti-American' seeking political asylum in the United States.

Within 24 hours Monique had joined him and he had held a meeting with the Chinese delegation to the UN. He refused to receive the Khmer Rouge, who had previously supervised his every move, when they begged to see him. By the end of the day he and Monique were admitted to Lennox Hill Hospital. One chapter in their life had ended.

Starting the next chapter was not as straightforward as Sihanouk had hoped. Despite his assurances to the Chinese delegation of his intention to return to Peking, Sihanouk did not wish to do so immediately. Lodged at American expense in the United Nations Plaza Hotel after his discharge from Lennox Hill, he received a visit from the US Secretary of State, Cyrus Vance. Courteous and solicitous though he was, Vance made no mention of Sihanouk's earlier request for political asylum. Faced with American silence on the issue, Sihanouk turned to France. Through the French permanent representative, he now sought Paris's agreement for a grant of political asylum and French passports for Monique and himself. Monique, he argued, was entitled to such a passport because her father was a French citizen. His own claim stemmed from his membership of the Legion of Honour and his status as a member of the French army reserve following his participation in two training courses at the cavalry school at Saumur.

When Ambassador Leprette received a reply to Sihanouk's requests, it was far from what the prince had expected. The embarrassed French permanent representative was instructed by his government to tell Sihanouk that he and Monique would indeed be granted political asylum, but that only Monique would be given a passport. As for the prince, the granting of asylum was contingent on his agreeing not to engage in any political activity nor to give interviews on any political matters. Sihanouk bitterly rejected these conditions, regarding them as extraordinary, coming as they did from a country which had offered much more generous hospitality to the Ayatollah Khomeini. 'Frustrated and humiliated', he turned to China, sure that Deng Xiaoping, who was visiting the United States, would invite him to resume his residence in Peking.

Sihanouk's assessment of how the Chinese government would behave was correct. When he dined with Deng, at Blair House in Washington on 31 January, the Chinese vice-premier duly invited the prince to take up residence in Peking. In doing so, he also urged Sihanouk to agree on a *modus vivendi* with the Khmer Rouge. As Deng and Sihanouk talked in Washington, the Chinese were preparing to administer a 'lesson' to the Vietnamese for their invasion of Cambodia. For China, to have Sihanouk once more associated with the representatives of Democratic Kampuchea, the Khmer Rouge, would have been of considerable utility. But when Sihanouk adamantly refused, Deng did not press the issue. For the moment, to have Sihanouk committed to taking up residence in Peking was sufficient for China's broader international aims.

Not until the end of February did Sihanouk finally reach Peking. In New York there were lunches and dinners to attend and a final banquet that Sihanouk gave for his American hosts. By now the 'old Sihanouk' was once more in the ascendant. His banquet, paid for by the uncomplaining Chinese, was *à la française*, with the dishes and wines chosen by the prince. Then, at last, the journey to Peking took place. It would be more than a decade before, finally, Sihanouk could go home.

Notes

Sihanouk's account of his first weeks of freedom after his departure from Phnom Penh, and in particular of his period in New York, is contained in his *Prisonnier de Khmers Rouges*. For a detailed account of Sihanouk's appearance at the United Nations and subsequent escape, the best source is found in Nayan Chanda, *Brother Enemy*, Chapter 11, pp. 363–9. Other useful sources for this period are reports and articles in *The New York Times* and the *Far Eastern Economic Review*.

20

Return to centre stage, 1979–93

When Sihanouk took up residence in Peking in 1979, few expected that he would ever again play a leading role in Cambodian politics. The odds seemed stacked against him. In the months following their capture of Phnom Penh in January 1979, the invading Vietnamese forces had gained control over the key lowland areas of Cambodia. China's efforts to administer a 'lesson' to Vietnam during February and March notwithstanding, there was no indication that Peking could force the Vietnamese out of Cambodia. Nor did it seem that continuing Chinese support for the Khmer Rouge could transform its defeated forces into a serious challenge to the regime Hanoi had installed in Phnom Penh. As Sihanouk once more experienced the 'gilded exile' of Peking—an exile varied by the extended periods he spent enjoying Kim Il-Sung's hospitality in Pyongyang—more than half a million Cambodians sought refuge in Thailand or along the Thai–Cambodian border. Some sheltered in the relative safety of camps under the authority of the United Nations High Commissioner for Refugees. Others eked out an existence in squalid border agglomerations, some with political affiliations, others dominated by rapacious warlords.

But there were forces in play that were slowly to change what seemed like a desperate and probably irreversible situation. Most importantly, the question of who was to control Cambodia became linked to wider geopolitical rivalries as China, in tandem with the countries of ASEAN (the Association of Southeast Asian Nations) contested the right of Vietnam, supported by the Soviet Union, to determine who should rule in Phnom Penh.

This was a situation shot through with moral ambiguities, a fact that Sihanouk readily recognised and over which he agonised. He had denounced the Vietnamese at the United Nations for their invasion of Cambodia, but like others, he could not ignore the fact that this same invasion had rid his homeland of the Khmer Rouge's terrible rule. Adding to the complexity of the problems associated with Cambodia was the indisputable conclusion that if there was to be any military challenge to Vietnam's occupation, the regrouped forces of the Khmer Rouge were the only troops capable of serious action against the invaders. Moreover, Sihanouk's Chinese hosts showed no reluctance to back the Khmer Rouge: Peking was ready to acknowledge that the Khmer Rouge had made 'mistakes', but much more important to the Chinese was the need to have a military tool that could make Vietnam pay for its disregard of Chinese interests. For the leadership in Peking, only the Khmer Rouge met this need.

The issue of what to do about Cambodia was seen from a different perspective by the ASEAN countries. They shared China's view that Vietnam's invasion of Cambodia and subsequent installation of a protégé regime was unacceptable, but they could not lend their public support to any program of resistance to the Vietnamese that depended solely on the Khmer Rouge. Not only had the Pol Pot regime been revealed as a murderous tyranny, but it also represented the antithesis of the anti-communist, market-oriented policies that, in their individual fashions, were the essential features of all the ASEAN countries. Though China felt no shame in supporting the Khmer Rouge, the ASEAN states, with Thailand and Singapore in the forefront, looked for other Cambodian elements that they could support. (This fact does not disguise the readiness of successive Thai governments to lend substantial covert support to the Khmer Rouge. Throughout the 1980s, the Thai military, acting as paymaster and supplier of materiel, became an essential link between China and the Khmer Rouge.)

The non-communist Cambodian elements were not hard to find, but initially it was far from clear that they could be transformed into effective fighting forces or be persuaded to work together. Factionalism, that old Cambodian enemy of any attempt to achieve effective, unified policies, had not disappeared in the face of disaster. In mid-1979 Sihanouk rejected overtures from the Khmer Rouge to head a united front aimed at driving the Vietnamese from Cambodia. At this stage he was not prepared to associate himself with those who had been his jailers and who had killed hundreds of thousands of his compatriots, including his own relatives. By October of the same year he proposed heading a neutral national front with its own armed forces, but nothing came of this proposal. Then in December 1979, another figure from Cambodia's political past, Sihanouk's former economic adviser Son Sann, presided over the formation of the Khmer People's National Liberation Front (KPNLF). Backed by Thailand and supported by a small number of politicians and military leaders from pre-1975 Cambodia, the KPNLF was never a major force in the political and military struggles of the next decade. However its formation did offer a rallying point for those Cambodians who were opposed to the Hanoi-backed regime in Phnom Penh, but who were unprepared to link their fortunes to either the Khmer Rouge or Sihanouk.

Throughout 1979 and 1980, international attention focused on the continuing outflow of refugees from Cambodia and the widespread, though by no means universal, shortage of food within the country. In the grim conditions that obtained, the bickering and manoeuvering of the anti-Vietnamese factions, and the fact that the Vietnamese-supported regime in Phnom Penh appeared to be consolidating its position, seemed to justify those observers who argued that acceptance of the status quo might be best for Cambodia and its people.

In all of this, there seemed little reason to believe that Sihanouk could achieve a political resurrection. He alternated between bursts of activity and periods of retreat. Initially, the prince insisted that the key to settling the Cambodian problem lay in reconvening a Geneva-style international conference and persuading the Vietnamese to leave Cambodia. After conceding in February 1981 that it might be possible to cooperate with the Khmer Rouge, he went on, in March, to found his own resistance movement, FUNCINPEC (the National United Front for an Independent, Neutral and Cooperative Cambodia). But much of his time was spent reliving past glories through showings of his films to diplomatic audiences in Peking or relaxing in the isolated calm of the North Korean capital Pyongyang, where Kim Il-Sung ensured that his every need was catered for.

As the months passed, with every sign that Vietnam's protégé regime was becoming more entrenched in Phnom Penh and that Vietnam itself was in Cambodia for the long haul, China and the ASEAN states intensified their efforts to promote a Cambodian coalition that would bring together FUNCINPEC, the KPNLF and the Khmer Rouge. The first real step towards this goal was achieved in September 1981, when Sihanouk, Son Sann and Khieu Samphan agreed to discuss the possibility of joint action. On-again off-again talks between representatives of these three groups were characterised by deep-seated antipathy and distrust, and nearly ten months were to pass before the three Cambodian factions were able to present a tenuously unified face to the world. On 22 June 1982, in Kuala Lumpur, they announced that they had formed the Coalition Government of Democratic Kampuchea (CGDK). The president of this new coalition, which now claimed to be the only legitimate representative of the Cambodian people, was Norodom Sihanouk.

Sihanouk has stated that he accepted this role 'without enthusiasm and with resignation'. Those who criticised him for associating with the Khmer Rouge had to accept that his action was a necessity, for it was the only way that Cambodia's 'nationalist' forces—his and Son Sann's supporters—could gain access to the United Nations, where the Khmer Rouge had represented Cambodia up till then. Sihanouk called the agreement enshrined in the formation of the CGDK a 'pact with the devil', but by 1982 he argued, *angkar*, the 'horrible power of the Khmer Rouge', was no longer the enemy. Since 1982, 'it was the Vietnamese coloniser who had become the enemy' and it was necessary to 'drive out and destroy' that coloniser.

This was an argument that Sihanouk and his supporters were to repeat many times, including during official Cambodian addresses to the United Nations in subsequent years. But his agreement to become the head of the CGDK was also a reflection of the brutal facts of *realpolitik*. Although the Chinese government treated the prince with every sign of honour and courtesy, its leaders made their commitment to supporting the Khmer Rouge perfectly clear. If Sihanouk wished China to provide material aid to the faction he headed, cooperation with the Khmer Rouge was the price to be paid. As for ASEAN, its policies were very much guided by the interests of Thailand as the 'frontline state', and the Thais were equally tough in their approach to Sihanouk. If he wished to travel through Thailand to see his partisans located along the Thai–Cambodian border, he had to accept the presidency of the CGDK. It comes as no surprise that Sihanouk, who deeply resented the pressure he was sustaining, found it difficult to absorb these blows to his *amour-propre* in silence. By the end of 1982, he was offering sharp criticism of his coalition partners, of ASEAN and of the Chinese.

The next several years had all the appearance of stalemate, a fact that led to Sihanouk's frequent public admissions of despondency. He was uncomfortable having the Khmer Rouge as allies, an arrangement that all too readily recalled his embrace of the communists' cause between 1970 and 1975. But at times it seemed that he reserved his harshest words for Son Sann and those who had rallied to that leader's side. Perhaps this was not so surprising, since among those who aligned themselves with the KPNLF were a number of Sihanouk's old political enemies, men who had welcomed his overthrow in the March 1970 *coup d'état.*

On many occasions, the prince expressed doubts that there would be a settlement of the Cambodia problem in his own lifetime. There seemed good reason for Sihanouk's pessimism. By 1984, Khmer Rouge forces were demonstrating a capacity to mount guerrilla attacks against Vietnamese and the Phnom Penh government's positions in western Cambodia and to establish bases in the fastnesses of the Cardamom mountains. But in the following year, what had seemed like an increasingly successful insurgency suffered a considerable setback as Vietnamese forces overran the major Khmer Rouge bases, pushing the guerrillas back into Thailand. As 1985 drew to a close, the prospects for the CGDK to become more than a symbol seemed bleak indeed. Meanwhile, and many thousands of kilometres away, another reminder of Cambodia's tragic modern history passed from the scene. Lon Nol, the general Sihanouk had trusted but who had then betrayed him, died in exile in California in November 1985.

Sihanouk summed up his view of the situation in his homeland in an interview with a journalist from *Le Monde* in December 1985. He had been joined in the Chinese capital by his coalition partners at the invitation of the Chinese government. As the Chinese leadership feted their Cambodian guests at banquets and receptions, their position was unwavering: for China, a settlement of the Cambodian problem depended on the total withdrawal of Vietnamese forces from the country. Talk of peace before that withdrawal was out of the question. Publicly Sihanouk had respected the Chinese position. This was despite the fact that only months before he had raised the possibility of a peace conference that would lead to an eventual coalition between the CGDK and the Phnom Penh regime headed by Heng Samrin and Hun Sen. He had refrained from talking about peace, Sihanouk told the *Le Monde* journalist, because 'the Chinese do not like people saying the things they don't want to hear'. Inimitably, Sihanouk then went on to do just that; for the Chinese to insist on the withdrawal of the Vietnamese was simply 'unrealistic'. They should recognise, Sihanouk argued, that 'time was not on their side'. Rather, it was on the side of the Vietnamese.

Within months of his delivering these gloomy prognostications, China showed that it was prepared to demonstrate some flexibility. In March 1986, the Chinese government sponsored a further meeting in Peking of the three factions making up the CGDK, at which an eight point plan to resolve the Cambodian problem was unveiled. Building in part on propositions that Sihanouk had put forward the previous September, the most important element in the plan was an acceptance that any settlement would have to take account of the existing regime in Phnom Penh: to that end, the plan proposed that an eventual solution should include the Phnom Penh regime in a four-part coalition. In terms of Sihanouk's past proposals, this seemed an advance. But later in the year he expressed reservations. Conscious that neither the armed forces linked to FUNCINPEC nor those associated with the KPNLF were a match for the Khmer Rouge's fighters, he now began to fear that the plan he had endorsed in March would open the way for a return to power by Pol Pot and his colleagues. But whatever the doubts that he now voiced, a more critical barrier stood in the way of a settlement. The Vietnamese government showed no inclination to withdraw its support from the regime in Phnom Penh, and the leaders of that regime remained unready to give up the power they exercised over the bulk of the Cambodian population. There still seemed little prospect for change or for Sihanouk's return to Phnom Penh.

As had happened many times before in Cambodia's history, external powers played a major part in shifting the country's politics from the position in which they seemed to have stalled. During 1987 it became clear that a whole range of countries that saw their interests involved in the Cambodian imbroglio were reassessing their policies. Central to this process of reassessments were the changes taking place in the Soviet Union, where President Gorbachev's foreign and domestic policies were leading to a rapid improvement of relations with the United States. But more than this, the Soviet Union was giving the first hints that it was no longer committed to providing Vietnam with indefinite support. As China and the Soviet Union inched towards healing the split that had divided them for so long, and as Vietnam counted the considerable cost in lives lost in its operations in Cambodia, other international actors resumed their efforts to find a basis for a Cambodian settlement. Among the ASEAN countries, Indonesia and Thailand were particularly active. So, too, were the foreign ministers of Australia and France.

Throughout 1986 and 1987, foreign governments continued to see Sihanouk as central to a settlement, a fact that led to his being sought out and asked to act in one way or another. At first glance this seems surprising, for his past record of governance had done little to inspire confidence, particularly during the 1960s. However Sihanouk was indisputably the best-known Cambodian leader, and there was good reason to be hesitant about most others who claimed a leading role. Son Sann and his KPNLF were only capable of generating lukewarm international support and only China was ready to be an unambiguous supporter of the Khmer Rouge.

Thus, in January 1987, President Ceausescu of Romania had approached him, Sihanouk said, with a message from Vietnam proposing talks between the CGDK and Phnom Penh. Nothing came of this as Hanoi disclaimed having made such a suggestion. Later that same year, while Sihanouk was in the North Korean capital, the PLO representative in Pyongyang asked Sihanouk to agree to meet Hun Sen, the prime minister in the Phnom Penh regime. Sihanouk at first agreed and then, while Hun Sen was flying to Pyongyang, he withdrew his agreement, probably because of Chinese pressure. By the time of this incident Sihanouk was no longer occupying his post at the head of the CGDK. In June 1987 he had stepped down as a protest, he said, at the fact that two members of his faction had been killed by the Khmer Rouge. A more likely explanation is that he sensed the international mood was shifting and he wanted to be free to pursue his own efforts towards a settlement.

In his search for a settlement, Sihanouk met the prime minister of the Phnom Penh government, Hun Sen, at the end of 1987 and in early 1988. The fact that these meetings took place at all was more important than the lack of any outcome, for they underlined the extent to which shifts were taking place in the international sphere that the contending Cambodian parties could not ignore. At times the significance of developments to the problems of Cambodia were not immediately apparent. Such a case was the Soviet Union's failure to offer either material or symbolic comfort to Vietnam in March 1988, when Vietnamese and Chinese forces clashed in the Spratly Islands. This lack of Soviet action served to remind Vietnam that it could no longer rely on its longtime ally, which was, in any case, now pressing Vietnam to withdraw a substantial number of its troops from Cambodia.

The combination of fast-moving international realignments and the pressures being applied to all of the Cambodian factions finally brought them together for their first quadripartite meeting, in Indonesia in July 1988. This Jakarta Informal Meeting—the JIM, as it came to be known among the many diplomats who now worked full-time on the Cambodian issue—was the start of a labyrinthine process of meetings and negotiations that initially raised hopes at a failed meeting in Paris in the summer of 1989 and continued for more than three years. During this time, the collapse of communism in Eastern Europe and the dramatic disintegration of the Soviet Union provided the backdrop against which the Cambodian endgame was played out.

In September 1989, Vietnam finally completed the lengthy complicated process of pulling its combat troops out of Cambodia. The end of Soviet aid had added to a recognition in the Vietnamese politburo that what the Vietnamese foreign minister Nguyen Co Thach had once described as the acceptable existence of shared poverty, was no longer a justification for the cost of maintaining occupation forces in Cambodia. Moreover, with the uncomfortable recognition that China's interests in Southeast Asia could not be endlessly ignored, the withdrawal was a first step towards a slow process of rapprochement with Vietnam's giant northern neighbour. Amongst the Cambodian factions themselves, many months were required to overcome resolutely-defended sticking-points. For the Phnom Penh regime, which felt increasingly isolated after the Vietnamese troop withdrawal and the end to support from the Soviet Union, a key concern was to avoid a settlement that would end its de facto status as the government that actually administered most of Cambodia's territory and population.

For many months, this issue, in various guises, stalled progress. The eventual solution, developed within a United Nations-sponsored plan for an overall settlement, and owing much to the initiatives of the Australian foreign minister, Senator Gareth Evans, involved the establishment of a Supreme National Council (SNC). Once a settlement was signed, this SNC was to symbolise Cambodia's sovereign identity. While negotiations continued, the SNC was to provide the forum within which the factions could meet.

Looking back over the complex steps that led to the eventual signing of a settlement agreement, two key events stand out as having had a major effect in shaping the eventual positive outcome. The first was the secret meeting between China and Vietnam held in the Chinese city of Chengdu in early September 1990. Until the time of this meeting, Vietnam had resisted the idea of the United Nations playing a major role in settling the Cambodian problem. It now accepted that this would be the case and it agreed, in effect, to apply pressure to its client, the Phnom Penh regime, to accept some form of power sharing. For all concerned, the Chengdu meeting underlined the fact that Vietnam now placed the improvement of relations with China above the giving of unwavering support to the regime it had installed in Phnom Penh eleven years before.

Hun Sen, now playing the most prominent part in the negotiating process for the Phnom Penh regime, made clear his unhappiness at the change in Vietnam's attitude. Interestingly, Sihanouk was also displeased by the deals he saw being struck over his head by his Chinese patrons. He resented the way external powers were setting the Cambodian agenda, particularly at a time when he was developing his own new strategy. Now that a settlement seemed a real possibility, even if still a distant one, he began to show signs that he was determined to be seen as a national rather than a factional leader. As a reflection of this aim, he had taken to signing press releases as 'former King of Cambodia'.

Fighting still continued in Cambodia as detailed plans for a United Nations Transitional Authority in Cambodia (UNTAC) were refined. For a period it seemed that Vietnam was prepared to risk its slowly improving relations with China by supporting Phnom Penh's refusal to contemplate the voluntary relinquishment of its authority. However, negotiations continued at various levels and at the beginning of May 1991 all the Cambodian factions said they would respect a United Nations' call for a ceasefire. Then, as the second key event, in June Sihanouk engineered the breakthrough the international community had been waiting for.

Building on the changed international atmosphere, in which both Moscow and Peking were concerned to end the Cambodian stalemate, Sihanouk took control of a meeting of the SNC being held in the Thai resort of Pattaya and succeeded in gaining the agreement of all factions to a set of broad propositions. The most important of these was the decision that in the future the SNC would meet in Phnom Penh and act as a kind of 'super' government. The agreement reached at Pattaya signalled Sihanouk's readiness to work more closely with the Phnom Penh regime than had been the case previously. The meeting also showed that

Sihanouk has recaptured some of the political skills and ebullience of the past. His press conference after the successful conclusion of the SNC meeting was like those of his earlier years in power. With the prospect of returning to Phnom Penh in November to live in the royal palace where he had been crowned king fifty years before, words mixed with laughter as the prince revelled in the attention he was once again receiving from the assembled representatives of the international media.

When Sihanouk returned to Cambodia on 14 November 1991, a peace settlement for Cambodia had already been signed by the nineteen nations participating in the Paris International Peace Conference of 23 October. Before that meeting, the five permanent members of the United Nations Security Council had settled the broad outlines of a plan that envisaged the disarmament of the forces of all Cambodian factions and the holding of elections during 1993. Until those elections, the SNC was to embody Cambodia's sovereignty. Sihanouk, who by now had declared that he was 'neutral' and no longer associated with his FUNCINPEC faction, had been designated chairman of the SNC.

Sihanouk, accompanied by North Korean bodyguards who were rapidly to gain a well-deserved reputation for brutality, returned to a tumultuous welcome. No effort was spared by the Phnom Penh regime to mark the end of the prince's twelve years of exile from his country. Before Sihanouk's return, Hun Sen had spoken of his hope that the prince would eventually be inaugurated as president of the government that would be established following the projected elections. He expressed this hope at a party congress at which he and his political colleagues announced that they were abandoning their communist affiliations and reconstituting themselves as the Cambodian People's Party (CPP). As the former King Sihanouk and the one-time Khmer Rouge leader Hun Sen rode together in an open limousine from Pochentong airport, it was clear that each saw considerable advantage in an alliance of more than usual convenience.

Events that followed swiftly on the heels of Sihanouk's return to Cambodia emphasised how deeply divided the country remained, a fact that boosted the prince's prestige as the one figure whom all were reluctant to criticise. November 1991 was marked by a dramatic attack on the Khmer Rouge leader, Khieu Samphan, when he returned to Phnom Penh as part of the peace plan. The attack was almost certainly orchestrated by the Phnom Penh regime and can be seen, in retrospect, as an early link in the chain of events that ended with the Khmer Rouge's refusal to participate in the UN-sponsored elections that finally took place in May 1993. Almost a month after the attack on Khieu Samphan, Phnom Penh was racked by savage rioting, which had as its cause widespread resentment of the rampant corruption at all levels of the Phnom Penh administration. For a time, the hopes that had been sparked by the Paris peace agreement seemed under serious threat.

Throughout the following year, as UNTAC started its operations and as it became increasingly clear that the Khmer Rouge were not ready to participate in the settlement they had signed, Sihanouk played his own hand. As had always been the case in his earlier political life, he was unpredictable, except in making clear his utter conviction that he alone had the capacity to save Cambodia from itself. Having led the coalition that had fought against the Phnom Penh regime for so many years, he now took to referring to its premier, Hun Sen, as his 'son'. His relations with his own natural sons, Princes Ranariddh and Chakrapong seemed more reminiscent of the unstable world of traditional Cambodian royal politics than of the needs of a country struggling to emerge from twenty years of war and destruction. Although Ranariddh had assumed the leadership of FUNCINPEC in 1989 after Sihanouk had resigned to show his political neutrality, and despite that faction's avowed support for Sihanouk's leadership, the prince frequently treated Ranariddh shabbily. Just why this should have been so has been attributed to many factors, perhaps the most persuasive being the generally agreed fact that there is no love lost between Sihanouk's consort, Monique, and Ranariddh, the son of an earlier marriage.

Prince Chakrapong, in contrast, seems to have enjoyed Monique's favour and to have continued to do so despite 'defecting' from FUNCINPEC to become a vice-premier in the Phnom Penh regime in January 1992. Deeply hostile to his half-brother Ranariddh and widely criticised for his pursuit of wealth by any means, it is almost certain that Chakrapong's decision to accept the vice-premier's post had Sihanouk's blessing, even if his appointment was not actually engineered by the prince.

When Sihanouk flew out of Phnom Penh in November 1992, few observers were confident that the United Nations' peace plan could be implemented within its prescribed time limit, with elections due for April 1993. The prince's own intentions were clear, up to a point. He had no doubt about his ultimate goal: to be once again the leader of an internationally-recognised Cambodian state. What was unclear was how he intended to achieve his aim. After a series of parties in Phnom Penh celebrating his birthday at the end of October, at which he once again sang sentimental songs, he left the country for medical treatment in Peking and rest in Pyongyang. The need for medical treatment was real and he did suffer a mild stroke in Peking in November, but there was much about his departure from Cambodia that recalled his earlier tactics of removing himself from the scene in order to achieve his political ends.

Most particularly, Sihanouk had lost patience with UNTAC, for its failure to disarm the armies of the contending Cambodian factions, its inability to stem the rising tide of political violence, and for the way in which its presence had led to the abuse of Cambodian women. Reacting to the killing of members of FUNCINPEC—the implication being that this was at the hands of agents of the regime headed by Hun Sen—Sihanouk announced on 4 January 1993 that he was ceasing all cooperation with UNTAC.

Sihanouk's shock announcement brought its intended effect. The head of UNTAC, Yasushi Akashi, led the succession of senior international figures who trooped to Peking to encourage the prince to remain involved in the Cambodian peace plan. Akashi persuaded Sihanouk to renounce his resignation from the chairmanship of the SNC, and a subsequent list of visitors, that included Hun Sen and the foreign ministers of Indonesia and Thailand, all assured Sihanouk that he alone had the prestige to act as Cambodia's leader. In a remarkable interview with Nayan Chanda of the *Far Eastern Economic Review* at the end of January 1993, the prince was frank in his own estimation of his indispensability. He was, he said, 'ready to exercise power even if I am called an autocrat'. Later in the same interview, he asserted 'People are very upset. They say only Sihanouk is clean, the only one is Sihanouk. He should be made to come back and take charge of everything.'

As he made his pronouncements in Peking, Sihanouk was anticipating that he would be elected to be president of Cambodia before legislative elections were held. In the event, as key international backers of the United Nations' plan hesitated to introduce this new element, Sihanouk once again distanced himself from the preparations for elections, expressing doubts that they could take place in the unsettled circumstances that existed. He was in a sceptical mood when he returned to Cambodia on 22 May, the day before polling started. Neither Sihanouk nor most observers expected the result that emerged from these elections and the high voter turnout that contributed to it.

The polling had taken place in the face of bellicose threats from the Khmer Rouge and a campaign of intimidation and assassinations for which elements of the Phnom Penh regime were clearly responsible. Nevertheless, more than 4.5 million registered voters went to the poll to record a surprise result. For all of the advantages the Cambodian People's Party possessed as the political arm of the Phnom Penh regime, it was beaten into first place by FUNCINPEC which polled over 45 per cent of the vote to the CPP's 38 per cent. But if the polling was remarkably smooth, and definitely fairer than any previous Cambodian election, the events that followed showed how fragile and vulnerable Cambodia's political culture really was.

As electoral officials were still counting the votes that led to FUNCINPEC's surprise success, that faction's officials in Phnom Penh were thought to be ready to discuss some form of coalition with CPP leaders. At the same time, the latter, shocked by their failure to win an outright victory, were beginning to argue that the poll results were flawed and could not be accepted. Then, in a totally unexpected intervention, surprising friend and foe alike, Sihanouk announced that he had formed a new interim coalition government in which he would hold the posts of president, prime minister and military commander. Claiming falsely to have Prince Ranariddh's agreement, Sihanouk named this son and Hun Sen as his vice-premiers. Within twenty-four hours the prince's gambit had failed. Faced with the reluctance of the party with which he had previously been associated to accept his proposal and a very cool reaction from UNTAC officials and foreign powers, most particularly the United States, he abandoned his plan and disappeared behind the high walls of the royal palace.

A week after Sihanouk's failed preemptive move, there was further drama. Still claiming the existence of large-scale election fraud, senior members of the CPP, including Prince Chakrapong, announced that they had organised the secession of six of Cambodia's eastern provinces, representing about 40 per cent of Cambodia's territory. This 'secession' lasted four days. If Chakrapong and his colleagues expected support from the Vietnamese government in Hanoi, as seems likely, they were sadly disappointed. The Vietnamese showed no inclination to again involve themselves directly in Cambodian affairs by lending their support to the would-be secessionists.

Despite the distraction provided by the attempted secession, the deputies elected in the May polls met as an assembly for the first time on 14 June and granted Sihanouk his deeply-treasured wish. The assembly unanimously declared that the actions of its predecessor in stripping the prince of his position as chief of state in March 1970 had been illegal. At the same time, the deputies voted to grant Sihanouk 'full and special powers . . . that he may save our nation'. This was sweet revenge for Sihanouk, who had never forgiven those of his compatriots who had stripped him of power 23 years before. The next day he went before the assembly to lend his approval to a power-sharing arrangement between FUNCINPEC and the CPP under which Ranariddh and Hun Sen would both act as co-presidents until a constitution was adopted.

The final steps along the path that led to Sihanouk's being installed once more as King of Cambodia were marked by a familiar pattern of alarms and excursions. Following his blessing of the arrangements that saw Prince Ranariddh and Hun Sen sharing power in the period before the adoption of a new constitution, Sihanouk again left Phnom Penh for Peking and Pyongyang. In doing so, he appears to have shrewdly judged that he could better orchestrate events from a distance, ensuring that Phnom Penh's politicians approached him in the role of petitioners. And this is exactly what happened.

When they journeyed to Pyongyang on 30 August 1993, Ranariddh and Hun Sen brought with them two draft constitutions, one restoring the monarchy, the other instituting a republic. Sihanouk commented publicly that the decision as to whether he once again became king was the Cambodian assembly's, but there was no doubt in the minds of those who had seen him that he expected to become king again. And, indeed, he is reported to have made many handwritten amendments to the monarchical constitution shown to him for his approval. Yet no sooner had the announcement of the intention to return to a government headed by a king been made in Phnom Penh, that Sihanouk called for the population to renounce the monarchy and his projected role as king. To further compound confusion, the prince also announced he was ending his presidency of the SNC. It was all very much of a piece with Sihanouk's behaviour in the past. Once the members of the assembly begged him to change his mind, he graciously did so. He had shown that he was truly wanted.

On 21 September 1993, the assembly adopted a new constitution which provided for Sihanouk to be king, to rule but not to govern, although as king he is commander of the armed forces and has a veto over the appointment of cabinet ministers and judges. Returning from Peking on 23 September, Sihanouk was once again instated as King of Cambodia in a solemn ceremony on 24 September, more than 38 years after he abdicated the throne.

As King of Cambodia, Sihanouk presides over a country that, in a very real sense, has lost its political nerve. The election process in May 1993, with Cambodians flocking to the polls in the face of threat and intimidation, was a testimony to hope and courage. But the disasters of the past two decades have contributed to a readiness of many of its politicians, and of the population at large, to risk Sihanouk's wilfulness rather than to try and develop their own plans and policies. What is more, he and those who have chosen to work with him still face the unresolved challenge posed by the Khmer Rouge who, as of early November 1993, were still not accepting the authority of the new government in Phnom Penh.

To add to the uncertainty surrounding Cambodia's future, there are grave doubts concerning Sihanouk's health. Ever ready to discuss his health in the most detailed fashion, he had announced in early September 1993 that his Chinese doctors had 'discovered a small tumour in my rectum, that is to say the end portion of the large intestine and not far from the anus'. Sihanouk later amended this diagnosis to say there was a possibility that he was suffering from cancer of the prostate. After surgery in late October, Sihanouk's Chinese doctors reported that they had removed a malignant tumour from near his prostate. Then in early November, Sihanouk, now undergoing both chemotherapy and radiation treatment, sent a message to Phnom Penh stating that he would not be returning to Cambodia until mid-1994. There must now be doubts as to whether Sihanouk can surmount his illness to return to Cambodia as its king.

Notes

There is no readily available general survey that covers the whole of the period dealt with in this chapter. David Chandler offers a reflective view of the period 1979–91 in Chapter 13 of the second edition of his *A History of Cambodia*. Sihanouk offers episodic coverage of some of the more important developments up to 1986 in the closing sections of his *Prisonnier des Khmer Rouges*, and his observations are supplemented by Simonne Lacouture. Nayan

Chanda provides an overview of developments up to 1986 in his outstanding *Brother Enemy.*

The problems associated with the massive outflow of Cambodian refugees in the period 1979–80 receives masterly treatment in William Shawcross, *The Quality of Mercy: Cambodia, Holocaust and the Modern Conscience,* London, 1984.

I was present at the foundation of the KPNLF, which took place a few kilometres inside Cambodian territory in December 1979.

For the general reader, the complex developments leading to the conclusion of a peace settlement in 1991 are best followed through the columns of the *Far Eastern Economic Review,* whose correspondent in Phnom Penh, Nate Thayer, has reported on events with diligence and insight. A useful account of the important Australian contribution to efforts to achieve a Cambodian peace settlement may be found in Gareth Evans and Bruce Grant, *Australia's Foreign Relations in the World of the 1990s,* Melbourne, 1991.

Sue Downie provides an account of the alternating moods of optimism and pessimism pervading Phnom Penh in the period 1988–92 in her *Down Highway One: Journeys through Vietnam and Cambodia,* Sydney, 1993.

Nayan Chanda's important interview with Sihanouk in Peking in early 1993 is in the *Far Eastern Economic Review,* 4 February 1993.

The quotation of Sihanouk's message concerning his health problems is from *The Australian,* 11 September 1993, in an article by Sue Downie.

21

Prince of light, prince of darkness

Throughout his long career, Norodom Sihanouk has been many things to many people, not least to himself. But crucially, in all the roles he has played, he has shown an inability to recognise that views and decisions other than his own were worthy of attention and that what he has cited as his positive achievements were often flawed or, worse, little more than fantasy.

Because this book has contained a critical evaluation of Sihanouk's life, it is important to note that other writers have presented him in a more favourable light. In particular, those who have written positively of the prince's achievements have tended to focus on two features of his rule. In domestic affairs, praise has frequently been bestowed on Sihanouk's support for education. In the field of foreign policy, his supporters point to the way in which, for so many years, he managed to preserve Cambodia from involvement in the Second Indochinese War at a time when conflict was taking place in neighbouring Vietnam and Laos. These are serious claims that deserve thoughtful consideration. But first, it is worthwhile tabulating some of the things Sihanouk was, and was not.

Sihanouk has said that he was, and is, in his own terms '*un bon Khmer*'. Literally translated, this means 'a good Cambodian', but a more accurate rendition of Sihanouk's meaning might be 'a real Cambodian'. His description involves more than a judgment on policies: it suggests that Sihanouk's character is essentially Cambodian. The dangers of ethnic stereotypes are great, but it is not hard to understand what Sihanouk means. Most important, he is defining himself in terms of his unwavering commitment to the pursuit of policies that have—in his judgment—been for the good of his country. Beyond any shadow of a doubt, Sihanouk has acted as he has, in a widely differing set of circumstances, with the good of his country in mind. If intention alone was the basis for judgment, it would be sufficient to record that Sihanouk was and is a patriot, and to say no more.

The problem has been that Sihanouk has always believed that he alone possessed the gift of knowing what was best for his country. His growth to political maturity in the early 1950s was accompanied by an ever-greater readiness to disregard the views of his advisers. It was a broader weakness of the world within which the prince operated that those advisers were seldom willing to express views that they felt he was unlikely to approve of. And, while believing in his own good intentions, Sihanouk had a fundamental character flaw in his inability to see dissenting views as other than expressions of criticism. Sihanouk was not Cambodia, but he thought he was. This belief has led to a basic lack of balance in his approach to issues great and small that has persisted throughout his life.

There are many examples of this. Friend and foe alike agree that Sihanouk was a thoughtful and gracious host, paying attention to the minutest points of detail. (When a member of the British royal family visited Phnom Penh as his guest he even ensured that the lavatory paper in the guest palace's bathrooms was of English manufacture.) But this concern to please, and other examples of attentive hospitality, were only parts of a personality that would embark on bitter personal attacks against any individual, whether Cambodian or foreign, who Sihanouk felt had failed to treat his country or himself—the two were not separate in his mind—with the deference they deserved. In such circumstances no statesman or government was exempt from his sharp tongue. This is not to say that in many cases, and in particular with regard to his neighbours South Vietnam and Thailand, Sihanouk did any more than give as good as he received. What has been important has been the lack of balance in his personality, which has led him to believe he should be exempt from criticism while not exempting others from it.

Hand in hand with this lack of balance has gone a tendency to ignore reality when that reality has not coincided with

Sihanouk's view of himself and his country. This is a harsh judgment, but it seems sustained by the facts. Indeed, it is possible to argue that Sihanouk has at various times gone beyond a refusal to face facts and acted in a way that suggests he is a fantasist. His reiteration of the claim that Cambodia was 'an oasis of peace' seems a case in point. Either the mantra-like repetition of this patently flawed description was a simple exercise in counter-propaganda or, as seems more likely, it was a case of Sihanouk's actually coming to believe that the description was true. The same characteristic embrace of fantasy was surely present in Sihanouk's view of his 'feature' films. Only by suspending rational belief could he accept that his film-making was of world class and deserving of the sycophantic praise heaped upon him in the Cambodian press and at the Phnom Penh film festivals.

If the suggestion of the prince's susceptibility to fantasy seems far-fetched, another less widely known example may reinforce the point. Believing as he did that the press in other countries was controlled by their governments, Sihanouk could not conceive that any media criticism of him could be other than a deliberate personal attack made with the approval of the government concerned. There is no more striking or absurd example of this attitude than Sihanouk's extended denunciation of Peter O'Toole's remarks after filming *Lord Jim* on location at Angkor, an episode mentioned earlier in this book.

The fantasy of a film star as the machiavellian agent of foreign powers working to bring Cambodia and its leader into disrepute was yet a further indication of serious weaknesses in Sihanouk's long rule. With all his talents, he lacked balance in his judgment and his actions. Personal enthusiasm for a particular policy or project was followed by a swift change of mood that pushed previous preoccupations into the background. All criticism was judged as of equal importance, and all praise equally welcome. This attitude severely affected Sihanouk's judgment of individuals. Just as he found the greatest difficulty in believing that any criticism could be other than ill-intentioned, so did he find it hard to accept that praise and adulation might be other than genuine and deserved. Only when the gap between proffered praise and contrary action was unmistakable could Sihanouk bring himself to believe that those who claimed to be his admirers might be dissimulating.

The levels of public adulation that Sihanouk was ready, and indeed expected to receive during the late 1960s challenge credulity. That the 'Prince Friend' or 'Papa Prince', as Sihanouk described himself, had the official news agency writing of his 'superhuman efforts' and of his 'ensuring the unique road to Cambodia's grandeur' might not have been harmful if these had been no more than words. But coupled with his expectation of undiluted praise—and the quotations in question come from 1969, when wide cracks had appeared in the edifice of Sihanouk's state— was his inability to organise a functioning system of government that involved the delegation of power.

In general, those prepared to risk criticising inadequacies in the Cambodian state found themselves excluded from positions of power. Moreover, the respect accorded Sihanouk and the power in his hands were so great that even his most vocal critics were reluctant, on those occasions when responsibility was thrust into their hands, to act boldly lest they offend the prince. This provides an important explanation for why a growing number of those on the left of Cambodian politics, from 1966 onwards, chose to go into clandestine dissidence rather than attempt to work through the existing system. Sihanouk's regime had many weaknesses, but it was capable of taking quick and sometimes fatal toll its perceived domestic opponents. Sihanouk's repeated denial of responsibility for the brutalities of his security services are self-serving and unconvincing, and are denied, particularly from 1967 onwards, by the evidence of his own speeches and by the testimony of those who survived the campaign against the left. Indeed, as Sihanouk's state entered its most dangerous period, from 1967 until his removal in early 1970, there was an ironical strengthening of the two tendencies just described. Dissent became more and more a matter for harsh repression while at the same time Sihanouk showed less and less inclination to share responsibility or to address himself to the critical problems that his government faced.

Despite Sihanouk's avowed concern with the need to respect the Cambodian constitution, and despite his sponsorship of various institutional innovations, he was unable to establish a form of government that was not dependent on his personal wishes. His failure to find a way to conserve the monarchy that would allow the Cambodian throne to be occupied was matched by his inability, or perhaps more correctly his unwillingness, to develop a way of maintaining control over the general direction of the Cambodian state while allowing the ebb and flow of politics. Some observers will find this a harsh judgment since it may be argued, and to some degree correctly, that Sihanouk alone should not be loaded with all the faults of a system of which he was only a part. The difficulty about this argument is that he was *the* vital part, the directing figure, and the political leader whose control of affairs was the major factor in determining the shape of Cambodian politics from the time of independence in 1953. His failure occurred within the system that he developed. Michael Leifer has neatly summarised Sihanouk's Cambodia in writing that his record 'suggests a greater facility for reigning than for ruling. He is more at home with the pomp and circumstances of government than with its good practice. His neglect of the latter when in power is part of the tragedy of modern Cambodia.'

In looking back at his years in power, both Sihanouk and his foreign defenders have made much of his efforts to transform and expand the Cambodian educational system. The claim invites debate, because there is no doubt that educational opportunities expanded in Cambodia, particularly during the 1960s. But, at the same time, there was an ever-growing gap between the numbers of pupils and students processed through secondary and tertiary institutions and the availability of jobs for those who had completed their education.

The issue of education, and Sihanouk's role in relation to it, is given further interest by the prince's own ambivalent attitude to formal learning. He has denied that he suffered from any sense of inferiority as a result of not having completed high school. At the same time, his actions and on occasion his statements have shown a curious blend of admiration for and distrust of the value of education. Publicly he could boast that he determined Cambodia's economic policies without caring 'a rap about political economy, political science or other subjects', and without having read any books on these subjects. But hand in hand with these views went his determination to found schools, colleges and universities. Moreover, few instances of criticism from his leftist opponents have so provoked his anger as the suggestion that his regime did not provide education for the masses.

The number of educational institutions and students in Cambodia increased dramatically under Sihanouk, particularly in the thirteen years between the founding of the Sangkum in 1955 and 1968. The number of primary school pupils mushroomed from just over 300 000 to over 1 000 000. But more spectacular still was the burgeoning of secondary and tertiary education. Some 5000 high school students attended institutions in 1955. By 1968 there were more than one million. No universities existed in 1955. By 1968 there were nine, with more than 30 faculties and a student population of nearly 11 000. The record, as Sihanouk has presented it, is a glowing one.

The reality involved low educational standards that became even lower over the years, and the inability of the Cambodian state to provide jobs for those who believed that the possession of a high school certificate or a university diploma guaranteed them employment. Some might argue that these developments were scarcely Sihanouk's fault; that the pursuit of expanded educational opportunities was an admirable aim; and that difficulties were inevitable in a developing state. The problem with this contention, and with almost every aspect of Cambodia so long as Sihanouk held power, was that until the closing months of his rule the prince's wishes determined the fundamental policies that were followed. In this, as in other matters of importance, Sihanouk was responsible. Convinced, according to Charles Meyer, by a visit to an Indonesian university campus in 1964 that tertiary education should be promoted, the prince ordered a rapid expansion of campuses and faculties but gave little, if any, thought to how these were to be financed, stocked with books and equipment and staffed, or to what would happen to graduates of these institutions.

Standards in most of the newly established faculties were deplorably low, not least because there were simply not enough trained university teachers. Meyer has written scathingly of what this hothouse approach meant in the case of the University of Takeo–Kampot. Started from scratch in the mid-1960s, it boasted from its inauguration a faculty of oceanography, despite being 50 kilometres from the sea, and a hospital for its 'medical faculty'. Most serious of all the shortcomings associated with Sihanouk's universities was the great imbalance between the numbers of students studying technical and professional subjects and those studying the humanities. In the closing years of Sihanouk's rule, Charles Meyer says, there were 131 students enrolled at the University of Agricultural Science, but the University of Fine Arts had no fewer than 787 students, of whom some 300 were studying choreography.

In education, as in so many other areas of Cambodian life under Sihanouk, the prince was more concerned with form than with substance. A more positive case may be made for the results of the prince's efforts to expand public health facilities in Cambodia. For here, again, the 1960s in particular saw a rapid expansion of clinics and hospitals, essentially because of Sihanouk's energetic backing. The fundamental problem in relation to the country's

269

health service, and one that was never overcome, was the lack of sufficient financial and human resources to keep it functioning effectively. In part this reflected problems common to all newly independent countries, but in part also, it reflected a mismanaged economy, a factor for which Sihanouk, again, must share a large measure of blame.

To some extent it is easier to reach conclusions about the success or failure of Sihanouk's domestic policies than to evaluate his conduct of foreign policy. Whatever his good intentions in relation to the internal affairs of the state, there was a yawning gap between the claims he made for the success of his policies and the reality of what was achieved. His disinclination to move beyond decision to implementation meant that, even when the goals he pursued were sound, they were seldom achieved. More open to criticism was his inability to subordinate his deep need for praise to an acceptance that even the descendant of god-kings could benefit from criticism. Failure to face fact easily slipped into acceptance of fantasy, so that Sihanouk not only believed his films were of world rank, but also thought they truly served the interests of the state. He could not recognise that they were an extravagant self-indulgence. At a more sombre level, Sihanouk's sanctioning of violence by his security services has ensured that no balanced account of his years in power can ignore this darker side of his character.

There is more room for argument over the prince's record in foreign affairs. This is so because his handling of Cambodia's international relations took place in circumstances that frequently offered him little leeway. Like his ancestors, he was the leader of a small country wedged between two hostile neighbours, and this was a geographical and political situation that he could not change. Certainly, he could have embraced policies towards both Thailand and South Vietnam that might have resulted in some diminution of the chronic tension that was such a feature of relations with his neighbours. But any lasting *modus vivendi* with those neighbours would have depended on their also having adopted different policies from those they pursued. Among the 'might-have-beens' of modern Cambodian history, one of the most desirable but unrealised, and unrealisable, possibilities would have been the ending of age-old inter-state and inter-ethnic rivalries between Cambodia and its immediate neighbours.

Might Sihanouk have played his foreign policy cards differently, to better effect, in relation to the United States? Here, again, a consideration of the record emphasises that he and his country confronted circumstances over which they had only limited control. There can be argument about whether or not Sihanouk was right to opt for a foreign policy that proclaimed Cambodia's neutrality, and just as sharp argument as to the extent to which his policies in fact deserved that description. Even allowing for the Sihanouk's flexible interpretation of the concept of neutrality, a case can be made that it was not, in itself, a foolish choice in a world divided into ideological camps.

Sadly for Sihanouk and for Cambodia, it was not a choice that fitted well with the aims of the United States in the 1950s and 1960s, nor, from a very different point of view, with the aims of the Vietnamese communist government in Hanoi after 1954. Given the world in which he had to operate, Sihanouk's decision to look to China as the guarantor of his country's sovereignty must appear, to all but the most biased observer, an understandable and, considering the time at which he made the decision, a logical one.

But of all his foreign policy decisions, none was more controversial than those which led him to enter into clandestine arrangements for the supply of Vietnamese communist forces in South Vietnam (the Republic of Vietnam) and then to accept, without protest, the large-scale presence of those forces on Cambodian soil. Given his conviction, which strengthened over the years, that the communists would be the eventual winners in the Vietnam War, his decisions did not lack logic. But in hindsight, these decisions can be seen to have involved risks that Sihanouk clearly did not consider when he countenanced first the supply of Chinese materiel through Cambodian territory and then the sale of Cambodian rice to the Vietnamese communist forces. Later, he clearly believed that permitting Vietnamese troops to seek sanctuary in his country would appease their leaders and that, once they had won the war, Cambodia's 'hospitality' would be remembered. He did not recognise, or perhaps initially did not care, that his right-wing critics within Cambodia were growing ever more concerned at what they saw as a loss of national sovereignty. And he failed to discern that this concern was joined to profound resentment of other aspects of his rule. Sihanouk's policies prolonged the years of peace within his country as he struggled to solve problems that were outside his control. But the policies he pursued to ensure that peace contributed to his personal downfall and

271

opened the way to the full-scale war that raged from 1970 until the Khmer Rouge victory of April 1975.

How should we judge Sihanouk's actions since he was thrown out of office? In particular, should he be condemned for lending his name to a Khmer Rouge–dominated national front when, from 1973 if not before, he must have been at least partially aware of its true character? Such a condemnation seems unfair. While one can accept that his profound hatred for Lon Nol and his burning resentment at having been toppled from office warped his capacity to judge his Khmer Rouge allies, it does not seem right to argue that Sihanouk knew what would happen once the Cambodian communists were in power. Being Sihanouk, and despite his talk of living as a simple citizen once the Lon Nol regime was over-thrown and his gloomy predictions of being discarded by the Khmer Rouge, it seems entirely likely that as he waited in Peking between 1970 and 1975 he thought it possible that he would eventually return to lead his country, even if it was a very different country from that which he had ruled before.

As for the period he spent as a 'prisoner of the Khmer Rouge', one probably cannot overemphasise the fear that was his constant companion during his confinement. Much of what he has written of this period seems—indeed is—self-indulgent. In contrast to the great bulk of his compatriots during that time, he lived in compar-ative comfort, but he could never be sure that he and Monique would not be taken away and killed. His deep-seated love for his country, and pressure from China, explain his subsequent readiness to go to New York in January 1979 as spokesman for Democratic Kampuchea to denounce the Vietnamese invasion of Cambodia. To unqualifiedly blacken Sihanouk's name because of his association with the Khmer Rouge is unjustified. Moreover, if one is looking for charges that can be sustained, there is no lack of these to be found in his long career.

Looking back over Sihanouk's career, one of its most notable features is that he was able to remain in power as long as he did. In leading Cambodia, Sihanouk had many advantages, not least the fact of his royal birth. But these had to be balanced against the severe disadvantages of a political system that used Western forms without the support of any political traditions that could easily accommodate the practices and institutions of the West. French colonial control had ensured the survival of the royal family and confirmed the importance of the great official families. It had not developed a system of administration, or a corps of administrators, that could confidently confront the problems of independence. Cambodia's lack of trained administrators, engineers and doctors was shared by many Third World countries emerging from colonial control. The difficulties caused by lack of personnel should, nonetheless, not be forgotten.

In the face of massive problems both external and internal, only a man of Sihanouk's great energy and ability could have achieved even a measure of success. But that success was always qualified by his failure to find a formula that would ensure the stable development of the state and the division of power between its leader and those who claimed the right to play a part in determining policy. The lack of a parliamentary tradition certainly contributed to this situation. But more important was Sihanouk's fundamental unwillingness to delegate authority. The prince's upbringing and his personality explain his intense dislike of criticism or disagreement with his views. The practical result of this was his refusal to delegate authority, since this could have led to the questioning of policies that he had proclaimed.

In delegating no authority, Sihanouk laid the foundation for disenchantment with his rule. Whether Cambodia could have avoided its economic difficulties is a matter for speculation. We know for certain that Sihanouk made the decisions that were followed by economic decline and stagnation against the advice of his advisers, and that he came to be seen as the man responsible for the parlous state of the Cambodian economy in the last years of his rule. It is doubtful whether any Cambodian politician, or group of politicians, could have eliminated corruption short of a genuine revolution. By insisting that he was the font of all power and responsibility, Sihanouk ensured that the politically conscious among his compatriots laid the blame for what they believed was Monique's corruption at his feet. In the field of foreign affairs, an area he claimed as his pre-eminent concern, when the prince was apparently unable to extricate his country from the difficulties it faced at the end of 1969 an important body of opinion came, not surprisingly, to blame him for what it saw as the decline in Cambodia's security.

Commentators will argue about how Sihanouk's leadership of Cambodia should be judged for many years to come. Because he was so overwhelmingly the dominant figure in his country, the prince will remain the lightning rod for praise and blame. Whatever measure he deserves of the former—and there are still those who are ready to overlook his faults in favour of praising his past achievements—my own judgment, reflected in this book, places strong emphasis on the negative side of his years in power. Even allowing for all the problems Sihanouk faced, it was his conviction that he alone knew what was best for Cambodia that fatally inhibited the kingdom's political evolution. Joined to that conviction was his dismissive contempt for the capacities of others. And contempt could be transformed into the condoning of brutal repression when the authority of his state came under threat.

So Norodom Sihanouk has been a Prince of Light and a Prince of Darkness. Perhaps, even more, he has been a Prince of Tragedy, the flawed leader whose own personal tragedies have been only part of a much greater, national Cambodian tragedy. In late 1993 it is still not certain that Cambodia's future will not be marked by further tragedy. The intentions of the Khmer Rouge remain unclear. The political alliances that have been forged may not last. And factionalism, fuelled by personal rivalries, could all too readily destabilise a country that is desperately impoverished both materially and politically. In making clear in February 1993 that he wished once more to be king, Sihanouk said, 'I must remain the father of the nation whose task it is to reunite the nation'. Seventy-one years old and in poor health, Sihanouk has been granted his wish and is king again. Should he triumph over his illness, no-one can be certain if he will be prepared to reign or demand to rule. In the years that have passed since his overthrow in 1970, Cambodia has changed radically. No-one can be sure if Sihanouk has changed too.

Notes

In writing this chapter, I have not hesitated to draw on my summation of Sihanouk's career, written more than twenty years ago, for the passage of time has not led me to make any substantial adjustment to the broad judgments I made then. I refer, in particular, to Chapters 7 and 9 of *Politics and Power*.

The attack on Peter O'Toole, Britain and the United States was recorded in *Receuil d'editoriaux du Prince Norodom Sihanouk, parus dans la revue 'Kambuja' de no. 1 au no. 9 de l'annéee 1965*, Phnom Penh, 1965, pp. 30–1.

The quotations praising Sihanouk in 1969 come from *AKP*, 17 April 1969.

Michael Leifer's comment comes from his article 'Sihanouk won't be a panacea', in *International Herald Tribune*, 17 February 1993.

For Charles Meyer's comments on education, see *Derrière*, pp. 162–5. For Sihanouk's own comments on education while he was still in power, see *Les Paroles de Samdech Preah Norodom Sihanouk*, October–December 1968, Phnom Penh, n.d., p. 626, a speech at the inauguration of the University of Battambang. See, too, *Prisonnier*, p. 239.

Sihanouk spoke of wanting to be king again to Philip Shenon of *The New York Times*, 13 February 1993. See, also, Sihanouk's remarkable interview with Nayan Chanda in the *Far Eastern Economic Review*, 4 February 1993, in which the prince said, 'I am ready to exercise power, even if I am called an autocrat'. And 'So everybody [including the Khmer Rouge] is rotten, everybody. They [the Cambodian people] say only Sihanouk is clean. He should be made to come back and take charge of everything.'

Further references

The endnotes to the chapters of this book list the sources that I have drawn on, both written and oral, in order to present a picture of Prince Norodom Sihanouk's life. Since my account of his career is often critical, readers should be aware of other, contrary views. Some of these have already been mentioned in the notes. Such is the case with Malcolm MacDonald's *Angkor*, the article 'Cambodia', by Roger Smith, which appears in G.McT. Kahin, ed., *Governments and Politics of Southeast Asia* and Michael Field, *The Prevailing Wind*. Other laudatory writing on Sihanouk may be found in Simonne Lacouture, *Cambodge*, Lausanne, 1964, and Jean Lacouture, *The Demigods*, New York, 1970. Another admiring view by a French scholar is Philippe Devillers's article, 'The dynamics of power in Cambodia', in S. Rose, ed., *Politics in Southern Asia*, London, 1963, pp. 143–63.

Readers who wish to delve deeper into Sihanouk's career and the country he ruled will be well served by consulting the bibliography in David Chandler's *A History of Cambodia*, 2nd edition, Boulder, Colorado, 1992, and his outstanding *The Tragedy of Cambodian History*, New Haven, 1991. A shorter bibliographical guide is contained in my own *Politics and Power in Cambodia*, Melbourne, 1973. The following short list of books dealing with broad issues of Cambodian politics and society highlights other valuable references.

Chandler, David, *The Land and People of Cambodia*, Philadelphia, 1972.
Chandler, David and Ben Kiernan, eds., *Revolution and its Aftermath*, New Haven, 1983.
Dauphin-Meunier, Achille, *Le Cambodge de Sihanouk, ou la difficulté d'être neutre*, Paris, 1965.
Delvert, Jean, *Le Paysan cambodgien*, Paris, 1961
Gour, C.-G., *Institutions constitutionelles et politiques du Cambodge*, Paris, 1965.

Further references

Kiernan, Ben and Chantou Boua, *Peasants and Politics in Kampuchea, 1941–1981*, London, 1982.

Migozzi, Jacques, *Cambodge, faits et problèmes de population*, Paris, 1973.

There is now a large and growing literature on the Pol Pot years and their aftermath, of which David Chandler's *Brother Number One* is the most recent and important. The following is a small selection of works not already cited.

Heder, Stephen, *Kampuchean Occupation and Resistance*, Bangkok, 1980.

Picq, Laurance, *Au délà du ciel, cinq ans chez les Khmers rouges*, Paris 1984.

Pin Yathay, *Stay Alive, My Son*, London, 1987.

Someth May, *Cambodian Witness*, London, 1986.

Stuart-Fox, Martin, *The Murderous Revolution: Life and Death in Pol Pot's Kampuchea*, Sydney, 1985.

Finally one book involving interviews with Prince Sihanouk which has been consulted in the preparation of this book but not cited in the endnotes:

Schier, Peter and Manola Schier-Oum, in collaboration with Waldrant Jarke, eds., *Prince Sihanouk on Cambodia: Interviews and Talks with Prince Norodom Sihanouk*, 2nd enlarged edition, Hamburg, 1985.

Index

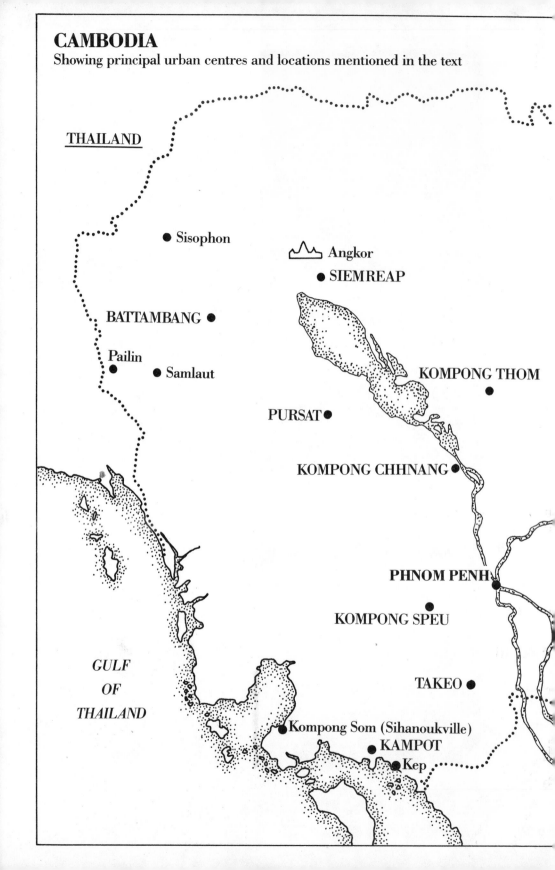

CAMBODIA

Showing principal urban centres and locations mentioned in the text

THAILAND

● Sisophon

Angkor

● SIEMREAP

BATTAMBANG ●

Pailin
●

● Samlaut

KOMPONG THOM
●

PURSAT ●

KOMPONG CHHNANG ●

PHNOM PENH

KOMPONG SPEU
●

GULF
OF
THAILAND

TAKEO ●

● Kompong Som (Sihanoukville)
● KAMPOT
● Kep